Digital Labor

Digital Media and Society Series

Nancy Baym, *Personal Connections in the Digital Age*, 2nd edition
Taina Bucher, *Facebook*
Mercedes Bunz and Graham Meikle, *The Internet of Things*
Jean Burgess and Joshua Green, *YouTube*, 2nd edition
Mark Deuze, *Media Work*
Andrew Dubber, *Radio in the Digital Age*
Quinn DuPont, *Cryptocurrencies and Blockchains*
Charles Ess, *Digital Media Ethics*, 3rd edition
Terry Flew, *Regulating Platforms*
Jordan Frith, *Smartphones as Locative Media*
Gerard Goggin, *Apps: From Mobile Phones to Digital Lives*
Alexander Halavais, *Search Engine Society*, 2nd edition
Martin Hand, *Ubiquitous Photography*
Robert Hassan, *The Information Society*
Kylie Jarrett, *Digital Labor*
Tim Jordan, *Hacking*
D. Bondy Valdovinos Kaye, Jing Zeng and Patrik Wikström, *TikTok: Creativity and Culture in Short Video*
Graeme Kirkpatrick, *Computer Games and the Social Imaginary*
Tama Leaver, Tim Highfield and Crystal Abidin, *Instagram*
Leah A. Lievrouw, *Alternative and Activist New Media*
Rich Ling and Jonathan Donner, *Mobile Communication*
Donald Matheson and Stuart Allan, *Digital War Reporting*
Nick Monaco and Samuel Woolley, *Bots*
Dhiraj Murthy, *Twitter*, 2nd edition
Zizi A. Papacharissi, *A Private Sphere: Democracy in a Digital Age*
Julian Thomas, Rowan Wilken and Ellie Rennie, *Wi-Fi*
Katrin Tiidenberg, Natalie Ann Hendry and Crystal Abidin, *tumblr*
Jill Walker Rettberg, *Blogging*, 2nd edition
Patrik Wikström, *The Music Industry*, 3rd edition

Digital Labor

KYLIE JARRETT

polity

Copyright © Kylie Jarrett 2022

The right of Kylie Jarrett to be identified as Author of this Work has been asserted in accordance with the UK Copyright, Designs and Patents Act 1988.

First published in 2022 by Polity Press

Polity Press
65 Bridge Street
Cambridge CB2 1UR, UK

Polity Press
101 Station Landing
Suite 300
Medford, MA 02155, USA

All rights reserved. Except for the quotation of short passages for the purpose of criticism and review, no part of this publication may be reproduced, stored in a retrieval system or transmitted, in any form or by any means, electronic, mechanical, photocopying, recording or otherwise, without the prior permission of the publisher.

ISBN-13: 978-1-5095-4519-3
ISBN-13: 978-1-5095-4520-9(pb)

A catalogue record for this book is available from the British Library.

Library of Congress Control Number: 2021951318

Typeset in 10.25 on 13pt Scala
by Fakenham Prepress Solutions, Fakenham, Norfolk NR21 8NL
Printed and bound in Great Britain by CPI Group (UK) Ltd, Croydon

The publisher has used its best endeavours to ensure that the URLs for external websites referred to in this book are correct and active at the time of going to press. However, the publisher has no responsibility for the websites and can make no guarantee that a site will remain live or that the content is or will remain appropriate.

Every effort has been made to trace all copyright holders, but if any have been overlooked the publisher will be pleased to include any necessary credits in any subsequent reprint or edition.

For further information on Polity, visit our website:
politybooks.com

Contents

Acknowledgments   vi

1   Defining Digital Labor   1
2   Exploitation: Digital Deeds Done Dirt Cheap   36
3   Process: Of Autonomy and Algorithms   69
4   Alienation: The Romance of Entrepreneurialism   100
5   Commodification: Affective Attachment and Inalienable Assets   133
6   Struggle: The Workers United(ish)   166
7   Conclusion: Digital Labor on the Edge   200

References   215
Index   242

Acknowledgments

Digital Labor was researched and written through a series of lockdowns during a global pandemic. These were emotionally challenging times as our worlds shrunk and became riddled with new fears and challenges. The book inevitably bears the traces of the isolation and anxieties of this context. It also bears the traces of the forms of solidarity and meaningful digitally mediated exchanges that were a feature of this grim period. It is these elements of lockdown life I wish to take with me as we (hopefully) emerge from under the shadow cast by Covid and which I want to acknowledge here. I am, of course, very grateful to all my colleagues whose insights have shaped my research and who have been instrumental in the making of this book, not least as it depends so much upon their excellent empirical studies. As with most things in this pandemic, though, these traditional considerations must temporarily take a back seat as I recognize the personal connections that have made the labor of this book possible.

I want to say a huge, heartfelt thank you to the Brexit in Space WhatsApp group comprised of Mary Gilmartin, Eoin O'Mahony, Sheamus Sweeney, Jorie Lagerwey, and Niamh Puirséil. Hilarious and heartfelt, the banter, love, and care experienced here – and during the occasional illegal bag-o-cans on the canal – got me through the long dark days of this pandemic. You are the very best of people.

Much gratitude also goes to the 3-Legged Stool WhatsApp – Gavan Titley and Stephanie Rains. We have been colleagues for what feels like forever and you never cease to encourage, support, and make me laugh. Thank you for all you have done to keep me sane these many years, especially the gossipy bits.

The other group of people whose presence (and prosecco) bolstered my flagging spirits was the Ballybough Pride of Place Community Group – Laura Williams, Ray McSweeney, Damo Byrne, and Aideen Leonard. As my people are known to say, "everybody needs good neighbors," and I clearly have these in abundance.

The most important group to acknowledge, though, is the great number of newly christened "essential workers" who continued to put themselves at risk to provide health and care services, sell us food, deliver goods, repair and clean, collect and process waste, or manufacture and prepare essential items. Workers in these jobs deserve everyone's gratitude and respect. Many of these workers are also the digital laborers who figure in this study, and I thank them for keeping everything afloat while so many of us had the privilege of staying safely at home.

Now more than ever I am grateful to have all these people in my world to help me live a rich life even when locked in my house.

Kylie Jarrett

I

Defining Digital Labor

Adorned in the teal livery of Deliveroo, Thiago Cortes rode his bike onto the quays running along the River Liffey in Dublin's city center one late August night in 2020. It was about 10.30 and the streets were quiet as a Covid-19 pandemic lockdown was in effect. Considered an essential worker, platform delivery riders such as Cortes were one of the few signs of life in the city. Like many other international students, Cortes worked for Deliveroo to meet the high costs of living in Dublin, riding his bike through the wet and windy city streets as a self-employed contractor for an average of €10.50 an hour, but sometimes for less. He had just completed what was likely to be his last delivery of the night and his fiancée expected him home as usual about 11 p.m. He was not to arrive. As he attempted to turn onto North Wall Quay, he was hit by a car traveling at speed. The car, its driver, and passengers then fled the scene. Despite being rushed to hospital, Thiago Cortes did not survive his injuries (Lynch 2020; Malekmian 2020). A few nights later, friends and fellow Deliveroo riders held a vigil both *in memoriam* and as a protest about the unsafe conditions experienced in their work, holding the platform to account. Deliveroo rejected this call, claiming that riders were "at the heart of Deliveroo and we prioritise rider safety" (Pollak 2020). At the same time, a crowdfunding campaign was set up on GoFundMe to raise money to repatriate Cortes's body to Brazil.

Directly across the Liffey from the site of Cortes's tragic death – and indeed spilling out onto the north side of the river – is the area of Dublin known as the Silicon Docks. Formerly the city's working port, and so associated with heavy industry, commodity trade, and blue-collar working communities, the area is now home to a significant number of the world's largest, and most famous, digital media companies. Lured by low tax rates and economic incentives, multinational companies such as Google, Facebook, Airbnb, and Amazon all have headquarters in Dublin's docklands (Jarrett 2021). Working in the towers of glass and steel that now comprise the Docks area is a range of full-time and well-paid engineers, programmers, marketing specialists, and game designers, along with a raft of less secure workers involved in content moderation, customer support, or software localization. State supported industry incubators foster digital technology startups in the docks who take advantage of the proximity to large, successful multinationals. Nearby co-working spaces also host freelance web designers, influencers, and podcasters, working their hustle in creative, entrepreneurial careers.

The morning after Cortes's accident, and not far from these centers of enterprise, I was scrolling through social media platforms when I spotted a news story about the incident. I clicked through the link onto an online news platform to read more just as a friend, also horrified by the news of another vulnerable worker being harmed, sent me a WhatsApp linking to another story about the incident. I spent time over breakfast clicking in and out of various applications, platforms, and news sites. In doing so, I was being put to work by the same social media platforms that reside in Dublin's docklands. Each click of a link, each moment spent reading a particular item on a feed, each time I reacted to a friend's post, I was generating data about my likes and interests that could be used to target advertising to me, which could be aggregated into marketing databases, or used to train algorithms and artificial intelligence. By engaging with the horrible story of a vulnerable worker's fatal industrial accident, I was creating the product upon which the economics of social media companies pivot: user data.

Defining Digital Labor

Unofficial "ghost bicycle" memorial to Deliveroo rider Thiago Cortes on North Wall Quay, Dublin. Source: Author's own.

At first glance, the experience of Thiago Cortes, the Silicon Dock's tech industry entrepreneurs, and me as a social media user seem to have little in common. The unsafe, low-paid, and marginalized work of a migrant student working for a delivery platform seems far removed from the clean, well-compensated, culturally esteemed careers of Facebook or Google's white-collar workforce. These kinds of labor are even further removed from me distracting myself by doomscrolling Twitter at the kitchen table. Yet Cortes, Google's programmers, and I are all engaged in what has become known as digital labor; work that has emerged since the transformation of society, culture, and economics by networked computerization. This book is about all these kinds of workers and the work they do. Its goal is to provide a critical overview of the defining characteristics of this form of labor and the challenges and pleasures it offers those who undertake it. It asks: How is such work compensated and managed? What makes such work desirable – or merely necessary? What are the negative consequences of how this work manifests and how do workers negotiate those dynamics? Its primary question, though, is: what does digital labor look like? However, as the divergent experiences of myself, Cortes, and the Silicon Dock's privileged programmers already flag, identifying commonalities between the many forms that digital labor can take is no easy task. What unites their experience and allows us to speak of their activity under the same umbrella? Is it even possible to talk about digital labor as if it was a single form of work?

To respond to these questions, the first challenge for this book is in defining what we mean by "digital labor". At first glance, that should be an easy task. The term is in common use. According to Google's Ngram Viewer which captures the relative increase in references to the term within the Google Books data set, there has been an exponential rise in its use since 2009. The study of digital labor is also a growing field of academic inquiry as the continually expanding array of publications addressing the topic attest. It also has international recognition. I belong to the European Network on Digital Labor, for instance which is affiliated with the International Network on Digital Labor. That you have picked up this book with the title *Digital Labor* speaks to a relatively wide recognition of the term and some conceptualization of the general field it describes. The term "digital labor" clearly has some legibility.

The increase in use of the term shown in the *n*-gram also indicates something more. It suggests that there has been the emergence of a type of labor that is somehow distinct from precursor forms, so much so that it warrants its own nomenclature. This can be tied to the growth of companies and sectors that are native born to digital environments – such as social media platforms and online retailers – and the transformation of existing industries through computerization. As Tim Jordan (2020) argues, while still recognizing the continuing importance of economic practices that do not involve computers or code, it is possible to distinguish a significant component of the global economy that pivots on information and communication technologies. The form and size of this sector are difficult to define, not least because there are many overlapping, parallel, and intersecting economic fields. However, he argues that there is a distinct area of economic activity that can be called the digital economy which has its own, quite specific processes and practices. These processes may not only be present in this sector, but their particular organization is part of what comprises it as a distinct field. With work being such a crucial part of any economy, some of these distinct features inevitably relate to how work is organized, managed, and exploited. Mapping the specificity of these processes within the emerging digital economy is at the core of this book.

Recent European data concretely demonstrate the growing importance of work in the digital economy and thus the importance of understanding it better. In a 2018 survey of 14 European countries conducted by the European Joint Research Centre, it was estimated that an average 10% of the adult population had been involved in some kind of work for digital platforms, with 8% being involved in this work frequently. About 2% of workers in the study were earning more than 50% of their income through this kind of labor (Pesole et al. 2018). Another 2016 survey of five European countries found widespread engagement with digital platforms to make money, whether that be through hosting on Airbnb, selling goods on eBay, or as "crowdworkers" for intermediating platforms. The data showed that 9% of the UK and Dutch adults in the sample, 10% of the Swedish, 12% of the German, and 19% of the Austrian had engaged in some kind of paid work for digital platforms (Huws, Spencer, and Joyce 2016). Importantly, these figures do not factor in all the workers formally employed by digital companies or creative freelancers in the digital media industries, or those working in various other guises in the sector. As this industry has grown – which will be talked about more below – so has its workforce in both primary and subsidiary roles. Given the growing significance of digital work revealed by even these limited statistics, it seems increasingly important to not only understand the digital economy but also the kinds of labor it involves.

But despite its wide brand recognition and economic significance, the term "digital labor" is ill defined and used to categorize and typify an almost bewildering array of activities, professions, and roles across a diverse range of sectors. Alessandro Gandini (2021) has pointed out that the term originated in the early 2000s to interrogate critically the exploitation of unpaid user activity within the emerging digital industries and to validate the incorporation of this kind of work into economic analyses. The more recent applications of "digital labor" to describe work mediated by digital platforms (which Gandini insists is a distinct category because it is paid work) or roles within the digital media creative industries have only emerged over time. Because of this over-extension, Gandini (2021: 370) argues that the expression "has acquired some kind of genericity, becoming a sort of umbrella term that is increasingly delinked from its origins as a critical Marxist stance on labour and value." He notes that "digital labor" has become an "empty signifier," a term hollowed out of any distinguishable critical or analytical purpose.

While I disagree with the narrow application of the term that Gandini advocates, he is right to argue that using the term requires specificity and that it is necessary to look beyond specific work activities or outputs in defining it. This still leaves us with the question: what on earth does "digital labor" refer to? Obviously, this must be answered before we can even get to the critical summary of its salient characteristics which is the purpose of this book. This introductory chapter then will answer this question and identify a working definition of "digital labor" that will be used in the following pages. In doing so, it will examine and discard a range of options before zooming in and contextualizing the definition it will adopt for the remainder of the book. It will then outline the analytical lenses that will be used to interrogate the bounded set of work practices that it will call "digital labor."

Digital? Labor?

A common sense understanding of the term would link "digital labor" to work activity which involves digital technology. The clue is in the name, right? But this would cover a vast range of occupational practices. Despite their many differences in terms of location, social status, labor mechanics, economic function, products, contractual arrangements, required skill sets, and worker profiles, the work of designing games, word processing, operating a mining excavator, or using a computerized industrial sewing machine could all arguably be defined as "digital labor." While these occupations differ markedly, all involve manipulation of some kind of digital system at some point. In fact, given the diffusion of computational systems throughout all industries, it would be difficult to find a worker today who was not, in some way or other, using a digital tool throughout the course of the day. To use the manipulation of computerized tools to set the parameters of this study would expand its scope to cover almost all kinds of labor and be utterly unworkable.

If defining the field by focusing on the tools does not serve, we could also categorize work by the nature of the product it produces; it would be considered digital labor if it produced a digital commodity. This would encompass all work that produces games, websites, or social media content, and so be reflective of how the term is commonly used. But if we follow the full length of the value chain, this definition might also include miners whose manual labor in mining minerals such as coltan ultimately leads to the production of our digital devices (Fuchs and Sandoval 2014). If, instead, we worked with a definition that limited the category to direct involvement in the immediate production of a digital technology, this definition would then exclude platform workers such as Ola

Cabs drivers, Deliveroo riders, or Handy cleaners who do not directly produce a digital product. However, these are the kinds of workers overtly associated with the term today. In this instance, the scope is both too broad and too narrow.

Another approach would be to consider only those industries that have been substantially transformed by digitization. It is useful here to draw on the description of "transmedia work" by Karin Fast and André Jansson (2019), which they describe not as a series of jobs or tasks but as a widespread social condition in which everyday expectations about media access and activity have had a transformative effect on the ways work – and society – is conducted. This includes traditional or everyday tasks such as sharing files or keeping in contact with an employer that have been reshaped by media systems. By this definition, though, we can include in the pantheon of transmedia workers the builder whose primary activity involves manual, non-digital activity but for whom there are firm expectations about mobile media access and whose work faces constant interruption from phone calls, texts, and messages on a variety of platforms. This builder's labor is profoundly transformed by digital technologies and yet they would fall outside of what is typically meant by the term "digital laborer."

To narrow this down, it would perhaps be desirable to include in our definition only those forms of work that have been *profoundly* transformed by access to and use of digital technologies. But as already noted, digitization has transformed almost all industries and almost all work practices. Such a definition would also need to include the printing industry workers explored by Shoshanna Zuboff (1988), whose everyday work activities and institutional hierarchies were fundamentally altered by the computerization of the factory. It would also need to include the farmer, who now manages their dairy herd through microchips and automated milking systems, and the mechanic whose assessments of engines are managed by digital machines. An argument could of course be made for including only types of work which cross a particular threshold for the degree of transformation. The question then becomes where that threshold would lie – a difficult line to draw in the absence of longitudinal empirical evidence about all workplaces documenting degrees of change. Yet again, this approach to defining the terms of this book would quickly become unworkable.

It might be possible to define the term by correlating it with a particular set of occupational conditions. However, there is still a remarkable diversity within each single digital labor sector in terms of work activity, products, and contractual relations that make this a challenge. To cite only one example of such typologies, in their study of work associated with digital platforms, Jamie Woodcock and Mark Graham (2020) describe a range of different forms: taxi and delivery work; domestic and carework; microwork; online freelancing. These forms differ markedly in relation to the required activity, skill levels, and their outputs. Labelling images for a company through Amazon Mechanical Turk is very different to driving a cab for Didi or building a website for a client contracted via Upwork, yet they are all instances of platform labor. These types of work also differ in terms of their relationship to geography, with Woodcock and Graham emphasizing the difference between work that is "geographically tethered", such as delivery services, to those that can span global geography, such as microwork for Fiverr. Perhaps more importantly, they also map the difference in how work is governed in each of these forms, exploring levels of control in terms of space, time, autonomy to set rates, capacity of work to be captured as data, barriers to entry, potential for repeat transactions, and degree of explicit coordination (2020: 63–9). Other theorists use different terminology and different categories to describe similar phenomena but also provide slightly different definitions and descriptions: Valerio de Stefano (2016), for instance, refers to "crowdwork" and "work-on-demand via app," while a study for the European

Parliament Committee on Employment and Social Affairs differentiates only between platform-mediated work that happens offline and online (Forde et al. 2017). There are important differences across even this narrow range of digital labor activities that make it difficult to find the set of occupational characteristics that can be used to define the field.

Beyond these pragmatic questions, there is also the very fraught question of whether all activity that occurs in the digital economy – and which is usually conceptualized under the term "digital labor" – can be defined as "labor" at all. As will be discussed further in chapters 2 and 3, many digital laborers are engaged in forms of self-employment or self-exploitation that place them outside of definitions of "labor" if that term is limited to work that is value creating and exploited by an employer. This is also a question regularly raised about unpaid work such as user activity on social media platforms. The absence of contractual relations, compensation, and coercion may suggest this is not labor. Much of user labor is, arguably, fun and so is more akin to play than work (see Kücklich 2005; Scholz 2013). There are also more complicated arguments about whether user activity is actually value generating because it is the labor of others such as marketing department employees and coders who parse the raw inputs from users into a money-making commodity (Bolin 2011; Meehan 1984). It has also been argued that value is actually generated in the stock market and not in user activity at all (Arvidsson and Colleoni 2012). An even more abstract argument is that social media platforms are, in fact, generating revenue from exploiting the natural resources of user affects and energies rather than being engaged in productive activity – exploiting rent – and so users are not engaged in value-producing labor (Caraway 2011; Pasquinelli 2009). Along with various colleagues, I have argued against such positions and made the claim that digital media users *are* engaged in value-generating labor (Jarrett 2016a; see also Andrejevic 2002; Fuchs 2008, 2009,

2014a; Fuchs and Sevignani 2013; Kücklich 2005; Scholz 2013), but nevertheless this persistent, unresolved question becomes another complication in defining "digital labor" for the purposes of this book.

With these various perspectives in mind, I am going to take guidance from Gandini and begin by providing some precision in my terminology and theory, not least so I can make my way through the tangled contradictions outlined above and find an object to focus on for this book. To do so, I will continue to draw on a commonsense usage of the term, but one informed by the literature in popular and academic fields of inquiry, to define the scope of what is in and what is outside my definition. By necessity, these boundaries will be relatively arbitrary and open to debate, and I certainly wouldn't propose them as the only way to define "digital labor." They will, however, limit the scope of the kinds of activities, workers, and workplaces across which I will be tracking commonalities in this book.

Labor context

My first intervention is to restrict the scope of the inquiry to "digital media industries." By this term, I mean the obvious sectors: the (in)famous multinational social media and technology companies such as Google, Amazon, or TenCent; the software, games, and creative sectors; and the Web 2.0 or social media sector, which includes its vast unpaid workforce of users. This term also includes platforms that broker various kinds of employment because, even if the specific labor activities they broker may neither be media work nor use digital technologies, the mechanisms that create the labor relationship on the platform rely on digital media platforms to exist and, effectively, create content.

The use of the term "media" here may be misleading due to its long associations with audio-visual entertainment and news industries, or "The Media." I use it here, though, to refer to mediating communication systems, and so it encompasses industries and labor involved with software, websites, platforms, apps, or the creation of content or data for these systems. This way, we can include coders building web-based health diagnostic systems, for instance, as part of the digital labor community, even though we would hesitate to call them part of "The Media." But we can also include factory workers employed by or subcontracted to Amazon as they are doing work for an online retailer within the digital media platform ecosystem, as well as data-center technicians sustaining the cloud infrastructure owned by digital media giants.

The focus on digital media industries is partly driven by its logic centrality to questions of *digital* labor. But it is also because this sector has been at the forefront of broader socioeconomic changes within the global economy and the changes to work that follow from them. To understand the emergence of digital labor thus requires sketching out the place of digital industries and technologies within the form of capitalism that emerged in the latter half of the twentieth century. There are many variations of this history across the globe that depend on the specific conditions and particular state of development of different places. Nevertheless, the story of socioeconomic change in the hegemonic, global North tells a useful story that exemplifies the increasing economic centrality of the digital and contextualizes some of the forms of labor we will see throughout this book. What immediately follows is a very sketchy but still quite lengthy socioeconomic history – which by necessity must reduce complex and entangled histories to a sentence or two – and which will take us quite some way from our central concern of digital labor. However, this history shows the evolution of some of the economic structures of the economy, and the digital media sector specifically, which directly influence the shape of the work it entails.

This narrative will begin in the 1970s as the economic fabric of the global North began to fray. The long boom of the twentieth century had been driven by the twin engines of mass production and a social compact relating to wages and economic security that enabled mass consumption. This logic was epitomized (if never quite actualized) in the idealized Fordist factory, where assembly lines of de-skilled but relatively well-paid and securely employed workers generated a raft of consumer goods that they were then in a position to purchase – a virtuous circle of production and consumption. Wage compacts between employers and workers, often brokered by relatively strong trade unions, and a broad social welfare safety net, funded by high taxation, sustained markets and enabled the emergence of new consumer domains as employment and wealth was spread. To keep the capitalist machinery ticking over, industry and society were focused on creating, shoring up, and innovating in relation to consumer demand (Harvey 1990).

By the 1960s, this mode of life and industry began to wobble as a youth-led counterculture began to reject the rigid modes of work associated with Fordism, but also began to query lives lived through consumption (Frayssé 2015). More importantly, though, consumer demand in the global North began to weaken as markets became saturated. The creation of global demand – expanding the consumer base – became necessary to continue growth. However, the relatively newly industrialized nations which were targeted as emerging markets also began to compete against global North companies for production activity. By the start of the 1970s, the mass production/consumption system in the global North became untenable, suffering from what became known as the "stagflation crisis." The ugly portmanteau refers to the dual problems of *stag*nant economies and rising *in*flation. The effects of this shaky economic context were exacerbated by the "oil shock" of 1973 in which Oil Producing Exporting Countries (OPEC) announced an oil embargo on a range of nations in response to their alleged support for Israel during the Yom Kippur war. The costs of production rose sharply as this vital component of almost all industry became scarce and thus more expensive.

The response to this economic crisis in the global North was to shift from focusing on demand to focusing on innovation in production: supply-side economics. Computerization and, in particular, digital communication systems were enrolled to produce greater efficiencies in production and transport and, importantly, flexibility in productive activity. The post-Fordist factory, typified by shorter production runs, more specialist goods, and a shift to economies of scope (selling fewer goods at a premium rather than masses of cheap goods) began to take shape. The emerging production technologies powered by computerization and electronic advances also enabled the widespread mobilization of the just-in-time production processes pioneered in Japan in the 1960s and 1970s. This model disaggregates the production chain so, rather than a factory producing all the components that comprise its final product, contributing components could be purchased elsewhere as needed, linking firms in extended supply chains (Tsing 2009). This allowed companies to shed inventory as well as elements of production – and the workers employed there – leading to leaner, more efficient corporate structures. What had once been the work of a single factory was outsourced to other, typically smaller, independent companies who, because they were typically in competition with other similar firms, offered lower wages and less secure conditions for workers. Computerized communication also allowed for organizational management across space and in real time to manage this distributed production. This also facilitated the offshoring of a significant amount of the global North's already outsourced manufacturing activity to emerging economies in the global South to take advantage of lower wages and often more lax regulatory environments. The effects of outsourcing and offshoring on workers in the global North were profound as downward pressure was applied to wages and employment became insecure.

Another element of the renewal of capitalism since the 1970s was the financialization of the economy. Rather than being entirely defined by their products and profit, companies themselves became commodities, floating on global stock exchanges (also facilitated by advances in communication technologies). They thus became targets of mergers and acquisitions by, sometimes predatory, companies speculating on abstract valuations rather than a commitment to the firm, its products, or its workers. Providing value for shareholders began to drive companies, leading to further rationalization of the labor force and bolstering efforts to increase productivity through more offshoring and outsourcing. Companies bought entirely with a view to profit were often restructured, broken up, and/or repurposed, creating insecurity for workers. With the "priority to sustain the confidence of investors, employers . . . were no longer in a position to promise lifelong careers to their employees" (Feher 2018: 18).

And so with financialization and supply-side innovation came the restructuring of the labor market – often supported by neoliberal state policy and deregulation – intended to enable more flexibility in hiring practices. The full-time, permanent job that had typified the Fordist era began to cede to more contingent, irregular labor contracts, including temporary, part-time, and subcontractor relations. These contracts allowed new temporalities in and organization of work to emerge, mapped onto the fluid industrial dynamics of the post-Fordist period (Harvey 1990; Standing 2016). For many workers, work itself also became fragmented into independent tasks or a series of varying gigs, demanding from them an increased flexibility and adaptability to circumstances and labor routines. As the twenty-first century has rolled out, the formal, permanent, contracted job has continued to decline in importance, with an International Labour Organization (ILO) report in 2015 finding that less than one in four jobs today follows this pattern. Additionally, persistently declining productivity across the globe has led to suggestions that increasing numbers of the world's workers will never be enrolled in the standard labor force.

Information intensive industries

The key to the economic transformation roughly sketched above was, arguably, digitization. Certainly, the innovations of the post-Fordist factory were materially enabled by it. But digitization also allowed for rapid production and circulation of materials and products in an "informational form" that has sped up and made more flexible the circulation of capital across the globe (Davis and Stack 1997). Additionally, the focus of economic activity has arguably moved from the manufacturing of material goods toward the production, manipulation, and distribution of knowledge, both in immaterial form – e.g. a patent or data stream – and when instantiated into an information-rich consumable – e.g. a game device or television program. Computerization has thus entrenched and increased the importance of white-collar labor. By comparison with the nineteenth century, today proportionally "fewer individuals manipulate *things*, more handle *people* and *symbols*" (Mills 1951: 58, original emphasis). This shift from secondary to tertiary industries – from manufacturing to service economies – is perhaps best understood as a change in which elements of value are understood to originate rather than a wholesale change in the amount of activity in each sector. Across the globe, manufacturing and primary industries continue to enroll a significant number of workers – particularly in lower-income countries – and continue to contribute substantially to national productivity (ILO 2020; OECD 2019). Nevertheless, industries "characterized in general by the central role played by knowledge, information, affect, and communication" (Hardt and Negri 2000: 285) have grown in importance in high-income economies, bringing increasing attention to – and privileging of – services and creative sectors, and rearranging other sectors in their image (Moulier Boutang 2011).

Media industries are right at the heart of the shift toward an innovation-led, information-rich economy. The twentieth century was typified by the growing importance of industries producing the symbolic content of goods: advertising, marketing, design, and media. These industries did not escape the transformations of the 1970s. As David Hesmondhalgh (2007) describes, creative and cultural industries also underwent a process of commodification in which media corporations became reconceptualized as assets to be traded on stock markets. They were, therefore, also at the mercy of mergers and acquisitions, with some of the largest mergers of the period occurring in this sector: Warner Communications (which had already been taken over by Kinney National Services) merged with Time in 1989 to become one of the world's largest media groups. This also meant that media companies and their workers were impacted by the processes of asset stripping, restructuring, and outsourcing that were a feature of the last few decades of the twentieth century, as well as some media firms becoming globe-spanning megacorporations, structured to maximize shareholder value.

In the 1990s, the internet emerged as another arena for the creation of cultural content. Initially conceived as a distributed communication system for military and civic purposes, the internet soon became home to a range of sites hosting political discussions and interpersonal engagement. From 1991, it also became home to commercial sites when the US National Science Foundation lifted the semi-official ban on such activity. A crucial point in the economic history of the internet was, however, the introduction of the Mosaic browser, which made easy, and thus popularized, access to the World Wide Web. Through this browser, the internet developed the kind of critical mass that indicated its potential as a site of commerce (Kenney 2003). This led to a dot.com boom where, supported by rivers of money from venture capitalists and investment firms, digital native startups began to emerge, particularly online retailers and community platforms. Various "old media" companies also began claiming space on the internet. They began developing portals and hubs as sites for both commerce and play, often drawing on a repurposed content from their offline products. A business model adopted by many of these sites, and in particular those with some longevity, was centered on advertising revenue. Echoing an approach familiar from broadcasting, access to sites was made free in exchange for user data and exposure to promotional material. In particular, the ability to collect direct data on audience engagement, from page views to click-throughs, was an extremely valuable innovation, overturning the vague mechanisms for capturing audience data used within the broadcast sector. Consequently, the first ads through which a user could click began appearing in the mid-1990s (McStay 2010).

As is the way with booms, the investment frenzy of the dot.com moment came to a sudden end. In 2000, the technology index the NASDAQ collapsed, taking with it not only the share prices of internet companies but also the confidence of potential investors. This was a double blow for the sector as a widespread recession also caused advertising revenue to falter just as seed funding and other forms of capital also dried up. Many internet companies failed during this time. Nevertheless, their economic model of reliance on advertising revenue survived as a core aspect of the internet economy along with some companies, websites, and platforms that continue in importance today, such as eBay and Amazon.

The digital media economy did rally relatively quickly but with a shift away from the proprietary walled gardens of portals such as Geocities and AOL toward the apparently open Web – led by Google and search – and to app development – led by Apple's decision to enable third-party application development. Legacy media companies' presence gave way to more digital native sites, bolstered by the emergence of what became known as "Web 2.0" (O'Reilly 2005) or the participatory Web. What we typically understand as "social media" (e.g. WeChat, Facebook, Twitter, TikTok) distils the essence of this shift. As conceived by technology publisher Tim O'Reilly, Web 2.0 marked a move from the publishing of static pages to sites and platforms that facilitated and encouraged user input and interaction. It was centered on conceiving of users as producers. O'Reilly argued that there were opportunities to build brand value and consumer loyalty by providing a platform for users' creative expression and interaction. Most importantly, Web 2.0 was also conceived as pivoting on the collection of user data which O'Reilly considered more valuable than hardware and software. In his depiction, then, we see the emergence of value creation centered on a new kind of worker: the digital media user whose labor would contribute both content and swathes of commodifiable data on consumer tastes and desires. Web 2.0 and its social media platform and app offspring are dependent on these contributions.

The key revenue source for the digital companies that have emerged since the 2000 crash has been advertising revenue and the aggregation of marketing data. It is this which makes user data a valuable commodity. Increasingly, though, digital companies are diversifying and moving into third-party service provision, for instance through becoming cloud-computing hubs or providing software as service. In this model, companies license access to infrastructure or software, offering online mechanisms for business and personal data management, process management, or analytic systems. Companies like Google or Amazon that have historically been associated with a single product – search and online retail respectively – have been able to parlay their technical expertise into new markets, diversifying revenue streams through licensing and subscription models. Advertising still forms a significant component of revenue for many large digital media companies though – Alphabet (Google's financial parent), for instance, still earned US$146.9 billion in ad revenue in 2020 despite a small loss for a quarter due to the Covid pandemic.

As the digital media economy has matured, new subsectors and new fields of work have emerged – such as app development, social media marketing, influencer talent management, and content moderation – generating novel forms of employment, professions, and roles within the increasingly broadly defined digital media content sector. More recently, a different form of internet-mediated site has emerged as an additional cog in the digital economy: sites and apps that broker exchanges between users (who become paid workers) and potential employers, with the site usually taking a percentage of the income realized by the worker. This is the growing range of intermediating platforms such as transport services Uber, Ola, or Grab, microwork platforms like TaskRabbit and Mechanical Turk, delivery services such as Deliveroo and Just Eat, and personal-service provision platforms such as Care.com and Handy. Capitalizing on the global economic crisis of 2008 and expanding on the already well-established trend toward outsourcing and economic deregulation (van Doorn 2017), the platform economy has emerged as a significant source of employment and economic possibility across the globe. As we will discuss in much more detail throughout this book, the economics of this subsector tap directly into the fracturing of labor security, providing additional gigs and income for many dispossessed within the current economic context.

As Nieborg et al. (2019; see also Srnicek 2017) argue, media production and computing more generally in the global North has also returned to being a proprietary walled garden as it is dominated by a relatively small group of powerful platforms who shape access to the internet and provide underlying software services: Google (Alphabet), Apple, Facebook, Amazon, and Microsoft, or the so-called GAFAM companies. In this concentration, there is more than merely platform dependency at stake. Nieborg and colleagues (2019) also describe the "platformization" of the creative industries as the governance, economic, and infrastructural frameworks of these online giants have come to influence production practices from product conceptualization onward. Media have become remade in the form dictated by the needs of platforms. This dynamic has also extended beyond the global North, with the Chinese government having linked its economic development to the potential of digital media industries for some time. China is also marked by a cadre of dominant digital media firms developed in parallel to those birthed in the United States and Europe – Baidu, Alibaba, and Tencent (BAT companies). These firms dominate a "hyper-platformized" economy, although greater competition and cooperation between the firms has created a less oligopolistic and diverse media platform environment than in the United States – or at least this was the case at the time of writing (Craig, Lin, and Cunningham 2021).

These leading digital media companies are not just dominant within media and creative production sectors but also within the broad global economy. Alongside the expected list of international banks, in May 2021 the GAFAM/BAT group of companies featured highly on the Forbes global 2000 list of the world's largest publicly listed companies. Apple was sixth, Amazon was tenth, Google/Alphabet thirteenth, Microsoft fifteenth, Alibaba twenty-third, Tencent Holdings was twenty-ninth, and Facebook was at thirty-three (Murphy et al. 2021). At the same time, Amazon founder Jeff Bezos was identified as the world's richest individual with a net worth of US$177 billion. Microsoft founder Bill Gates was fourth on this list, with Mark Zuckerberg of Facebook behind him at fifth, Google/Alphabet's Larry Page and Sergey Brin at eighth and ninth respectively, Microsoft's Steve Ballmer at fourteenth, Ma Huateng of Tencent at fifteenth, and Alibaba's Jack Ma was listed as the twenty-sixth richest person on the planet (Dolan, Wang, and Peterson-Withorn 2021).

This status of the GAFAM/BAT digital media companies and their founders seems the logical outcome of the processes begun in the 1970s which emphasized technological solutions, privileged sectors involved in information and symbolic production, and sought new ways to exploit – and provide opportunities for – workers impacted by labor insecurity. The digital media industries, and the labor they rely on, arguably epitomize contemporary economic logic so this type of work and its management also exemplify general trends within the economy. Labor within the digital media industries and the experience of its workers are thus important to understand not only because the sector is economically significant – although that is certainly relevant. It is also important to analyze for what it can reveal about the broader workings of contemporary capitalism; exploring digital labor becomes a lens to look at contemporary labor relations. Using work within the digital media industry to embody the scope of this study is thus more than merely a useful mechanism for creating a working definition of digital labor for the purposes of this book.

The labor triptych

To refine the definition of digital labor further than "work in the digital media industry," I will also restrict the scope of the inquiry to three broadly defined categories of workers within this sector. These categories are differentiated not by role or sector, outputs or inputs, but more by the nature of their relationship to the employer – although these dynamics are entangled. Using this triptych of workers to define the extent of that which is understood as digital labor means that the term is no longer directly linked to the types of tools, products, activities, or occupational conditions associated with work and all the complexities that involves. Nevertheless, this approach allows for the mapping of commonalities across a range of digital media work environments, rather than the single form implied in the original use of the term. This opens up a wider range of digital work forms to the critical lens associated with the concept "digital labor."

The first category to fall under the conceptual umbrella is *user labor*. This describes the unpaid, uncontracted work on social media platforms from which economic value is extracted and about which the term "digital labor" was originally developed. Some of this work may take place with a view to compensation or monetization, but much of it – such as tweeting a joke, sharing an image on Pinterest, or organizing a political protest via WhatsApp – has no such pretension. Nevertheless, economic value is still created from these interactions either because such work provides the content that makes a site desirable or because data are extracted and exploited within the advertising economy (Fuchs 2014a; Terranova 2000). It is this extraction of value from user contributions that transforms such activity from work – activity creating objects with embedded, meaningful value to the user (use-value) – into labor – activity producing goods defined primarily by their value in a marketplace (exchange-value) (Fuchs and Sevignani 2013).

The second group is comprised of *platform-mediated workers*, although I will adopt an expansive and perhaps novel definition of this term. The term "platform worker" is often instinctively applied to those workers in the gig economy who work in a series of jobs, sometimes simultaneously, rather than in a single career or profession. Often platform economy and gig economy are used interchangeably in the literature in the field (see Woodcock and Graham 2020, for instance). Specifically, though, "platform workers" refers to people employed through intermediating platforms such as Deliveroo, Didi, or Amazon Mechanical Turk that connect workers with employers to undertake discrete tasks. It also refers to careworkers or home helpers employed through sites such as UrbanSitter, Care.com, or Helpling, forms of platform work which have until recently had little or only cursory exploration (see McDonald, Williams, and Mayes 2020; Ticona and Mateescu 2018, for instance). The tasks undertaken by these workers are diverse and depend upon the platform. They may be physical and material – deliveries, driving a car, doing home repairs, or childcare – or they may be entirely informational – web design, filling in surveys, or answering questions for supposed artificial intelligence systems. Such workers are typically self-employed – or involved in bogus self-employment where the reality is that they are employees but are not contracted in this way (see chapter 6 for more exploration of this issue).

To this definition of platform worker I want to add creative and technical workers in the social media economy such as influencers, cammers, beauty bloggers, and live-streamers. In the digital labor literature, there is a peculiar schism between studies of "gig work" and creative "social media work," with very little cross-fertilization of ideas between the two fields. There may be a range of reasons for this, but the divide seems to fall on gendered distinctions between private and public activity. In the studies of Deliveroo and Uber (which are the dominant gig-economy studies), we see work happening, often literally, in public. Even cloud-based microwork that happens in people's homes becomes public because of its easy correspondence with what we understand as "work." On the other hand, social media creative work has less correspondence with the traditional masculinized ideas that define labor. This is work that typically involves subjectivity, embodiment, and intimacy. It is less public, more private, and happens conceptually, and sometimes literally, in intimate, domestic spaces. Consequently, it is readily relegated to the feminized sphere of social reproduction and considered unproductive activity in many orthodox interpretations of labor.

Whatever the reason for this division, gig workers and social media workers are similar kinds of worker. They are both involved in commercial, but not waged, relationships with platforms (Feher 2018: 176). Social media sites such as YouTube or Kuaishou function in similar ways to other labor-mediating platforms as they draw on a large and scalable freelance workforce and use automated management systems for organizing and controlling that labor (Niebler and Kern 2020). Like work-brokering platforms such as Foodora or Upwork, social media platforms such as Instagram or Twitch broker relationships between creators and clients, which in these latter instances are brands, advertisers, marketers, and/or other digital media users. As we will see later in the book, both types of workers are also impacted by the algorithmic systems used to manage various aspects of their labor. Consequently, creators who generate incomes via social media platforms can, and I believe should, also be described as platform workers. Consequently, the category of "platform-mediated worker" spans a range of workplaces and work activities from driving for Didi or riding for Deliveroo to influencing on Instagram or sex work through a compensated dating forum on Baidu Tieba (Chu 2018; Tan and Xu 2020).

The third kind of worker I will refer to as the *formal worker* to capture paid workers engaged more or less full-time, or on an ongoing basis, within the digital media industries. This includes those involved in sustained, elite, professional careers such as design, programming, or marketing in the GAFAM/BAT companies, games companies, or in digital media industry startups. There are, unfortunately, very few academic studies available that explore the labor of these workers. This is primarily because limited access has been granted to undertake research in these workplaces and due to the impact of non-disclosure agreements imposed on workers. My primary sources for understanding these laborers have thus been a range of studies in the popular business press as well as industry memoirs. Some of these reports need to be read circumspectly as many are excoriating documents, written in the spirit of grievance. Nevertheless, they have provided fascinating and important insights into the dynamics of this work and the experiences of such workers.

As I am using it, the formal worker category also includes professional, but less secure workers, such as web designers or game developers who may be freelance or employed through a series of contracts, but whose work is not mediated primarily through digital media platforms. These workers may be self-employed, work for small companies, or be hired only for specific projects, but the types of work they do, and their ongoing professional status, accords with that extended to more permanent employees. These workers may supplement these formal gigs with work secured through platforms, but at these moments they slip from one category to another.

Finally, and possibly more contentiously, this category also includes more marginal workers who are paid employees in less elite positions such as content moderators, Amazon fulfillment center workers, data-center workers, or game testers. While their work conditions may correspond more with those in the platform economy than those in elite positions in the same firm, such workers sit in this category because they are formally employed by digital media companies – or formally subcontracted to them from other firms. Throughout the analysis that follows, attention is paid to the differences in these labor situations, but for now it is appropriate that these workers are drawn under the umbrella term as they are formally employed by firms within the digital media sector.

As already flagged a few times, the user, platform, and formal worker groupings are non-exclusive categories. Almost all workers are digital media users at some point, engaging in unpaid contributions to the digital media economy, and some kinds of platform work can bleed into formal work, particularly if the client and worker move off the platform. Unpaid work can become monetized and vice versa. Consequently, the subcategories remain flexible and are intended to be loosely defined. Most importantly, the capacious definition of "digital labor" articulated here is broad enough to cover the wide spectrum of labor conditions, work activities, and final products of the kind we intuitively understand as connected to the digital economy. We are able to incorporate, for instance, the prestigious, salaried labor of professional game developers along with the unpaid labor of a Facebook user whose interpersonal relationships are gathered as data points and the physical exertions of the supposedly self-employed Uber Eats rider whose work is waged, but whose income is unfixed and uncertain. At the same time, we have some clear parameters about what forms of work fall under the rubric of this book.

What this framework leaves out is the wide range of work practices and roles that have been transformed by digitization. For instance, this means I will not include office work involving computers, unless this office is itself part of the digital media industry. I will also not include our aforementioned builder and their mobile telephone or the home careworker whose patient allocations are organized via a database and who is required to remain in contact by mobile phone. We will, however, consider the builder and the careworker whose labor is brokered and managed by digital media platforms, focusing on how that intersection enacts a particular set of social relations. We will also include the craftsperson whose work may be manual – knitting, for instance – but whose income from that work is mediated by a platform like Etsy and therefore whose work is reshaped in accordance with the dictates of that platform (to return to Nieborg et al.'s concept of platformization). These are perhaps arbitrary distinctions, and a case could be made to include within the term all work that requires a substantial amount of interaction with digital devices and which has been fundamentally transformed by this demand. However, as already discussed, this would dilute the concept of "digital labor" to the point of meaninglessness, and we would return to the confusion that started this chapter.

This definition also leaves out the many people involved in the hazardous work of mineral extraction, manufacturing, and e-waste disposal that support and are also necessary for the digital media industries to function (Fuchs and Sandoval 2014). The people who produce the raw materials and the hardware that go into those objects are an important group of workers. However, while they may map onto some aspects of digital labor – although arguably for many their conditions are far worse and they experience other social relations, such as slavery (Qiu 2016) – they do not strictly work in the digital media industries that have developed in conjunction with the changes of post-Fordism which is informing the framework of this book. Such work may be reshaped by digitization – which includes exposure to new dangerous chemicals required for digital systems or be intensified due to an increase in demand – but it is not part of the industry per se; arguably, the work would continue in the same form without digital technologies. This is perhaps the most unfortunate and difficult exclusion to make as the appalling labor conditions for these workers deserve a good deal more attention. Their labor contexts, though, are quite distinct from what is captured in the definition we are mobilizing and so they are removed from consideration.

It is difficult to distil this discussion into a single, coherent, defining sentence of how I will use "digital labor" for the rest of this book without reducing some of the complexity that has required this extended explanation. However, it still seems essential to propose a clear working framework to inform the discussion in what follows. And so, with full knowledge that each of these words requires the clarification that precedes this sentence, I will define digital labor as *the work of users, platform-mediated workers, and formal employees that generates value within the digital media industries.*

Critical frames

Thus far, though, we have only satisfied one of the concerns raised by Gandini. I have described the scope of the study but not yet stipulated the critical frameworks I will use to identify and interpret the salient qualities of digital labor. For me, the only obvious choice is to draw on Marxist – or Marxian – frameworks. There has been a resurgence of interest in Marxist approaches to the economy and these have been a dominant feature of existing studies of digital labor (Fuchs 2014b). Marx's thinking provides a powerful – and still salient – critique of labor under capitalism, not merely as an activity but as a suite of inequitable social relations. His understanding of capitalist dynamics – and the refinements and extensions of that thinking by various scholars – has provided a set of orienting concepts that point to the important qualities that define work in capitalist economies. This book will therefore draw on some of Marx's key critical concepts to pull out what is important to know about digital labor. It will look at dynamics of how labor is *exploited* for profit, how work *processes* are organized to maximize the extraction of value, the *alienation* that is caused by work's exploitation, and how subjectivity itself subsequently becomes a *commodity*. But, as an historical materialist approach advocates, it will also focus on workers' *struggle* as this drives the ever-changing form of capitalism.

The discussion in this book, though, is also shaped by feminist principles which demand that any study of labor focus not only on that work which is defined as productive or directly generative of value. To do so assumes a fully formed worker who enters a work environment, labors, leaves, and returns the following day, remaining unchanged by events beyond, or even within, their workplace. However, decades of critical scholarship by feminist scholars such as Mariarosa Dalla Costa, Selma James, Leopoldina Fortunati, Angela Davis, and Silvia Federici argue for the importance of also considering the dynamics of the reproductive sphere in order to understand how that worker is produced and reproduced as a worker. This is not only about drawing attention to the unpaid, domestic, and volunteer labor that allows capitalism to function – although that is important. It is also about understanding workers as products of ongoing social processes and interrelationships that happen in and outside the formal work context and interrogating how that shapes the form of capitalist enterprise.

Informed by this perspective, this study will also draw on social reproduction theory (SRT) which, despite the name, is really a methodology for its application defines the object of study. It is, as Tithi Bhattacharya (2017: 2) notes, an approach "that is not content to accept what seems like a visible, finished entity – in this case, our worker at the gates of her workplace – but interrogates the complex network of social processes and human relations that produce the conditions of existence for that entity." SRT views workers as unfixed and in a state of becoming and suggests that if we are to understand their labor, we also need to explore more messy dimensions of selfhood and self-making. This takes us beyond moments of commodity production where labor is producing goods or services that are sold in the marketplace to other places where other activity produces self, subjectivities, and bodies that sustain and support capital. The analysis that is to come will be inflected by this feminist Marxist framework and so will consider various cultural formations that are formally not work but are part of the constitution of digital labor and the digital laborer.

Bringing orthodox Marxism and SRT together, each chapter will draw on a key concept in Marx's critique of capitalism, inflected by SRT, to identify and critically interrogate the nature of the social relationships associated with digital labor. It will then identify manifestations of these dynamics within each of the three subcategories of digital labor being examined in this book. The goal, though, is to look for commonalities that span across the various types of activity in order to provide critical insight into the holistic object "digital labor." This is not a direct application of Marxist economics to digital labor and is not intended to provide a detailed exploration of its theoretical paradigms – I direct your attention to the various works of Christian Fuchs (e.g. 2008, 2014b; Fuchs and Sevignani 2013) for that kind of analysis. It is instead a heterodox critical approach to the topic, using the lens provided by Marxist thought to illuminate specific digital labor dynamics. On the way, it will critique, extend, and sometimes refine the key Marxian concepts it draws on to render them more appropriate or useful for understanding the dynamics of an emerging form of work shaped by forces that Marx was unable to predict.

About this book

But first a caveat: this book does not contain primary research. The data for this critique are instead drawn from a wide-ranging survey of existing scholarship on the digital economy, digital labor, social media, media economics, and surveillance processes, and include examples from a variety of national contexts. As already noted, another key source is business press and corporate memoirs which provide very useful insights into labor within the GAFAM/BAT companies and startups which are often difficult for scholars to access. Given the breadth of the definition of digital labor used here, a significant range of source materials and academic studies have been synthesized in this analysis – my groaning bookshelves are testimony to this. Accordingly, there is a large amount of citation throughout, but this has been consciously included so that the reference list can serve as valuable resource for further research. The scope of the sources has, unfortunately, been limited by my shameful monolingualism, but I have taken care to seek studies that range beyond the usual suspects of the North American giants. Labor practices and the digital economy function very differently – but also in ways that are alarmingly similar – in different jurisdictions, and some of this diversity needs to be captured. Despite its range, though, this book does not claim to be a comprehensive survey, not least as the field is flourishing and it is impossible to keep up with the large number of publications that emerged even in the year it took to write this book. There will, necessarily, be omissions and the analysis can only ever be partial. It is, however, an extensive overview of key approaches and findings across the range of labor forms.

Chapter 2 takes on the question of labor economics and maps the various ways the exploitation of workers manifests in digital labor environments. In particular, it draws on the association of digital labor with a state of precarity or instability not merely to indicate *that* such work is exploitative but explore how this exploitation is typified by income insecurity, entangled with job and employment insecurity. It examines the chronic under-compensation of the sector – including aspects of wage theft and extended unpaid working hours – but also considers how work being apportioned through algorithms and unilateral policies has implications for workers' incomes. It makes the case for understanding such work – even in its elite forms – as cheap labor, locating it in the social imaginary of Asian labor as interpreted by Minh-Ha Pham (2015).

The next chapter – focused on management of the labor process – picks up the thread of job and labor insecurity again to explore the organization and management of work and how that has far-reaching impacts on the experiences of digital labor. It describes how the informality that pertains in the sector in a variety of ways establishes a degree – or at least a sense – of autonomy and agency for workers. This, however, is offset with enhanced control mechanisms that diminish that autonomy, creating a dynamic of cruel optimism (Berlant 2011) that produces workers' ongoing consent to their exploitation.

The optimism of digital labor is picked up again in the fourth chapter – "Alienation" – which explores the promise of dis-alienated work in the digital media industries. However, rather than seek to prove or disprove the existence of such a dynamic, it instead examines how widespread cultural and social discourses about "good work" put a premium on the kinds of entrepreneurial dynamics seen across digital labor forms. Drawing on the work of Luc Boltanski, Laurent Thévenot, and Eve Chiapello (Boltanski and Chiapello 2005a, 2005b; Boltanski and Thévenot 2006 [1991]) on the spirit of capitalism, Colin Campbell (1987) on the Romantic ethic, and Adam Arvidsson (2019) on "industrious capitalism," it examines the normalization and valorization of hustle within the digital media industries and society as a whole. In contrast to the previous two chapters which describe a variety of iniquities and assumptions about the exploitative nature of work, this chapter posits that digital labor is, in fact, desirable and pleasurable.

The next chapter also challenges an orthodox Marxist reading – this time of the idea of commodification. It explores how digital labor involves exploitation of the whole of the self – from the intellect to embodied performance to affective states. Using the concept of "human capital," it documents the different ways value is drawn from those aspects of self typically considered inalienable or outside capitalism. It links these processes to the feminization of the economy and the increased demand for reflexivity in the workplace. However, rather than lament such incorporation as the commodification of subjectivity in the service of capitalism, it proposes interpreting this as a process of assetization as described by Michel Feher (2018). It thus offers a re-reading of the exploitative dynamics of digital labor through a more agential lens.

The final chapter engages again with agency and is focused on workers' resistance to the inequalities and exploitation within their labor contexts. It describes the variety of forms such struggle is taking as the digital media industry matures and increasingly formalizes. It explores the challenges of formal worker organization but notes that this is nevertheless growing, documenting a range of industrial actions and expanding unionization. However, it also pays positive attention to more individualized acts of resistance that lack the scope of formal organization and its class consciousness but which nevertheless speak to worker agency. Moreover, it also suggests the importance of such tactical resistances for the kinds of assetized workers found in digital labor.

The concepts examined in each of these core chapters are quite entangled. It is difficult, for instance, to clearly separate the dynamics of how labor is exploited for profit from how work is arranged. The sense of autonomy that workers experience in their labor processes is difficult to clearly differentiate from the entrepreneurial self-actualization that drives the digital economy. It has been a challenge to create false distinctions that allow these aspects of work to be discussed separately and to keep the chapters contained and cogent. This means there are echoes and correspondences between chapters and the same instances of digital labor are sometimes interpreted from different angles to provide multiple insights. But the unclear demarcation between the chapters is also valuable as it allows them to nest together, building a holistic picture of digital labor.

The central argument of this book, though, has application beyond the confines of the digital media industries and the particular kinds of work explored there. Throughout the analysis, there is a series of arguments drawing links between the characteristics of digital labor and racialized, gendered, and sexed modes of work that have historically been pushed to the fringes of the formal economy. The conclusion brings these threads together but also pans out from the specificity of this work to explore what these dynamics can tell us about contemporary capitalism more generally. It returns to the designation of digital labor as cheap, to the connection between the assetized worker's reflexivity and gender performance, and the social history of industrious hustle to place digital labor within a longer history of marginalized work and workers. It concludes by asking questions about what happens when the edge cases of labor relations become the center, but also what this means for how we can understand contemporary capitalism. It suggests the need to inflect our critical analysis so that it fully appreciates the features of the economy that digital labor reveals.

Ultimately, the conclusion of this book will pose more questions than it can answer – or that can be answered at this nascent stage of digital capitalism. It will, however, provide a useful picture of what digital labor is today and open up some tantalizing and perhaps challenging questions about the nature of a mode of accumulation that centers work within the digital economy.

2

Exploitation: Digital Deeds Done Dirt Cheap

It is very tempting to make a chapter titled "exploitation" a list of examples of profiteering or wage theft by digital media companies. Such stories are, unfortunately, plentiful. Outsourced contract warehouse workers at Amazon receive fewer benefits than full-time, permanent employees doing the same work (Jamieson 2015). Dynamic pricing systems leave Australian food delivery cyclists underpaid by up to AU$322 per week (Karp 2019). The *Huffington Post* was bought out by AOL for US$315 million but failed to distribute any of this money to its unpaid contributors (Kirchner 2011). Google has systematically been underpaying temporary workers in Europe, Asia, and the United Kingdom (Wong 2021). However, from a strict Marxist perspective, it would be the height of banality to offer these examples and conclude that digital labor is exploitative. To make this chapter about that conclusion would not actually advance our thinking beyond pointing out that digital labor occurs in a capitalist context.

According to Marx's labor theory of value, exploitation occurs whenever a worker produces more value than they receive as compensation for their labor whenever a capitalist employer generates surplus from a worker's activity. This is the basic relationship of capitalism. The logic goes as follows: a widget maker is hired for an eight-hour day at a rate of €10/hour. They are able to create 10 widgets in the course of the average day which are then sold by their employer for €12 each, generating a total revenue of €120. The worker, though, is only being compensated €80 of that revenue, meaning that the remaining €40 is surplus value retained by the employer.

This can also be presented in terms of labor-time. To produce value to the equivalent of their salary, the widget maker only needs to work for just over 6.5 hours a day. However, they work for eight hours, meaning there is an hour and a half of work each day for which they are not compensated; work undertaken during this time is, effectively, unpaid labor. The existence of such unpaid work is what constitutes an exploitative labor relationship. Exploitation of workers is thus one of the foundations of value creation in the regime of accumulation that is capitalism – see *Grundrisse* (Marx 1993 [1939]) for more explanation of this economic concept. Consequently, it would not be surprising to document the economic relations of the digital media industries and find that digital labor is exploitative because all waged labor under capitalism is exploited.

However, there are important questions about whether the framework of exploitation as understood via this labor theory of value applies to all forms of work under consideration here. Not all digital laborers are, formally, waged workers, and so their labor is not able to be interpreted this way. As we will discuss further in the next chapter, there are three main forms of contractual relation between digital laborer and employer across the forms of work under consideration in this book. The first takes the base form of traditional waged labor, which may be linked to an hourly rate or annual salary. This form is commonly experienced by elite, full-time industry professionals as well as some lower-status formal workers. Yet these contracts sometimes reflect non-standard labor relations such as the offsetting of salary into share options. This practice also makes these workers investors in a firm, rather than merely employees, complicating their relationship to value creation. The second form of labor contract in fact has no contract and is the unpaid work associated with users which is typically undertaken during leisure time. While I argue this *is* exploited labor, this status is contentious because of its uncontracted and uncoerced nature

– something we will discuss further below. The third form is self-employment, such as that associated with freelance creative workers, startup entrepreneurs, or platform workers where they are not hired as employees despite experiencing many aspects of a standard employment relationship (see chapter 6). In all three instances, we are looking at some level of self-employment or self-exploitation – where the extraction of surplus is not undertaken directly by an employer – which means that the strict application of the labor theory of value becomes complicated.

Also, the term "exploitation" is often used beyond the formal, structural definition associated with this theory. It is regularly invoked normatively to describe the degree to which surplus value is extracted and/or the cruel, coercive, or cynical conditions through which this extraction occurs. Analyses of exploitation are often focused on describing unfairness and brutality in the work regime under question and speak to the suffering of workers. A useful illustration is in the long-running debate about whether user activity on social media platforms can be understood as exploited labor. In querying this association, Hesmondhalgh (2010: 271) asks "are we really meant to see people who sit at their computers modifying code or typing out responses to TV shows as 'exploited' in the same way as those who endure appalling conditions and pay in Indonesian sweatshops?" Here he equates exploitation with degradation within the workplace, rather than referring to a structural relationship to surplus value creation. This discursive slippage of the term complicates whether it is feasible to describe all the work we are examining as exploitative. While Deliveroo riders like Thiago Cortes, whose untimely death at work begins this book, most certainly qualify to be described as exploited workers, it is less easy to reconcile other digital labors – such as Silicon Valley's young programmers playing foosball in their hip open-plan office and the unpaid users of QQ chatting with each other from their sofas – with this understanding of exploitation.

However, if we shift the central framework of this exploration of digital media labor economics from questions of exploitation to questions of income instability and the precarious labor position that creates, it is possible to combine these two perspectives and develop a more meaningful understanding of what digital labor looks like. Labor insecurity is related to the structural economic relations of work but also to degraded material and psychic conditions for workers; it reflects both the formal and normative definitions of exploitation. I suggest that, rather than trying to understand whether digital labor is exploitative, it is more valuable to consider the various mechanisms through which incomes are made unstable and uncertain by the systems of value generation in the sector. This brings attention to where and how digital labor is made precarious as both cause and effect of the exploitative machinery of the digital media industries. By moving us away from the fiscal accounting of the labor theory of value, this perspective allows us to develop a richer understanding of the qualities of exploitation, even in the contexts of self-employment.

This chapter will thus consider the relationship between precarity and digital labor in more detail before mapping the chronic under-compensation that manifests within the kinds of work under consideration here. It will also consider how this income insecurity is entangled with job insecurity and how these dynamics feature in digital labor. Through this, the chapter will map an exploitative regime that, using a framework from Minh-Ha Pham (2015), imagines digital labor as "cheap." In approaching the topic through the lens of precarity, this chapter does begin on the side of criticism, failing to adequately explore those instances where digital labor – particularly in the form of platform labor – offers opportunities and raises incomes for workers. It also doesn't adequately engage with the high salaries of some formal workers in the tech sector, although as we will see high or better incomes do not insulate workers from the dynamics of instability associated with precarious labor. Some of the desirable aspects of this work are discussed later in the book – particularly in chapter 4 – but for now the focus is on those mechanisms through which surplus value is generated, bringing attention to the tendency toward undercompensation and precarious conditions.

Precarity and digital labor

Central to the changes wrought by post-Fordist and neoliberal economic policies for workers is increased *precarity* or the condition where instability is so normalized it becomes the basic state: the condition of "stable instability" (Heidelkamp and Kergel 2017). The demand for flexibility in the organization of work, the decline of unions, and the collapse of the industrial compact that promised secure, full-time employment over the latter half of the twentieth century have eroded security for workers. The condition of precarity thus relates to wages that are not secure but also to work contracts and conditions that are moveable and uncertain. Guy Standing (2016; Kalleberg and Vallas 2018; Lorey 2015) takes this further, drawing on the increasing insecurity of social welfare and a generalized pervasive sense of insecurity that typifies neoliberal societies to describe instability as a broadly experienced social malaise. He contends that this experience of precarity is so widespread that it is the foundation of a new class formation: the "precariat." As the exemplary form of labor in the post-Fordist economy, digital labor is fundamentally tied to the emergence of the precariat.

As Greig de Peuter (2011) reminds us, the precariat is found in three distinct forms across information-intensive industries such as the digital media sector. Emerging out of Ursula Huws's (2003) important foundational analysis of digital labor, the first form – the "cybertariat" – refers to a class of workers whose work has been reorganized so that networked capital can exploit their (immaterial) labor and generate value from the impermanence of their employment. It includes the exploitation of unpaid work such as that provided by the users of digital platforms. The second group is comprised of autonomous workers which, as the name suggests, is a concept associated with autonomist Marxism. For this worker, work is marked by flexibility, which may be undertaken for reasons of self-determination but may also align it with responsibilization and the devolution of risk to individuals that has marked neoliberal capitalism. In this group, we find the platform workers involved in various forms of self-actualizing or self-exploiting employment. The third form is labelled the "precog," which is a term de Peuter borrows from an Italian activist collective and applies to the "nonstandard cognitive worker [who] might have a prestigious occupation but labors under classic precarious conditions" (2011: 420). These are the formally employed workers driven into freelancing or contracted work. Like Standing, de Peuter is talking about a broad class formation, but if we look more closely at the work of these different types of workers, his triptych usefully ties together three kinds of labor formations being discussed within this book – unpaid work, gig work for digital platforms, and the formal labor of digital media industry professionals. The connection between digital labor and precarity is profound.

Standing offers a broad definition of precarity. It is, he says,

> not just a matter of having insecure employment, of being in jobs of limited duration and with minimal labour protection, although all this is widespread. It is being in a status that offers no sense of career, no sense of secure occupational identity and few, if any, entitlements to the state and enterprise benefits that several generations of those who saw themselves as belonging to the industrial proletariat or the salariat had come to expect as their due. (Standing 2016: 27–8)

He goes on to identify various forms of labor security that were available during the period of "industrial citizenship" after World War II, but which have since been eroded to create the conditions of precarity. He lists the following:

> labor market security – adequate income-earning opportunities within a society;
> employment security – workplace protections against unfair dismissal and hiring practices;
> work security – protections that create workplace safety;
> skill reproduction security – opportunities for skill development;
> representation security – the capacity to have a collective voice;
> job security – the ability to retain a secure position with opportunities for upward mobility;
> income security – the assurance of a stable income.

Through income insecurity, precarity is directly linked to questions of how labor is exploited at a structural level, but in its various other dimensions it creates the kinds of negative working conditions associated with the qualitative definitions of exploitation. All these dimensions are interconnected with the stability of a worker's income, but wages are most obviously entangled with job and employment security; when jobs are not protected, pay is necessarily impacted. Consequently, examining the ways in which incomes are rendered insecure in digital labor working environments, along with some mechanisms through which job insecurity is tied to this uncertainty, will show not *that* labor is exploited but what forms this takes.

Working for free

One of the key trends within the global economy is an increasing use of unpaid labor to directly generate value, and this is at the core of the exploitative dynamics associated with digital labor. Capitalism is marked by competitive relations between firms which increases pressure to generate higher rates of profit – to increase their take of surplus value – without increasing costs to consumers. This is most often achieved by increasing productivity (the number of widgets produced in eight hours), typically through technological change, or by reducing labor costs (increasing the length of the working day). As described in the introduction, responses to economic crisis within firms – first, the 1970s stagflation crisis and, more recently, the 2008 global economic crash – have placed a particular emphasis on using non-standard and contingent labor contracts to reduce costs and increase profit. In digital media environments, some of the increase in profitability has happened through reducing salaries by moving staff to unfixed and less well-remunerated contracts with fewer benefits, but also through the bleeding of surplus value extraction mechanisms into formally uncontracted work time.

While capitalism has long saturated the lifeworld and indirectly exploited labor that formally sits outside the realm of work (Jarrett 2017, 2018; see also ch. 5 below), the rise of economies rooted in culture and knowledge production has arguably increased the direct exploitation of such work. This is most obvious in the use of user labor to create content for digital platforms. From the user-generated content of sites such as YouTube or TikTok, the peer ratings on sites such as eBay and reddit, and the work involved in managing and sustaining social bonds on various social network sites, users are key providers of the material that draws people to these platforms, engages their interests, and sustains their involvement. Not only are users doing voluntaristic, uncompensated work by populating these sites with content for free, by building affective and social bonds through them they are also making them "sticky" for themselves and other users. This stickiness is important for sustaining user traffic but also key to the brand value of the platform itself. This can then be leveraged on financial markets or in the ongoing hunt for venture capital. The time users spend being social on many platforms is thus a form of surplus creation and, so, unpaid work. The economic value of this unpaid labor was made stark in October 2021 when a 7.5-hour outage at Facebook – which took down Facebook, Messenger, WhatsApp, and Instagram globally – was estimated to have cost the company US$99.75 million in revenue (Morris 2021).

A more contentious proposition is that users are also engaged in unpaid labor when these same unpaid activities are mined for data, aggregated into meaningful marketing formats, and either sold to other firms or used directly to generate advertising opportunities. In an industry driven by advertising revenue, data on users' consumption habits, leisure interests, or political leanings are extremely valuable commodities. Christian Fuchs (2014a, 2014b) has been the strongest advocate of the conceptualization of users as exploited when their activity is reconstituted as marketing data. His argument draws on Dallas Smythe's (2014 [1977]) famous description of the audience commodity in broadcast contexts. For Smythe, the most valuable product of the television industry is not programming. TV series, he argued, serve as merely a lure for attracting audiences whose viewing activity is captured as ratings data. This renders those audiences the product of the television industry that actually has value in the advertising marketplace. Sut Jhally and Bill Livant (1986) finesse this argument, claiming that audience activity is labor "bought" as watching time by the broadcaster for the nominal "wage" of media content, emphasizing that watching is a form of value-creating labor as they do so.

This same dynamic of extracting value from audiences and attention has been replicated across the digital media industries, with (typically) free access to content and platforms offered to attract and compensate users for the exploitation of their data and to enable their exposure to advertising. In interactive, digitized environments, though, the ability to capture audience data, to generate more targeted – and thus potentially more valuable – advertising, or to collate audience tastes into marketing insights becomes immediate and highly detailed. Fuchs argues that not only does the capturing of audience labor seen in television also occur in digital media, but that it is extended through the totalizing capture enabled by digital systems. He says: "[a]ll hours spent online by users of Facebook, Google and comparable corporate social media constitute work time, in which data commodities are generated, and potential time for profit realization. The maximum time of a single user that is productive (i.e. results in data commodities) is 100% of the time spent online" (Fuchs 2014a: 115).

There is a vast array of arguments against defining this form of value creation as labor – for instance, many insist that it is a process of rent extraction or that value is created by others in the value chain – and I won't rehearse these arguments here (see Jarrett 2016a for a summary and argument for defining the exploitation of user data as labor). However, if it is accepted that all users' everyday engagement with digital media that are capturable by the platform is labor, then the implications are significant. The saturation of digital media platforms with mechanisms for data capture and the penetration of these systems into formal working lives *and* our social lives mean we are constantly producing value for digital media platforms. In the absence of any formal compensation, this constitutes digital media users as deeply exploited workers.

But unpaid work is also a feature of other kinds of digital labor. The most alarming version is direct wage theft which is all too common in task-related platform work. Non-payment of cancellation fees and inaccurate payments that do not reflect the jobs taken have both been reported by Uber and Deliveroo workers (Cant 2020; Rosenblat 2018). Online task workers may also complete a job as assigned by a platform like Fiverr but find the payment is not forthcoming as the client rejects the product (Berg et al. 2018). In these circumstances, the worker rather than the platform is asked to absorb the sunk costs of time, energy, and material resources that have gone into producing the rejected work. *Gonghui* multichannel networks have been noted as taking the vast majority of the income generated through tipping by the *zhubos* or live-streamers they manage (Craig, Lin, and Cunningham 2021: 126–7), and many influencers report struggling to receive payments from both clients and management companies, with some having to take court cases to get paid. Platform workers may also be summarily locked out of their accounts, suspended, or banned from the platform, for transgressing opaque rules or through technical glitches, typically losing any income that may have been accrued there (Blunt et al. 2020; Gray and Suri 2019).

But there are more subtle ways that unpaid work is exploited in the digital media industries. Internships are a widespread corporate trend often supported directly by government policies in education and welfare. They also have particular purchase in the digital media industries in both creative and technical fields (Corrigan 2015; Xia 2019) and may involve either unpaid roles or pay at substantially lower rates than that offered permanent employees. In *Intern Nation* (2012), Ross Perlin describes the growing normative pressure on young people to work without pay, either as part of their programs of study or in supposed apprenticeships or skills development programs within white-collar professions. Accurate data are difficult to come by, but Perlin estimated that in the United States in the 2010s between one and two million people annually were undertaking internships. Sixty-two percent of the graduating class of 2017 in the same country reported doing an internship during their college degree. Only 17 percent reported the same in 1992 (Waxman 2018). In China, internships are an extremely common – and sometimes coerced – feature of undergraduate and postgraduate education (Xia 2019). Internships have alternately been seen as positive experiences for both the worker and business and as sites for egregious exploitation of a vulnerable workforce, riddled with inequalities, and rarely manifesting the workplace learning and career opportunities they boast (Frenette 2013).

There are also a range of informal working practices within digital labor environments that mimic the experience of internships in that they are about gaining industry experience and contributing unpaid labor, although they are not formally defined as such. Creative professionals have long worked without compensation with a view to establishing themselves within a field and generating a range of experience and outputs that they can showcase to future employers, funding bodies, or clients. Such future-oriented, unpaid work is what Kathleen Kuehn and Thomas Corrigan (2013: 10) refer to as "hope labor"; the "un- or under-compensated work carried out in the present, often for experience or exposure, in the hope that future employment opportunities may follow."

Such activity is common in the digital media creative sector where breaking into elite industries can be difficult but also where there are particular pressures to be proven before you are able to secure employment. Producing online magazine articles for "exposure," generating hours of video on YouTube in the hope of securing a following and subsequently advertising revenues and brand deals, and taking up unpaid internships in the games industry to increase your personal networks are all mechanisms by which unpaid work is exploited. With its orientation toward future gain as opposed to being merely for fun, such work differs from other forms of unpaid user labor, but these boundaries are particularly porous. Because of affective investment in the practice, craft, or outcomes, creative labor that can be monetized (either by the worker or the platform) can be simultaneously play and labor. As the title of Brooke Duffy's (2017) book on beauty bloggers says, workers are (not) getting paid to do what they love. With the growing extraction of value from these kinds of formally unpaid work, there is arguably a race to the bottom for wages in digital media industries.

Linking internships to user labor and to other exploitation of unwaged work, Andrew Ross (2013: 25) argues that today there is a widespread consensus about what constitutes fair waged labor, with people able to recognize the inequities of sweatshops, for instance. He adds, though, that we still have "very few yardsticks for judging fairness in the salaried or freelancing sectors of the new, deregulated jobs economy, where any effort to draw a crisp line around work and pay (not to mention work and play) seems to be increasingly ineffectual."

Going above and beyond

Even in formally paid contexts, under-compensation through exploitation of unpaid time is a theme of digital labor. Workers within digital industries are typically required to take on work outside their officially contracted hours. In the games industry, for instance, such extensions happen during the notorious "crunch time" when a product is due for completion. Game workers – and famously their families (Bulut 2020; EA spouse 2004) – report working grueling, long hours during these common, high-pressure periods in the production cycle of the industry. Beyond these specific moments, cultures of overwork – tied to questions of passion, dedication, or corporate fit – are also common in the games sector. Commitment to the craft of game development is often flagged through being willing to stay at work after formal closing (Bulut 2020; see also ch. 5 below). The highly competitive employment context of many high-tech companies also encourages extended overtime as evidence of commitment (Xia 2014). Flexible working schedules within digital labor professions foster this holistic absorption into work. The supply of food, laundry, and other perks in elite digital workplaces encourages the extension of the time spent working, extending the working day and increasing the amount of surplus value that is able to be extracted from workers' labor. Sometimes this strategy is overt: in 2006, Mark Zuckerberg announced a US$600 a month subsidy to Facebook employees who lived within a mile of the office and thus were able to be on call at any time.

The uncompensated extension of the working day is also a particular feature of work for freelance, short-term contract, and platform workers. Various studies of influencers and YouTubers show the significant amount of preparation from scouting locations to building sets to perfecting skills in performance and equipment use that is required for each post. Hours, even days, of planning, preparation, and rehearsal can go into creating content for a short piece – such as a 60-second TikTok video – much of which is not recouped from monetization strategies (Bucher and Shannon 2020; Cunningham and Craig 2019; Duffy 2017; Pham 2015). The time sunk into developing their craft is typically not factored into the already meagre incomes many workers generate in these sectors. For these and other self-employed or contract workers, their working day is also extended through the need to constantly re-skill and/or update knowledge during their private time and at their own expense. For those in the constantly changing digital media environment, where programming languages, platform settings, and device parameters are constantly shifting, keeping up to date can be very costly (Kotamraju 2002; Neff, Wissinger, and Zukin 2005). These are skill reproduction expenses that might once have fallen under the remit of the employer and be accounted for during paid working hours. Now these costs fall to the worker. For freelance or self-employed digital laborers, it is also not only the cost of the education that they must bear but also the time such training takes away from potential paid work time.

The working day is also extended into leisure time in many paid digital labor contexts. For many freelance or entrepreneurial digital laborers, employment often follows informal social networks or emerges from interactions with clients in otherwise non-work hours of the day. As in various cultural industries where moving from gig to gig through word of mouth recommendations has a long history, in many digital industries a premium is placed on building and maintaining social relationships outside and inside work. As Neff and colleagues (2005: 321) say: "A fluid boundary between work-time and playtime is shaped by compulsory 'schmoozing,' 'face-time' or socializing within the industry after the workday." In some emerging and small-scale industry contexts, such as the sub-Saharan digital entrepreneurial environment described by Friederici, Wahome, and Graham (2020: 100), "painstaking and time-intensive" relationship building is also necessary to secure funding, build and sustain a client base, or to support a product. Whether through face-to-face industry events, personal meetings, or carefully curated social media profiles, networking becomes a requirement which extends the working day but also demands the adoption of a self-promotional stance to the world. Aspects of self, including interpersonal and affective relationships, become instrumentalized as part of work, even when not consciously conceived as such. As one of the interview subjects of Rosalind Gill's (2011) study of new media workers in Amsterdam noted, there was no outside of work for them: their whole life was a pitch. This enrolling of a worker's entire subjectivity into work dynamics is troubling and will be returned to and explored further in chapter 5. What it demonstrates for us now, though, is how the particular demands of digital labor, particularly in its creative modes and in its freelance structures, extend the actual working day beyond formally contracted hours. It is difficult to charge clients or add to your contract the time spent on managing your sense of self, so this remains uncompensated work.

Unpaid work also emerges from the competitive environment of digital labor. Gill describes "bulimic" work patterns – and therefore incomes – for freelance, contract, and platform workers. Such work is typified by periods of intense overwork, followed by fallow periods of underemployment. She also notes that many of the workers in her study consistently underquoted for their work. Pressures to secure gigs ahead of competitors, particularly when launching a career, as well as a common underestimation of the work required to create products of which they could be proud, often led to freelance digital media workers logging hours well beyond those for which they were contracted. Gill (2007: 17) notes: "Without an intervention such as fixed union rates for the job – as exist in the highly unionized film industry, for example – it might be expected that the freelancer who pitched at the appropriate level would simply not get the job. Interviewees were painfully aware of this." Platform workers who are able to set prices for their labor also experience this dynamic (Graham, Hjorth, and Lehdonvirta 2017). It is also notable that these pressures are gendered and raced. Gill's study recognizes the domination of the creative digital media sector by white workers and that women secured fewer contracts than their male counterparts, partly due to the ways in which informal networks create exclusions. These dynamics persist in a variety of digital labor environments, ranging from microwork to platform-mediated carework to influencer blogging to web design.

Wobbly wages

These demands for unpaid work are particularly pernicious in creative platform work where incomes are often dubious and unstable to begin with, particularly when they rely on advertising revenue. Low barriers to entry generate extraordinary levels of competition for the key source of revenue – partnerships and brand sponsorships. This dilution of the market has, in turn, reduced the value associated with audience share. On YouTube, for instance, AdSense revenue has collapsed over recent years, with the standard rate for a million views dropping from US$25 to US$2. This has created an industry in which only a few elite creators have YouTube as their single income source (Cunningham and Craig 2019). Substantial revenues may be generated through merchandising or licensing, but this avenue is typically only viable for well-established and famous players.

Another revenue stream for content creators is via crowdfunding, patronage, and subscription systems. A third option is through online tip jars. Various social media platforms, particularly those involving live-streaming such as Chaturbate or Inke, broker direct relationships between creators and fans, allowing followers to send tokens or gifts that can be redeemed as cash or goods (Hernandez 2019; Zou 2018). While not as common in "western" social media, such exchanges are well integrated into the Chinese social media economy and these streams provide an important element of platform workers' incomes (Craig, Lin, and Cunningham 2021). These systems, though, make income contingent and directly reliant upon sustaining the goodwill of audiences, fans, and followers. The "relational labor" (Baym 2018) required to satisfy individual audience members when working for patrons in this way can be time consuming and require a significant affective commitment from digital workers that may never be redeemed. Patronage models also come with high expectations from followers. This was the experience of singer-songwriter Amanda Palmer, who encountered hostility from Patreon subscribers after announcing her pregnancy not long after setting up her account. In an angry response to the singer, one fan asked: "Are your patrons paying for new music, or are they paying for a new baby?" (Palmer 2015). At the mercy of potentially unreasonable follower demands, viable incomes for creative digital laborers can be difficult to generate and sustain consistently (Bonifacio, Hair, and Wohn 2021).

Digital laborer incomes are also rendered fundamentally unstable by non-human actors such as algorithms – although it must be noted that algorithms are created by corporate policy and human agents and so reflect the designs and goals of the company. The use of automated and computerized management systems for managing, allocating, and rewarding workers is a particular feature of the platform economy. While some platform workers, such as Meituan delivery riders, are provided with a base salary, for most workers a significant part of their income depends on ever-changing rates for individual work actions such as a successful delivery, customer journey, or completed task. These rates are often dynamic, shifting over time and between jobs, and are dependent on complex calculations of competition, organizational policies, and market elasticity, all of which are encoded into platform algorithms. Alex Rosenblat (2018) offers valuable insight into the impacts of these algorithmically actualized rules for North American Uber drivers. An "algorithmic manager" enacts company policies, such as the changing pay rates, controls dispatch, and measures and assesses drivers' compliance with Uber's suggested behavior. The app also enacts penalties, such as the withholding of tips or jobs, and is instrumental in determining when a driver's account will be deactivated. Driver incomes – which are already unstable as demand and growing competition within the driver pool cause trip rates to fluctuate – are also dependent on satisfying the dictates of the app. These technologies function as black boxes, with neither client nor worker typically knowledgeable of, or able to intervene in, the automated decisions that manage their economic exchanges. In this opacity, actual incomes become impossible to predict.

Similarly, the wages of freelance and pro–am creators involved in producing monetized content for platforms such as YouTube, Instagram, or Twitch are determined by audience traffic flows. Consequently, they are susceptible to the ways algorithms and system settings make their content visible and thus able to capture views or engagements. This puts these workers' incomes at the mercy of the automated dynamics of the host platform. They must be perpetually guessing the logics that animate the system and constantly adapting and calibrating their performance, content, and marketing tactics to fit with its imposed dictates (Cotter 2019; Duffy 2017; Gillespie 2014). Sophie Bishop (2019a: 21) puts it succinctly: "To be a successful vlogger (video blogger) on YouTube, one must make oneself legible to the site's algorithms." Failure to be promoted to viewers or to prospective advertisers can be fatal to YouTuber or influencer income streams but because these all-important algorithmic rules are not transparent, digital laborers toil in constant, murky flux. As Duffy and colleagues (2021) argue, the precarity of their visibility makes online creative work particularly uncertain.

Platform workers and creative content producers are also at the mercy of unilateral changes to organizational policies that can reduce incomes or end someone's employment in the field. Sometimes this is driven by shifting legal contexts, such as the 2018 FOSTA-SESTA laws which made platforms liable for sexual content or the Chinese government's increasing regulation of content (Craig et al. 2021). At other times, it is more an effect of direct economic concerns, such as the need to placate advertisers. Whatever the reason, any amendments to the visibility or appropriate labelling of content can have a significant impact on the incomes of workers. Illegibility to the algorithms or the socio-technical policies of the site can trigger the flagging and removal of content, either by automated systems or human actors, removal of advertising partnership options for the content or the site (demonetization), user banishment, or the insidious practice of shadowbanning, in which content remains published – it is not formally censored or removed – but is not rendered easily visible to users (Are 2021).

Platforms can also unilaterally alter compensation rates and change conditions, a practice for which ride-sharing and delivery platforms are notorious. Uber is a regular offender. When it enters a new market, driving for Uber is typically a good employment option. The platform pays relatively high rates to encourage a critical mass of drivers as part of a strategy to create a quasi-monopoly. However, as drivers in Kenya found too late, the conditions under which they work can change dramatically. After a few years in the country, and facing new competition from a rival firm, Uber reduced its fares by 35 percent, increased the number of drivers by changing entry requirements, and set up fare options that further increased competition among drivers. This left many drivers with large debts from their initial investment in vehicles and with inadequate income to service those obligations and/or provide living expenses (Sperber 2020). This pattern has been repeated in a number of nations or cities in which Uber has sought to generate a presence, with declining incomes a feature of work in this sector.

A prominent example of such instability is YouTube's "adpocalypse," which was both a change in algorithmic systems and a policy change that severely impacted incomes for many digital laborers. In 2017, a range of companies became outraged about the inclusion of advertisements for their products next to objectionable, violent, or sexual content on social media. Demanding guarantees that the platform was safe for their brand, almost 250 large multinational companies, like AT&T and Proctor and Gamble, threatened a boycott of YouTube and other sites. YouTube's parent company Google acknowledged the issue and responded by enabling more conservative advertising settings but also, and most importantly for our narrative, excluding certain kinds of content from its advertising revenue models. The changes implemented by Google increased content moderation, allowed advertisers to exclude certain kinds of content more readily, made it more difficult for creators to enter the YouTube Partner Program (YPP), and used filters to demonetize content and channels that it did not deem "advertiser friendly." The introduction of these unilaterally imposed changes was devastating for some YouTubers; some creators reported over 90 percent losses in revenue (Caplan and

Gillespie 2020; Cunningham and Craig 2019; Hill 2019). The new eligibility criteria for the YPP – 1,000 subscribers and 4,000 hours of watch-time over the previous year – also made it almost impossible for small-scale channels or amateurs to monetize their content. It demanded a much longer time commitment before revenue generation was possible, leaving amateur creators to absorb the costs of production equipment, skills development, and work time for much longer (Kumar 2019). For many, this bar was simply too high and they were forced to exit the platform, taking with them the sunk costs of developing their brand and their follower base. At risk of losing profit by losing advertisers, YouTube/Google sacrificed its ordinary users, their cultural expression, and their income and job stability.

Importantly, the impact of these algorithmic and policy exclusions is not distributed evenly. The inequalities that unfairly direct financial rewards to white, cis, heteronormative, able-bodied people persist in the online creative world. The sanitization of content that occurred during the adpocalypse was based on conservative principles – particularly around sex, sexuality, and politics – that effectively targeted fringe communities and creators. The introduction of a tiered system of monetization privileges also made it more difficult for members of smaller, marginalized communities to be considered for inclusion within the YPP as they were less likely to reach the eligibility thresholds (Cunningham and Craig 2019; Kumar 2019). Trans, queer, and sex-positive YouTubers – along with YouTubers of color – have all reported challenges in generating revenue via the platform (Bishop 2021; Caplan and Gillespie 2020; Cunningham and Craig 2019). For many marginalized creators, their existing income instability is routinely compounded by algorithmic and policy interventions to the extent that it intensifies job insecurity.

Beyond YouTube, shadowbanning and demonetization processes have disproportionately impacted marginalized bodies and subjects on various platforms (Are and Paasonen

2021; Blunt et al. 2020; Carman 2020). African-American fashion blogs, for instance, are not listed highly in search results even when their online traffic is higher than their white counterparts (Carman 2020; Pham 2015: 23). As Francesca Sobande (2020: 83) describes, anyone whose existence "due to racism, sexism, homophobia, fatphobia, transphobia, and other types of intersecting oppressions, is often demonised and a source of moral panic" is disproportionately affected by these practices. Content engaging with non-normative practices and embodiments that are marked as "other," such as people with disabilities, plus-size models, sex workers, black women, sex and body positivity movements, and trans communities, are often censored or demonetized in an increasingly conservative commercial Web environment. Customer ratings systems that feed into employability and thus incomes for various platform workers also often reflect racist and sexist principles of the offline world. These workers are also more likely to encounter the types of online harassment and hate that can render working and generating audiences in online environments more difficult, if not impossible (Are 2020; Paasonen, Jarrett, and Light 2019; Siapera 2019). This is a cause for concern for its chilling effect on public discourse, for how it perpetuates exclusive, racist, homophobic, transphobic, and ableist ideologies, and for the psychic impact on the individual creators and their communities of practice. But it is also a problem for how it impacts the livelihoods of creative workers within these already economically marginalized communities.

Creative pivots

For elite digital workers in formal, full-time employment, income instability would not seem to be a concern. With secure, formally contracted work not directly tied to the whims of algorithms or user attention, the instabilities that bedevil freelance or platform workers do not appear to apply.

However, the common practice of offsetting a portion of salary into company shares introduces a significant degree of instability for those workers who undertake this gamble. In availing themselves of stock options and decoupling their immediate salary from their work time, they effectively bet their wages on the future success of the company (Adkins, Cooper, and Konings 2020: 46–7).

A reliance on stocks for income is a particularly risky strategy. The startup business model often depends on a successful initial public offering (IPO), or less ideally being acquired by a larger firm, to recoup money for shareholders. If a startup fails before going public, there is often little but debt and whatever can be raised from the sale of legacy technology to distribute among stakeholders, including workers. Alternately, a startup's IPO may fail to reach projected targets, at which time it is typically ordinary employees who take a higher proportion of that loss. Founders are typically able to sell personal shares at any time and so may have already accrued income from their investment prior to an IPO. Investors and venture capital companies are generally protected by various guarantees that ensure their initial investment is, at the very least, recovered in a less than stellar IPO. They are also protected from the impact of a single startup failure by virtue of a diverse portfolio of revenue-generating companies. This does not apply to most of the workers within the company though, especially if they were later hires during the startup phase. These workers are more likely to feel the full force of any corporate failure. In a lackluster IPO, they are typically some of the last to see benefits; if a startup fails to launch at all, they completely lose out. Moreover, with part of their salary sacrificed to stocks, and with these digital workers typically only able to activate their investment past particular time thresholds, they are usually unable to afford to leave an obviously failing company without incurring significant losses. Alternatively, for workers forced out of a successful company before an IPO, like Noah Kagan (2014: 97), who was fired from his role as product manager at Facebook in 2006, the worst thing can be "thinking of all the money I would never see." Having been employed for less than a year, none of the 20,000 shares he was offered in lieu of salary had vested and so he was left with no stake in the company. Writing in 2014, he calculates that at the current market valuation those shares would be worth US$170 million.

Not all startups become a mega-corporation like Facebook, however, and this produces another set of uncertainties for elite workers. Startup culture emphasizes creative destruction, risk taking and, in chasing the payoff of being bought out by a larger company or an IPO, a perpetual state of impermanence. This makes it a particularly volatile work environment and leads to income and job insecurity. Various studies – and a truism of the industry – suggest a failure rate of 90% for startups, with between 20% and 30% failing in the first year and about 60% by the third (Bryant 2020; Calvino, Criscuolo, and Menon 2015; Kepka 2020; Mahr 2020). A startup founder interviewed by Ben Tarnoff and Moira Weigel (2020) blames the high failure rate on market uncertainty caused by constant change both in technology and consumer demand. While big players in Silicon Valley might enable failure – the founder notes that everything he has worked on has failed but he has still been rewarded and promoted – for those working in small startups, the economic and emotional fallout from these collapses can be difficult to absorb. Even the successful founder in Tarnoff and Weigel's account recognizes the demoralizing effects of failure and its role in burnout for tech workers. Even in more established companies, overwork and a ruthlessly competitive environment create a "burn and churn" (Kantor and Streitfeld 2015) dynamic, considered a feature rather than a bug of the elite digital media industry. The promise of new opportunities in the ever-growing sector also creates flux in employment as elite workers readily exit of their own accord.

The instability in employment leads to income instability over the course of a career. This is partly caused by the influential business model of Silicon Valley which adopts a scatter gun approach to funding as venture capitalists (VCs) bet on the next big platform and privilege growth (or scale) over profit. This often leads to companies running large deficits, even those considered successful. These "thinly capitalized" (Styhre 2019) companies are built on shaky foundations with direct consequences for the stability of employment in the sector. A useful example is short-form video platform Vine, which was bought by Twitter in 2012 for a reported US$30 million and once claimed a user base of 200 million people. Despite this early success and its role in the creation of memorable memes, it was unceremoniously shut down by its parent company in 2016. With Twitter struggling to turn a profit, the under-supported Vine became a casualty of cost cutting. This included staff retrenchment (9 percent of its global workforce was cut) and corporate restructuring (Newton 2016). This sudden closure obviously disrupted the careers of Vine and Twitter staff – although many Vine senior executives had already fled the company – but also impacted its pro–am content creators who were generating income from branding deals and using the site to launch their creative careers. For some of these platform laborers, their income stream and career pathway vanished almost overnight. While Vine, and the range of workers it employed, may be small fry in the big pond of the digital media industry, it is also notable that at the time of writing the collapse of the much larger Twitter remains the subject of business gossip as it fails to sustain profitability.

The story of Vine is a common narrative in the creative industries whose products have a high failure rate, not least because their audiences are unpredictable. In legacy media sectors such as Hollywood or the publishing industry, the risks of failure are offset by producing a large catalogue of goods; if only one product is a significant success, it can offset the losses made on the others. However, in the digital sector, labor is often arranged through outsourcing, so workers are often freelancers or contracted in small companies which restructure depending upon the contract. Such companies do not typically have a suite of products upon which to defray the losses of a failed product; a failure to launch, reach its market, or even to be paid by a contracting firm can hit these companies very hard, with flow-on effects for workers' salaries and careers. The potential for failure is one of the many risks that digital laborers such as web designers, software engineers, and content producers are asked to take on (Neff 2012; Styhre 2019). But it is also taken on by platform workers such as Didi drivers and Rappi riders whose livelihoods are tied to the fortunes of the platforms that mediate their labor. As the Vine example shows, investment in the demands set by a particular platform, such as taking out a loan to purchase a vehicle for ride-share driving or redesigning your home for potential renters, can be almost instantly rendered worthless. Unilateral changes to compensation systems, a surge in competition after a recruitment drive, or a platform's corporate restructure that causes the company to pivot and change direction can all alter the landscape of work in ways that negatively impact, or even destroy, livelihoods. Even natural disasters can impact incomes, as many Airbnb and other house-sharing platform hosts found as the 2020 Covid crisis decimated tourism. In much platform work, all the risks posed by such pivots, policy, code changes, and divine acts are borne by the worker, a point poignantly made by a series of suicides in 2018 by Uber drivers no longer able to service loans on their vehicles due to changes the company made to the revenue distribution model (Pager and Palmer 2018).

The risks of corporate and product failure are further exacerbated by the mergers and acquisitions that have typified creative industries as cultural products have become important and valuable commodities, an effect sent into overload by the financialized dynamics of Silicon Valley. Not only are companies bought and sold, the drive to achieve profitability often generates destabilizing structural and production shifts that impact the career development and everyday work of digital laborers. In an industry based on the plasticity of digital code and working in perpetual beta mode, digital industries are "clearly very comfortable with regularly 'rebooting' (starting again), 'iterating' (trying again), or 'pivoting' (changing direction)" (Cunningham and Craig 2019: 47). This kind of flux in which a restructure renders someone's career or position within a firm untenable is a common feature in stories from Silicon Valley. The struggle to find meaningful work in a company that no longer values your contribution or whose direction or product you no longer believe in is one side of this story. Being forced out of a firm as it pivots outside of your skill set is another (see García Martinez 2016; Kagan 2014; Lyons 2016).

In *Blood, Sweat, and Pixels* (2017), Jason Schrier documents the development of ten significant games in ten different video game companies. Among the familiar narratives of crunch time and fulfilled or frustrated creative expression is also a latent but unsettling sense that each role in the industry is built on merely illusory foundations. The sector is driven by hits, led by share prices, and manifests the creative destruction dynamics that dominate the tech industry. This leaves workers and their working lives simultaneously at the mercy of audiences and corporate maneuvers (Bulut 2020). Leadership flux or financial instability in a parent company, publishers' conservative tastes, clashes of vision within a development team, developer burnout, or a product pivot in response to market demand could all lead to the abrupt cancellation of a project resulting in, at best, a sense of insecurity about a worker's place in the company or, at worst, sudden unemployment for any game worker.

An apparently unlikely site for such instability was LucasArts which, despite being part of the Lucasfilms empire responsible for the *Star Wars* mega-franchise, was repeatedly reshaped by shifting leadership and management structures, and put in a weak market position due to poorly produced games. Some way into the production of the *Star Wars 1313* console game, founder George Lucas intervened to insist the main character be changed to Boba Fett, an existing character within the franchise. This required undoing months of work and fundamentally disrupted the planned and worked-through story line. Lucas insisted. Schrier summarized the vibe in the company, overtly describing the kinds of animating anxieties documented throughout all the companies he describes:

> Maybe it'd be worth the stress, though. The *Star Wars 1313* team knew they needed to impress people. Even within LucasArts, there was a concern that the hammer might come down at any time – that the studio's parent company, Lucasfilm, would cancel the game; that they'd suffer more layoffs; that Paul Meegan might be another casualty of the cursed title "LucasArts President." (Schrier 2017: 261)

Soon after this shift in the game design, Lucasfilms was bought by Disney. This created new flux as it put on hold the hiring necessary to complete the game. More importantly, it also came with a decision to shift away from console games, such as *1313*, toward social and mobile gaming as well as the licensing of game production rather than in-house creation. At the mercy of these top-level, strategic shifts, and despite significant fan buzz from industry showcases, game production slowed.

Then, in April 2013, the full extent of game-developer precariousness manifested: Disney shut down LucasArts entirely, along with all its internal projects, leading to the layoff of a rumored 150 staff. Lead development staff who had not already left the company during the preceding turmoil tried one last pitch to EA-owned developer Visceral to save the game and the employees, but to no avail. Many of these workers left, with a few taking interviews for another Star Wars-themed game at Visceral. While highly specific, this narrative is nevertheless instructive of general trends. Within it, we can see how even relatively privileged workers can experience a workplace featuring the entangled dynamics of income and job insecurity. That the LucasArts story is one of ten in the book that document similar dynamics – albeit the most dramatic – is also instructive. No digital laborer can be assured of stability; nobody is safe.

Cheap labor

The various insecurities associated with precarity and connected to questions of economic exploitation manifest differently across the three main groups of labor practices we have been exploring. Elite, full-time tech workers experience some kinds of income instability but not of the magnitude suffered by influencers or microworkers who are, in slightly different ways, at immediate risk of losing jobs and whole incomes from tweaks to policy or algorithms. The limited scope of their contracts or ostensible self-employed status often makes these latter workers even more vulnerable and needing to absorb all kinds of economic risks. Nevertheless, formally employed workers also function in sectors where churn and flux – the much-vaunted creative destruction of the tech sector – ensure a wider range of instabilities in that employment. Finally, there are users whose labor often underpins the incomes of the other workers but who are entirely unpaid and lack any certainty about the stability of platforms or the conditions of that activity beyond ever-changing and unilaterally determined use agreements. Yet these workers do not experience income instability and certainly not in the same way as platform workers or Silicon Valley programmers, for whom platform viability becomes an existential problem.

Nevertheless, I suggest that a commonality of the instabilities in the exploitative regimes of the digital media industries is that they frame labor as *cheap*. By this term, I don't mean that it doesn't cost a great deal – although that may certainly be important – but that it is disposable and treated with contempt. The refusal to provide adequate income, career stability, and/or future pathways within digital labor environments articulates a view of workers and their labor as something to be exploited but not valued, respected, or invested in. Like throwaway consumer goods, cheap labor is readily discarded and replaced with little thought for the human who stands behind it. Obviously, this disposability is not evenly distributed, but even in the world of internet celebrity or star brogrammers, the dignity of work is cheapened when its exploitative dynamics lead to the chronic instabilities and under-compensation documented across the chapter.

This is not a novel conceptualization of labor – arguably Marx's entire point about capitalism is how it cheapens labor – but it has a particularly gendered and racialized history that is worth noting. In using the term "cheap," I am drawing on Minh-Ha T. Pham's (2015) insightful study *Asians Wear Clothes on the Internet*. She describes how the exploitative conditions experienced by the predominantly Asian style bloggers of her study "resurrects the specter of Asians' historical role in capitalism and, more specifically, in the fashion industry as unskilled, cheap labor" (2015: 189). From the association of badly produced consumer goods with the Made in China or Taiwan stamp to the denigration of "Chinese gold-farmers" in digital games (Nakamura 2009), "Asian labor" has a long history of being synonymous with degraded work conditions, trivial and poorly manufactured products, and low pay. Growing up in the United States, Chinese artist and coder Xiaowei Wang describes their relationship to this sentiment:

> Made in China became seared into my psyche as a symbol of corruptness. The phrase meant something shoddily crafted, made by people who were mindless drones in a factory bent on gaining profit by cheating foreigners out of an extra cent or two . . . . [cheap products] reflected the laziness of the Chinese, who were unwilling to be diligent about work and always wanted to cut corners. (Wang 2020: 121)

Pham argues that this labelling of products and labor as cheap must be understood as a practice of economic racialization, a mechanism through which racial difference is produced to justify and support the division of labor that reduces costs. She says that "dividing labor into hierarchical categories (cheap labor, low-level labor, domestic labor, and so on) has an ethnicizing effect that marks certain workers as socially inferior" (Pham 2015: 72). To treat labor as cheap is to place it in this history of global, colonial exploitation.

This labelling is also gendering because cheap labor is also feminized labor. As Pham (2015: 73) notes, the stereotype of the docile Asian worker is encoded as feminine, and this is mobilized to associate both Asian women and men with feminized labor markets such as cleaning, cooking, and laundry services. The connection to domestic labor – which under capitalism has long been considered "women's work" – is also important. Women's labor has long been associated with lower wages, casualization, and fragmented labor experiences – it has long been precarious, unstable work, and the first to be discarded in times of economic crisis (Mies, Bennholdt-Thomsen, and von Werlhof 1988; Morini 2007). Like the racialized labor of Asian workers, women's work both in and outside the home has historically been separated out from legitimate, valuable productive labor and devalued accordingly. Such racial and gendered divisions between forms of labor – whether the work is deemed productive or unproductive, valuable or cheap – are vital to the functioning of capitalism. In Marxist terms, such divisions help create an industrial reserve army of unemployed or underemployed workers who generate competition for jobs and drive down wages. The racial and gendered division of labor is thus not an accident of geographic conditions or solely an expression of racism or patriarchal logics. It is the entwining of these dynamics with economics in a mutually reinforcing relationship.

It is fairly uncontentious to label user labor, platform work, and subcontracted formal work as cheap; the precarity associated with these forms of labor is already well acknowledged and the entire economic logic for using work in this form is predicated on its relative cheapness to other forms of labor. However, it is more difficult to place full-time, elite Silicon Valley work into the racialized and gendered category of cheap labor, particularly with its persistently white, middle-class, and masculine workforce, as well as its socially privileged status. Nevertheless, the financialization of the sector and the emphasis on share price devalues the importance of all workers to the sector and its economy. Digital labor can be well paid and socially valorized but still be treated as disposable as share prices wax and wane. This logic is embedded deeply in startup culture, and startup culture is embedded deeply in the mature digital media industry. If we understand cheapness to be on a spectrum with being valued, the digital labor of full-time tech workers is tending toward cheap. This is not to directly equate such work and such laborers with objectively disenfranchised and vulnerable workers, but to acknowledge the socioeconomic tendency that unites their exploitation by capital. Understood as a socioeconomic imaginary of labor actively mobilized in the service of profit, cheapness becomes a useful framing.

Categorizing digital labor as cheap seems to capture the dynamic of how it becomes exploited. Arguably, I could have retained the term "precarious" to describe the phenomena I have examined here; the two concepts are very similar. However, the term "cheap" reminds us that this labor condition is not new nor entirely specific to digital labor contexts. Cheapness is evocative of the long, brutal history of labor exploitation across the globe and its racist and misogynist qualities. Drawing this history into our understanding of contemporary digital labor conditions ensures we reject claims to the novelty of such processes of devaluation, remain mindful of the uneven distribution of exploitation, and remain cognizant of the structural violence entailed in these processes. It also reminds us that the degradation of labor has always been conservative. It has historically been about the re-inscription of power within the global North and so asks us to question who benefits when even elite work manifests as cheap labor.

3

Process: Of Autonomy and Algorithms

Labor is the most uncontrollable part of the capitalist process. Workers, replete with human frailties and idiosyncrasies, can disrupt production through incompetence, resistant tactics, sabotage, industrial action, or simply by rejecting their subordinate role. Consequently, for the efficient running of capitalist enterprise, to keep costs to a minimum, and thereby increase profit, control of workers is essential. This can be done through direct coercive mechanisms such as violence and physical and social constraints as seen in slave labor contexts. More often, though, it is achieved through the systematic organization or management of the labor process. This has become the key mode for controlling workers in liberal, democratic states. The formal and informal ways work is managed are thus closely linked to the ways work is exploited.

Harry Braverman's (1998 [1974]) famous *Labor and Monopoly Capital* uses Marxist critiques to describe the reconstitution of work through the organization of the labor process; referred to as labor process theory. For Marx and Braverman, once labor begins to be performed according to the needs and desire of the company that buys the labor of the worker – when it becomes entangled within capitalism – it will inevitably be degraded in the search for profit. The most common mechanism for this degradation is the division of labor. This is not the division of labor between productive and unproductive categories (although it relates) but the breaking up of a particular process of production into smaller, discrete units which are then distributed among workers.

This practice, arguably to introduce efficiencies, ends the need for skilled workers able to execute a task competently from beginning to end. Instead, it only requires workers able to perform individual, simpler, standardized tasks, demanding much less skill, education, or experience. Less-skilled workers are less expensive than well-trained artisans, saving the capitalist money. This process, though, reduces all workers to functional cogs within a production process with no ownership of their labor and the products it produces.

As Braverman argues, as this organization of labor became widespread in industrial capitalism, workers became permanently de-skilled, no longer needing to develop deep knowledge of a craft, making them easily replaceable. It also created a hierarchy of workers – those who were involved in complex labor and whose time was "infinitely valuable" and those involved in simple labor whose time "is worth almost nothing" (1998 [1974]: 58). Particularly when coupled with assembly-line structuring and scientific management techniques – that identified and then broke work into the most efficient, discrete units of activity – the division of labor reduced the autonomy, creativity, and ultimately the agency of the worker. No longer in control of the scope and intensity of their labor activity and with work activities executed at preset tempos and patterns, it became increasingly difficult for workers to limit and shape the nature of their workloads.

The strict organization of a worker's movement serves as a mechanism of general control. Workers' specific and skilled labor activities – right through to individual gestures and motions – are reorganized as a mirror of the company's needs. In doing so, the discipline and dictates of capitalism are embedded in the body and consciousness of the worker. Control in the Fordist factory was thus not only exerted through corralling into a shared space but was exerted holistically through the capitalist's monopoly over the steps of the labor process and the ways these became inculcated into the minds and body of workers. In this process, Braverman suggests, workers become dehumanized. Involved in repetitive, mindless tasks over which they have no control, rather than creating products over which they can take ownership or in which they have any pride, they become a tool within the pursuit of profit rather than active, autonomous creators. In Marxist terms, they become alienated workers – a point we will return to in chapter 4.

However, for digital laborers involved in information-intensive knowledge production, their work typically involves activity that makes management of the labor process more difficult. Action involving knowledge, affect, or creative expression as is common in the digital media industries has long been considered too difficult to measure, record, and instrumentalize through Fordist techniques. More often than not, digital labor requires embodied knowledge and craft skills that cannot be broken down into discrete units or which demand the kinds of flexibility and autonomy that Braverman's managers actively sought to replace with replicable, standardized activity. This means that in digital labor, the exploitation of workers requires very particular modes of management. As Huws (2014) points out, what animates labor focused on creativity or innovation is a dialectic of autonomy and control which differs from that in industrial capital.

Consequently – and following suggestions by both Nicole S. Cohen (2012) and Gandini (2019) – this chapter will explore the processes that organize the working activity of digital laborers and, in particular, the tension between autonomy and control that is mobilized within them. Some of what we will focus on below is about what workers are asked to do – the organization of their work time and processes. This will involve us returning to some neglected dimensions of precarity outlined in the previous chapter – specifically employment, work, skill reproduction, and job insecurity – to see how these qualities of precarity emerge from the modes of management we find in digital labor. But underlying the analysis is how digital laborers are encouraged to act so that their activities are in concert with the goals of their employer. It is, effectively, about the mechanisms by which digital laborers are disciplined as particular workers and ultimately consent to the processes of their own subjection in the workplace (Burawoy 1979). This chapter is thus not an exhaustive or detailed study of the production relations that organize specific labor processes, companies, or industries – the diversity of workplaces under consideration makes that impossible. It is, though, a study of some general mechanisms that shape the labor experiences and everyday working conditions of digital laborers. It explores how degrees of autonomy are enacted through contractual relations and workplace informality, but also how management creates worker compliance through the supposedly objective mechanisms of workplace cultures and algorithms.

Contractual and conceptual independence

A striking feature of digital labor is how many workers have some form of independence from their employer, although this articulates differently across various sectors. This variation can be mapped, at least initially, through the differing contractual frameworks that form the foundations of the work. As we will go on to see, some of this autonomy is illusory or offers contradictory outcomes, so this section is riddled with qualifiers. Nevertheless, the degree to which digital labor contractual relations link to autonomy is noteworthy. Some of this agency is hinged to the irregularity and informality of the contracts that typify digital labor environments, while for other workers it is related to their relatively elite, white-collar status.

As already indicated in the previous chapter, there are three key forms of labor contract associated with digital labor. The most informal of these – if it can even be called that – is associated with unpaid user labor. The social relationship between user and platform, app, or site is formalized through End User License Agreements (EULAs) and Terms of Service (ToS) which tend to describe rights over data – the product of this labor – but also circumscribe some aspects of user conduct – the labor process. Although they rarely overtly direct the actions users can do or the time in which they can undertake them, these contracts do organize some aspects of their creative activity. Nevertheless, as opposed to the traditional labor contract, unpaid users are contracted with a meaningful degree of autonomy over the hours of work and the nature of the content they contribute; Twitter, for instance, does not tell you when and how often you should post. Also, given the reliance on clicks, likes, and all kinds of raw data for their incomes, many advertising-supported digital media companies really do not care what users do – although as we will see there are inconsistently applied rules about this – or how they go about that activity. They only care that users do this work while tethered to their platforms. Perhaps because they are not formally a workforce, unpaid users are the most autonomous of all digital laborers.

Many workers occupy a second category: self-employed workers. These may be freelancers, or in short-term, project-related posts for a larger firm, or working for digital platforms. For a corporation or a platform, hiring ostensibly self-employed workers reduces costs in a variety of ways. In fact, the business model of most platforms depends on positioning the bulk of their workforce, especially those actually engaging in the activity that is brokered via their site, as independent contractors and denying their status as employees. As Nick Srnicek (2017: 76–7) summarizes, for work-mediating platforms this practice "enables the companies to save around 30 per cent on labour costs by cutting out benefits, overtime, sick days, and other costs. It also means outsourcing training costs, since training is only permitted for employees." A lean company with low production costs is the result. For workers, though, self-employment often means zero-hour contracts

– in which the time engaged in paid work and thus income per week is unfixed – and/or a reliance on commission, piece rates, or short-term, insecure contracts. At times, this self-employment is bogus and contested – as we will see in chapter 6, which describes a range of legal challenges to this contractual arrangement. At the time of writing, though, and despite some success in securing employee status for some digital laborers in a few jurisdictions, platform workers are usually formally classified and employed as freelance, independent contractors. Consequently, according to the law, they are outside the company's direct control.

This means that platform workers and some other freelance or subcontracted digital laborers can potentially exert a good deal of autonomy within their working conditions. They are, ostensibly, able to choose their hours of work and the place and rhythms of their activity while thus engaged. They may choose when to log in to the app; they may be able to select which jobs to bid for or accept; they can devise and design their own content based on their own tastes or desires; set their own prices; or take initiative in how they create and deliver their products or tasks. Which aspects of independent activity they can manifest is dependent on the nature of the platform and the kinds of work for which they are contracted – influencers working for Instagram have a different set of activities over which they can exert control to microworkers on Fiverr, which is again different from a freelance web designer – but there are usually many aspects of their work that self-employed workers are formally allowed to control.

This autonomy is also a key selling point of work within the digital platform economy. Many platforms promote the idea of signing up to their workforce by appealing to ideals of autonomy that come from being only loosely tied to an employer or being self-employed. Promises may be made of economic independence or agency based in the control the worker will have over their work environment, particularly the scheduling of work. Deliveroo's rider recruitment page exhorts potential riders to "find work that suits you," talks about making money "on your own schedule," and working "when you want to" (Deliveroo n.d.). Home-maintenance broker Handy sells flexible scheduling as part of its pitch to its pool of home-help professionals: "You choose when you want to work and how much. Build a full schedule of your customers or simply add a few jobs on the side" (Handy n.d.). Upwork emphasizes growing *your own* business or career but also the freedom to choose work tasks. The platform offers the "freedom to work on ideal projects" (Upwork n.d.). UK carework platform Swarme (n.d.) promises that careworkers can work how and when they want and set their own pay rates, describing this multiple times as "taking back control" not merely of work but of all life.

For freelance workers, the autonomy espoused in their contracts can be actualized in the day-to-day management of work time, space, and activity. Similar kinds of autonomy are also often granted to the final category of digital laborers – formally employed workers. While hired under contracts that put them under the direct control of their employer, many workers in this group are nevertheless granted the kinds of creative autonomy and occupational independence in the workplace that have historically been associated with creative workers (Huws 2010; Ross 2003, 2009). Even though some knowledge work – such as white-collar office work – has been subjected to Taylorist regimes, broken up into small slices of optimized activity and closely managed, in industries thriving on innovation and disruption such control is deemed counterproductive. "To exercise creativity, workers need to be at liberty to imagine new possibilities, to exercise curiosity, to be able to access a wide range of information freely, to have the resources to experiment with new ideas and to 'think outside the box,' as the management jargon puts it" (Huws 2019: 800). Consequently, elite workers, particularly if they are involved in creative or high-concept roles, are often granted significant latitude in the management of their work rhythms and patterns. In Silicon Valley, workers typically determine their own working hours, their office environment, and the pace and goals of their daily activity. They may also have some autonomy over the longer-term goals of their work as in Google's allowance of "20% time," in which workers can pursue personal projects. The flat hierarchies that are emblematic of Silicon Valley's approach to management, at least ideally, further articulate the degree of independence and autonomy ostensibly granted to elite workers. Bosses are not remote figures of control, with work often conducted in project teams of peers. Moreover, the entrepreneurial spirit that animates the tech industry, which will be discussed further in chapter 4, is a discourse predicated on independence of thought, action, and subjectivity. Principles of autonomy, whether realized or not, permeate the relationships between many workers and employers in the digital media industries.

Of course, not all formal workers in the digital media industries are granted independence in their labor environment or their contractual relations. Some formally employed digital laborers – such as Amazon's fulfillment center workforce – have little to no control over their working hours, working practices, or processes. Similarly, content moderators, community managers, and game testers may be formally employed on a full-time basis but do not experience the same conditions and autonomy as programmers and designers for the same companies. Such workers are often managed at a granular level and without pretense to independence. They more closely resemble the laborers of Braverman's industrialized workplaces than they do many of their colleagues in the same company. Independence from an employer is thus merely a *tendency* within digital labor or, at the very least, an aspiration. The autonomy experienced by many digital laborers is not available to all and, as this chapter will show, may well be illusory for all. Nevertheless, for many digital laborers, some form of autonomy over when and how they work is extended to them via their contracts or their elite status. The model digital laborer thus seems far removed from Braverman's alienated factory worker.

Informality and insecurity

Autonomy and independence as a management principle does not necessarily create workplaces that are entirely happy, though. In digital labor environments, the organizational structures that foster independence can also feed into the kinds of skill development, job, and occupational insecurities that make work precarious and workers anxious. Perhaps ironically, these structures thus become mechanisms for controlling the workforce, not least because insecurity of tenure can render a worker more inclined to align his or her interests to that of the employer. This exercise of soft power – or hegemonic despotism (Wood 2020) – is a powerful tool in ensuring compliance with organizational demands and thus to manage the workplace. An overt example of such systems of control is the offsetting of wages into share prices in elite digital workplaces that directly invests the worker in the success of the company. However, many other techniques of securing consent to regimes of control are less obvious. Central to these is corporate informality.

In Silicon Valley, workplaces are famously informal, both in the sense of business attire and in how work is organized. Part of the spirit of startup culture is a rejection of traditional corporate conventions and their attendant bureaucracies, with these often considered a barrier to innovation (Gallagher 2017: 184). This is both an attribute of the freewheeling, often libertarian, corporate ethos of many companies and an inevitable effect of exponential growth. It may also be an effect of founders who are inexperienced in management processes or whose primary skill is code rather than organizational leadership. For many companies, this means little investment in human resources (HR) and other systems of staff management, development, or support, leading to chronic problems of work, employment, and skill-reproduction insecurity.

Being HR-lite is logical and manageable when a startup is only a handful of employees but, as companies grow, the absence of such formal management systems leads to problems for employees and often for the company. For Uber founder Travis Kalanick, a "big company" feel – which meant formal systems and processes – was anathema, even when the company had more than six thousand direct employees (not including millions of drivers across the globe). He believed it would disrupt the ethos of quick-fire innovation the company alleged to embody. Being a "big company" included having a meaningful HR department which, to Kalanick, meant "behavior codes, sensitivity training, sexual harassment policies, misconduct reporting procedures, formal reviews – all things that make a hard-charging young man roll his eyes" (Isaac 2019: 217). The absence of effective, formal systems ensured that when employee Susan Fowler encountered inappropriate sexualized conduct from her manager on her first day at Uber, she was left with little to no support. She documents this story in her 2020 book *Whistleblower*, which followed a 2017 blog post that was influential in propelling the emerging discussion about gender inequality in high-tech industries. It also helped bring about the changes in Uber management that dethroned Kalanick and introduced a more formalized set of institutional structures. Nevertheless, limited, under-resourced, or ineffective HR departments are regularly noted in reports from Silicon Valley.

For platform workers and other contracted digital laborers, the informality of their employment status means an almost total absence of formal mechanisms for providing work and skill reproduction security. These are responsibilities devolved to the individual worker. As already described in relation to wage instability, for freelance creative workers or platform laborers there is little formal accreditation or employer-supported skill development on offer, and such activity must take place in the worker's unpaid personal time. As Cunningham and Craig (2019) describe, pro–am YouTube creators rarely have training before and during their time as content creators for the site. More often than not, they are self-taught, using video tutorials as guides. There are also rarely formalized divisions of labor in content production, with creators regularly taking on all roles from location scout to composer, visual effects, makeup, editor, and talent, as well as being responsible for managing advertising and marketing deals. The rise of multichannel networks has formalized some of the top-tier roles, especially those associated with monetization, yet many content creators on YouTube and other platforms still work with informal structures that involve them in all phases of production. Those with formally defined crew often use family members or intimate partners as their production team, partly to retain the "authenticity" demanded by followers and fans. Even as the digital content creation sector formalizes, the onus for skill development and reproduction remains firmly with the individual worker.

A more troublesome responsibility that is devolved to contracted workers is ensuring occupational health and safety. For workers hired as contractors, there is no obligation to provide appropriate provisions or training to ensure a safe workplace. Reports abound of food delivery riders or ride-sharing drivers being assaulted, injured, or even killed while fulfilling their work responsibilities – the story of Thiago Cortes that starts this book is not an isolated incident (Gregory 2021). A 2019 report on delivery riders for Rappi in Colombia found that almost none of the 50,000 workers were covered by national safety and health laws. Work-related accidents had been suffered by 63.2% of riders, and over the last two years 67% had suffered an occupational disease. At least three riders were killed in 2020 (Connell 2020). Only in very few instances have platforms accepted full responsibility, provided compensation, or adequately acknowledged injuries or harms to their workers. In November 2020, food-delivery company Hungry Panda failed to turn up to an Australian state parliamentary inquiry examining the death of one of their riders. Their contracted worker Xiaojun Chen was killed in a collision in September only two days after an Uber Eats rider, Dede Fredy, was also killed in another road accident. Hungry Panda's disavowal of responsibility was astonishing. Not only did they not report the incident to Safe Work NSW – the government agency responsible for workplace safety in the state – their failure to front the inquiry was described by the committee chair as "the height of disrespect." It did not, he said, "inspire much confidence in their ability to support workers" (Zhou 2020). In such instances, life itself become part of the insecurities associated with digital labor.

This devolution of risk and informal, if not irregular, contractual relations is a feature of the flexible accumulation model of the economy that emerged out of the collapse of Fordist production and under the hegemony of neoliberal dogma. Demands for greater flexibility and adaptability by workers were part of the supply-side innovations of the post-Fordist factory. It was important not only to be able to retool a production line but to retool the workforce in relation to fluid production processes. The outsourcing and just-in-time production models, as well as the view toward immediate profit driven by financialization, placed a premium on an unfixed and flexible workforce in terms of its work time, work hours, and work practices. To facilitate this reorganization of the economy, neoliberal states' regulatory capacity becomes focused on facilitating the adaptability and fluidity of a company's workforce through processes of labor deregulation. Across a large number of jurisdictions in the 1980s and 1990s, policies were introduced that scaled back protections for workers. Laws were changed to make it easier to fire or redeploy staff and to enable non-standard work contracts. Corporations took advantage of this trend to embed insecure contracts and divest themselves of responsibilities for many aspects of occupational and skill reproduction, as well as dimensions of workplace safety. This effectively ended the compact of the industrial economy which offered job security, potentially for life, in exchange for various forms of alienated labor. Today, no job is expected to be permanent but rather one in an ongoing series of gigs, and often an overlapping series of gigs, as wages drop below sustainable levels. This has made temporary and casualized work, including zero-hour and other irregular, more informal contracts which do not guarantee any particular hours of work or pay, an increasing feature of the global economy. For workers in all industries, occupational or job insecurity and informal employment relationships have become a normalized feature. Digital labor, though, exemplifies this trajectory even in its most elite forms. While corporate needs often dictate these arrangements, worker compliance with such regimes is also generated through normative models of activity, enacted through indirect mechanisms.

Getting in and staying put

In Silicon Valley, where workers may well be hired on what are secure, permanent, and formal contracts, the power of management tends to be exerted through informal relationships and "culture." This system of normative control (Wood 2020: 16–17) begins with the hiring processes and tracks throughout the career lifecycle of elite digital laborers. Like the gig work of freelancers described in the previous chapter, success in securing and sustaining employment in Silicon Valley is often driven by the informal logics of social capital. Hiring from existing social networks is common (Cohen and de Peuter 2020). The drive to "move fast" in tech startups often means a rejection of time-consuming, external, and perhaps objective hiring processes in favor of interpersonal recommendations. Key staff members, particularly in the early days, are often hired for their similarity to the founder, both physically and in terms of personality. Detailing hiring practices at Uber, journalist Mike Isaac describes how the tone for the company culture was set by founder Travis Kalanick. "Kalanick knew what he wanted in his employees – who were mostly white, male, and in their twenties – and made his hiring decisions based on that instinct" (2019: 194). The economic logic of this homophily in hiring was articulated by Peter Thiel, co-founder of the notoriously homogeneous PayPal (cited in Chang 2019: 50). He argued that the pace of startup work places a premium on employees having a shared worldview so that limited time and resources are not wasted on arguing between alternate visions or processes. Like Thiel, venture capitalist and investors also recommend founders hire experienced people they already know in the early stages of a company based on the idea that interpersonal norms make it more likely that they will be convinced to take on the risks of these roles. It is suggested that to specifically seek more diverse employees may slow down a company's growth (Pisoni 2017). This in turn creates "dynastic privilege," in which successful founders in one startup draw on that initial success in selling their next venture. They then compound advantages by hiring the same "winning" team and placing those people in senior roles from which they accrue further privilege to take into the next venture. In this way, the cycle of homogeneity continues (Chang 2019: 56; Pisoni 2017). Through this mechanism, money and career success flow through informal, interpersonal networks, making personal relationships important tools of management.

This form of management is, however, prone to producing and reproducing inequalities throughout the employee lifecycle. Anna Wiener's (2020) account of working within a Silicon Valley software company describes the problems of homophily in hiring, promotion, and salary negotiations and its impacts on career advancement. "For years, my coworkers explained, the absence of an official org chart had given rise to a secondary, shadow org chart, determined by social relationships and proximity to the founders. . . . Those with the ear of the CEO could influence hiring decisions, internal policies, and the reputational standing of their colleagues" (2020: 175).

A technical writer interviewed by Tarnoff and Weigel (2020) also points out that in the flattened hierarchies of the tech industry, line managers are given a significant agency, including over remuneration. Rarely adequately trained, these managers can readily retrench their own prejudices and interpersonal affiliations in their decision making.

These effects are exacerbated by the principles of meritocracy that form part of the cultural norms of some high-tech companies, particularly those that have emerged out of the libertarian traditions of hacking and computing cultures (Chang 2019; Liu 2020; Streeter 2011; Taplin 2017; Turner 2009). This underlying principle means that employment and work insecurity impact elite digital workers across existing race and gender lines. As Gill (2014) describes, when narratives of neoliberal bootstrapping and individualized entrepreneurialism shape the subjectivities that enable success in an industry, structural patterns of discrimination such as racism, sexism, or homophobia become unspeakable. Discourses of meritocracy disguise the disadvantages of workers from minoritized groups by replacing questions of uneven access and structural inequality with narratives of inherent talent or personal ambition (Bulut 2020: 24–5; Liu 2020). For many of Wiener's white, middle-class, male colleagues and for her employers, "the meritocracy narrative was a cover for lack of structural analysis. It smoothed things out. It was flattering and exculpatory, and painful for some to part with" (2020: 182). This means that the inequalities embedded in the hiring processes are reinforced by becoming measures of success which fail to recognize disadvantage and continue to reward homophily.

However, interpersonal networks and cultural fit are a particularly unstable foundation upon which to base a career, and business memoirs recount many tales of workers pushed out of work through conflict with a founder or dis-alignment with the ethos of the company (Chang 2019; García Martínez 2016; Losse 2012; Lyons 2016). Additionally, systems where control is exerted through patronage are difficult to resist as they allow only informal and/or individual responses such as "outmanoeuvring the boss, using personal charm or manipulation, using gossip networks to shame and blame, or simply walking away" (Huws 2010: 516). This type of system can also enact brutal, but subtly articulated, forms of exclusion. The workplace culture of Silicon Valley that privileges superstars and fetishizes youthful exuberance and blind loyalty creates an industry which can and will readily shed staff who no longer fit with that norm. Workers' interests are thus best served by ensuring they meet those expectations in terms of work practices, outputs, and personal dispositions.

In elite digital labor companies, staff churn is high as "stars" seek better deals in fresh pastures but also, and primarily, because experienced, mature, and more cautious staff become expensive both fiscally and to the corporate image. "As soon as someone better or cheaper comes along, your company will get rid of you. If you turn fifty, or thirty-five; if you demand a raise and become too expensive; if a new batch of workers comes out of college and will do your job for less than what you are paid – you're gone" (Lyons 2016: 116–17). As one tech company founder noted, nobody seems to know where all the old programmers go (Tarnoff and Weigel 2020). Workloads and hostile work conditions also generate churn in staffing. In companies that pride themselves on disruption and novelty, uncertainty is the base ground of company culture. Amazon quite famously adopts a "purposeful Darwinism" in its annual culls of white-collar staff who fail to reach its high standards, regardless of reason, and fosters peer surveillance and aggressive critique, leading to high staff turnover and burnout. A 2013 survey by salary analysis firm PayScale found the median employee tenure at

Amazon was only a year and was one of the shortest in the Fortune 500 (Kantor and Streitfeld 2015). There is a "general nonchalance about retention policies" in favor of extracting as much from workers as possible in the immediate term (Chang 2019: 213). While these dynamics are not unique to this sector, according to industry insider Dan Lyons (2016: 116), Silicon Valley "has become a place where people live in fear." This chronic insecurity perpetuates the culture of overwork that feeds the productive machinery of Silicon Valley. In effect, it manages workers into replicating toxic labor dynamics.

Informality in workplaces – particularly the "cool" workplaces of Silicon Valley – is, perhaps counterintuitively, also a means of managing the times in which work takes place. Elite workers, along with platform workers, are typically allowed to determine their own hours. However, workplaces use various mechanisms to encourage or enforce extended worktimes. The provision of food, gyms, washing facilities, and other lifestyle services within the workplace not only *allows* workers to remain in the office but *encourages* them to do so. Describing Google's package of workplace perks, Susan J. Stabile (2008: 100) notes "Google provides the level of benefits and amenities it does, not out of altruism, but as a matter of business interest." While the packages Google and other tech firms offer do technically allow their staff to spend more time with family, in reality they are designed, and function, to maximize time spent in value-producing activity; making caring for life's details easier quite simply gives employees more time for work. At times, the strategic function of these facilities is not subtle. For a long period, Uber quite famously would not serve its evening meal until 8.15 p.m. to encourage/enforce its culture of overwork (Isaac 2019: 119; Chang 2019: 212). Nevertheless, even when this imposition of extended work time seems more organic, it is difficult to opt out. In a competitive and insecure workplace environment, pressure is on to be a team player, to adapt to the long hours, and to be seen to be doing so. This organization of work time and the pace at which work happens are not rigid or formal rules set by the employer, but they do exist, informally enacted through culture, norms, and the counterintuitive mechanism of employee perks.

The invisible manager

In this process, workers are being effectively managed without impacting their sense of autonomy in their work. Silicon Valley's informality can thus be understood as a management tool, but one that works at a remove. It works in alignment with the principles of autonomy by not directly and overtly prescribing actions, but it nevertheless creates a context in which the insecurity it engenders drives and shapes the everyday labor experience of workers. This is a strategic approach to managing creative labor. In the case of Amazon's elite programmers, with its vicious performance reviews and long, grueling hours, these brutal conditions discipline workers to work hard, to remain aligned with corporate ideals of industriousness and creativity. For some workers, though, being challenged by their work in this way is a key motivator, and some have reported finding the punishing Amazon routine an addictive way of working. As one former executive says, "it's the greatest place I hate to work" (Kantor and Streitfeld 2015). In striving to satisfy the self-realization that comes with the entrepreneurial, creative autonomy ascribed to their roles, Amazon's elite workers become their own managers.

This model of management acting at a remove is also enacted in different digital labor contexts via indirect and opaque actors such as code, affordances, and (supposedly) technical surveillance systems. It also is enacted through bureaucratic means. As has already been flagged, for users the key mechanism that controls their labor is the EULA or the ToS – the legal contract that users are required to agree to when signing up for a new service. Many users, myself included, often simply click acceptance of these contracts rather than wading through pages of sometimes incomprehensible legalese. These contracts are often experienced merely as an annoying barrier to accessing the rich affects and information of the platform. Related mechanisms for managing the labor of users are community guidelines, content policies, or app store rules, all of which also outline the scope of permissible activity. More directly impactful on some digital laborers are the policies relating to what or who will be able to monetize their content. YouTube's Partner Program, discussed in the previous chapter, is one such example of a policy which positively asserts control over digital laborers by determining employability and, more passively, by encouraging the production of content that is advertiser- and eyeball-friendly in order to reach the benchmarks that enable monetization. You *can* produce any content you like, but it is not necessarily advisable.

Together, these contracts and policies stipulate many things, including and especially the right to capture, use and reuse user data – the lifeblood of the digital economy – and copyright over content produced on the site. These contracts may also provide codas that inoculate the platform against responsibility for harms related to the nature of the content or the user experience of the site. Most importantly for the sake of this argument, they also set limits to the actions of the user, effectively providing a set of controls over the labor of these workers. These contracts and other use policies are often framed as "guidelines," maintaining the assertion of user autonomy, and they may be further softened with the suggestion that they emerge from an amorphous and unfixed "community." Nevertheless, they set increasingly rigid boundaries on which kinds of activities are allowed and which are open to censure. Sexual content, for instance, is increasingly subject to controls, including removal and blocking (Blunt et al. 2020; Paasonen et al. 2019; Tiidenberg and van der

Nagel 2020). Such content, and the users who create it, are regularly banned from platforms while applications that enable its distribution are removed from various app stores. Other users are encouraged to flag breaches of content rules to the platform, which then activates increasingly opaque "community" guidelines in punishing the supposed miscreants.

Platforms also hire a particular group of digital laborers – community managers or content moderators – to process these flags and make decisions on the propriety of content or user activity. This work, as Sarah T. Roberts (2019; see also Buni and Chemaly 2016; A. Chen 2012, 2014, 2015, 2017) has described, is emotionally and mentally taxing. These marginalized workers are required to trawl through reams of often violent and distressing content, assessing its validity against opaque and inconsistent rules imposed by the platform. Importantly, though, these workers are often invisible, with companies distancing themselves from their impact by suggesting that such moderation work is performed automatically and through supposedly objective algorithms (see Tubaro, Casilli, and Conville 2020 for discussion of the human digital laborers that underpin supposedly automated systems). This obfuscation of the agency of platforms in setting limits to content is part of the way the illusion of user autonomy is maintained. It is true that the scope of what they allow is broad. Nevertheless, these rules are a mechanism for controlling the labor of users, proscribing the scope of acceptable activity, and punishing those in breach that work just as effectively as a daily allocation of tasks in a Taylorist office.

Even more effective in managing the work of users is the control exerted through a platform, website, or app's technical affordances – the ways in which the underlying infrastructure of a site can allow or disallow various kinds of activity. The code underlying a platform provides much more rigid policing than the interpretation of content guidelines by moderators as it can make some actions simply impossible. For instance, the character limit on Twitter sets parameters on the length of individual tweets, serving as a hard limit on what a user can post. But the ability to either reply or add tweets in a thread which are also an affordance of the platform allows the tweeter to create lengthier forms of expression. Technical affordances such as this work to both enable and constrain the possibilities of action. In doing so, they create a context akin to an assembly line where a worker's ability to manipulate an aspect of the product will be limited by the tools and goods allocated to their workstation. Again, the scope of these affordances is typically broad – platforms want a user to stay connected for as long as possible so it is in their interest to enable a range of activities – but, nevertheless, no user is entirely free to act as they choose when engaged with any platform. Moreover, the working of these systems is opaque, creating an information asymmetry that weakens the capacity of digital laborers to understand and intervene in the mechanisms that shape their actions. These technical systems often work in concert with bureaucratic norms set by EULAs and ToS to impose shape on the work of digital laborers.

The managerial role of these automated systems of control becomes more pernicious when we consider their impact on marginalized paid workers within the digital media industry, particularly in the platform economy. For these workers, there are often more direct mechanisms of control than that of platform affordances or community guidelines, although they are often given the same veneer of indirectness through attribution to mysterious and supposedly objective algorithms. Automated systems are attributed with determining various aspects of platform workers' everyday conditions, "invisibilizing" the actual managers of that work (Gandini 2019). For instance, in the previous chapter, we explored how algorithms can determine the visibility of content and shape audience traffic in ways that have significant effects on the ability of influencers, YouTubers, or *zhubos* to generate revenue. But it also organizes what these workers do in their everyday working practices. Mapping the nature of content, posting schedules, and pace of production to the logics of opaque algorithms is essential for these workers to secure the all-important legibility to these computation logics that enable their visibility (Bishop 2019a; Bucher 2012; Cotter 2019; Duffy 2017; Guo and Lee 2013; Hardy and Barbagallo 2021). Consequently, like one of Ford's factory workers, the tempo, practices, and temporalities of their labor are fundamentally organized by the platform's production system.

Similarly, computational dynamics such as algorithmically determined "surge pricing" in ride-hailing and delivery work not only have a direct impact on incomes as described in the previous chapter, they can also set the pace and intensity of a worker's labor. Notification of temporary price increases or busy periods are used to encourage more drivers onto the application, adding pressure to adopt working hours that suit the platform (Cant 2020). Uber and Lyft apps, for instance, regularly message drivers, nudging them to keep driving through a sometimes pleasurable gamified system of rewards and punishment (Attoh Wells, and Cullen 2019; Mason 2019; Rosenblat 2018: 135). Similarly, work-on-demand platforms can automatically generate short deadlines for both accepting and completing many jobs, imposing an "artificial time squeeze" that creates a high-pressure work environment (Chen and Sun 2020; Gray and Suri 2019: 77). Workers in various platforms are also typically penalized if they refuse too many jobs, which limits the control they can exert over their working activities and times. Contrary to how it is sold to potential workers, Gray and Suri contend that on-demand labor is not a space of autonomy and flexible working conditions. Rather, it "more closely resembles the infamous *I Love Lucy* television comedy sketch with Lucy and Ethel working on the assembly line at a chocolate factory. As they scramble to keep pace, the pace of work comes faster and faster" (Gray and Suri 2019: 77). This description is telling as it locates platform work in the same context as the de-skilled factory work of Braverman's description in which control over almost all aspects of work is removed from the worker.

Digital systems also provide a great variety of tools for on-the-job worker surveillance – many of which function at a granular level of detail – as well as enabling the automation of discipline both by management or through processes of self-disciplining (see Ball 2010; Rosenblat, Kneese, and boyd, 2014). These mechanisms saturate many digital labor workplaces. In environments where all tasks are digitally mediated – which means recorded and calculated – there is scope for detailed oversight of activity, allowing many points of intervention for either reward or punishment. Upwork, for instance, captures screenshots of workers' computers in real time and may penalize them for undertaking non-work activity during paid time (Anwar and Graham 2020). For drivers and riders in the delivery and ride-sharing sectors, the applications downloaded to their phone not only provide instructions on work tasks – deploying workers to the next pickup – they also feed back to the platform real-time metrics on workers' activity that allow for ongoing oversight and correction. Ride-sharing service DiDi Chuxing, for instance, captures information about drivers' speed and location in three-second intervals, integrating this into its Tides information system which maps and calculates transport demand in real time. It also draws on data about driver movements through accelerometers embedded in the app, identifies location through GPS, and may monitor driver fatigue and customer interactions through a dashboard camera. Individualized trip histories are also fed into the system and can be used to allocate jobs to particular drivers, based on algorithmically calculated assessments of previous behavior (J. Chen 2017, 2018; Chen and Qiu 2019). This kind of surveillance and micromanagement is widespread in the platform economy and structures the tempo, processes, and tasks undertaken by workers (see also Chen and Sun 2020; Irani 2015; McGregor et al. 2016; Rosenblat and Stark 2016; Veen, Barratt, and Goods 2019; Woodcock 2020).

It happens, though, in an ostensibly voluntary context, where workers supposedly decide for themselves when and for how long to be engaged with the app or the platform. They are always *technically* free to log off, even though there are typically negative consequences for disengaging in terms of rankings or the apportioning of work. A less voluntary environment is that within Amazon warehouses where individual, wearable technology tracks and monitors the location and micro-movements of workers. The random inventory distribution system used to store goods is not based on logical organization or grouping of items. Rather, items are placed wherever there is space, with the location digitally recorded. Pickers are guided to each item in order via handheld digital systems. In 2013, BBC journalist Adam Littler took a post in Amazon's Swansea fulfillment center and documented how his handset allocated a fixed number of seconds to find each item (usually 33 seconds), counting them down as he worked, alerting him to errors or time overruns, as well as documenting his performance for oversight by managers (*BBC News* 2013). Workers whose picking rates were deemed too low by the system's calculations faced disciplinary action or sacking. Toiling in shifts spanning at least 10 hours and in which they typically walk over 10 miles, workers' breaks were also scheduled, timed, and monitored by these same systems (Baraniuk 2015; Cadwalladr 2013; Geissler 2018). Even though there is detailed and direct control of workers' activity, their automation places management at a remove from actual managers.

Automated, or quasi-automated, systems are also used within performance review across the platform economy. On many platforms, the job of assessing worker compliance is outsourced either to users through ratings systems which register the legitimacy of a worker's actions or are generated by automatic calculation. Job acceptance, rejection, and cancellation rates are monitored consistently by many apps, and non-compliance often generates an immediate suspension or cancellation of the account and work contract. This is typically coupled with end-user ratings systems that evaluate performance. For instance, on the various careworker platforms explored by Julia Ticona and Alexandra Mateescu (2018), workers are measured in terms of response times to queries, how many job requests they have accepted, and how often they are rehired by the same family. They were also rated by their employers in ways that were often experienced as arbitrary but which, nevertheless, had significant consequences. One careworker noted that minor mistakes, such as being a few minutes late, could result in a negative rating, impacting the capacity to secure further work. While word-of-mouth recommendations have long been a feature of carework, Ticona and Mateescu (2018: 4396–7) argue that, "Poor ratings have greater visibility than off-line circulation of reputation, such as through written letters or by phone, over which careworkers have greater control."

As Rosenblat (2018: 149) points out, the mobilizing of ratings systems not only turns customers into middle managers involved in evaluating workers but also makes management omnipresent within the workplace. Uber drivers, for instance, are rated by passengers on a five-star scale after each ride, so that customers are effectively evaluating worker performance (Rosenblat and Stark 2016). Drivers can have their accounts suddenly deactivated or suspended if they fall below arbitrarily declared thresholds relating to user ratings, ride-acceptance rates, or cancellation rates. Despite being considered independent contractors, Uber's digital laborers must consequently "deliver a standardized experience to passengers or risk suspension, deactivation, or loss of pay" (Rosenblat 2018: 150). Drivers are thus disciplined to temper their affect, identity, and working practices in line with the expectations of passengers (Raval and Dourish 2016; see also ch. 5 below). Uber is also notorious for its failure to respond quickly or effectively to appeals against deactivation or suspension, often leaving drivers without incomes for extended periods. The kind of job insecurity created by the widespread use of such automated systems encourages, or perhaps enforces, self-discipline and alignment with the required norms of the platform.

Christopher O'Neill (2017) has argued that such systems – even the brutal regimes imposed upon Amazon factory workers – are not examples of the imposition of management rule associated with Taylorism. Because they seek to optimize capacities at the level of individual bodies and subjectivities, rather than being imposed upon the whole workspace to optimize productivity, such measures are more aligned with the European Science of Work approach to organizing labor which was designed to humanize the effects of Taylorism. In this model, managers seek to work with and adjust workers' psychological and social rhythms rather than impose an alien structure upon them. Through the apparent voluntarism associated with many digital labor management tools, but particularly because they appear to manifest as instructions generated autonomously from digital systems or from customers, such workplace surveillance and worker management tools are amorphous, generating a "more 'organic' evolution of workplace management" (2017: 616). Such systems, O'Neill argues, are a form of soft domination which is a more legitimate exercise of power in liberal contexts than direct, forceful coercion. The diffuse nature of this power also makes it more difficult to resist.

The cruel optimism of the management minuet

O'Neill may be overstating the case when we look at the treatment of Amazon pickers or social media content moderators – the control of their practices does seem more like a direct, coercive imposition of hard power. Nevertheless, the use of automated surveillance and work allocation systems, as well as extensive regimes of user or peer ratings, exerts a degree of control over the activity of workers of which the floor manager in a Taylorized factory could only dream. Control mechanisms saturate the digital working environment and are used to rationalize but primarily to intensify work (Warin and McCann 2018). Describing these processes as automated or algorithmic is also a useful mechanism for platforms to deflect their role in managing and controlling workers. This is important because these workers' claims to employee status often pivot on the degree of autonomy in working conditions; without clear lines of control over workers' actions, the claims to their self-employment become stronger. It also provides a useful scapegoat for worker or regulator concerns. Management through technical mechanisms allows content creation platforms to assert their status as a neutral provider that is ultimately not responsible for any harms caused by their products. These are either attributed to users or to the black box of algorithms. Uber, for instance, adopts language referring to "server errors" or "glitches" to "mask its manipulative activities," such as wage theft and the overpromising of incomes to drivers (Rosenblat 2018: 115). This has led to the peculiar situation where workers who are some of the most minutely managed are being presented as not managed at all.

But this is really the point. In the deployment of informal systems that create job insecurity, the use of informal guidelines to police creative activity, the reliance on user or peer evaluation of workers, and in control via algorithms, codes, or computation, there is one common thread: disavowal of the direct control of the digital laborer. Braverman (1998 [1974]: 118) notes that the goal of industrial capitalism was for management to grasp the whole labor process and control every element of it. In digital labor, though, the impetus changes. Management processes still want to exploit the whole labor process – and much more besides as my discussion of exploitation in the previous chapter indicates – but it does not seek to directly control every element of it. Instead, it provides at least the semblance of autonomy and agency, allowing room for intellectual engagement, creativity, or entrepreneurial innovation, not least as this is part of what it seeks to monetize. This disavowal is what sustains the sense of autonomy and agency that is associated with the work and allows the figure of the creative, entrepreneurial worker to flourish. Sustaining the myth of workplace autonomy is also one of the non-coercive mechanisms used to produce consent and minimize resistance to workplace control (Burawoy 1979; Purcell and Brook 2020). It makes work desirable and worthy of investment, ensuring greater alignment with the needs of the firm. This autonomy, however, is always tempered with novel systems of indirect intervention to manage and limit that agency, amplified by the capacity of digital systems to gather, capture, and track granular aspects of behavior. There is both freedom and fetters in digital labor. Effectively navigating this dialectic of autonomy and control is the management minuet (Huws 2010), the delicate dance between providing agency and retaining discipline that is typical of creative and knowledge-intensive work.

For workers, though, this dance is shot through with what Lauren Berlant refers to as "cruel optimism" or the state of being attached to a potential or possible future, but one which, when realized, is "discovered either to be impossible, sheer fantasy, or *too* possible, and toxic" (2011: 24). In a study of women running online craft micro-enterprises such as Etsy shops, Susan Luckman (2018) describes this state as the "new normal" for self-employed digital laborers. But it is also the new normal for many other digital laborers. The currency of digital labor is hope. For game testers, the hope is that their temporary position will be a stepping-stone to a more permanent, more creative job in the industry (Bulut 2020: 124). In *Ghost Work*, Gray and Suri (2019: xxvi, original emphasis) note that all the platform workers they interviewed in their five-year study expressed hope, despite differences in geography and the platform(s) for which they worked: "They *hope* to use on-demand jobs to control when they work, who they work with, and what tasks they take on. They *hope* to stay close to their families. They *hope* to avoid long commutes and hostile work environments. And they *hope* to gain experience that refreshes their résumé or opens a door to new possibilities."

In the elite work of the digital media industry, hope is also essential. Startup founders hope to find an amenable VC with deep pockets. A VC hopes to find that startup that can return their investment tenfold upon IPO. Everybody hopes that this bit of tech will be the next killer app. The possibility of a big IPO is dangled in front of engineers as a powerful recruitment tool. With salary often deferred or sacrificed to stock options, workers in tech startups must remain hopeful about the economic future of the company in which they invest all their time. The fantastic nature of tech sector optimism is summed up by the term "unicorn" to describe companies valued at over US$1 billion. The perpetual promise of catching a ride on such a mythical beast drives work in the sector, occasionally bolstered by the stories of those lucky few who succeeded in attaching themselves to mega companies like Google or Facebook at the right time.

This hope is not only cruel because the likelihood of finding the unicorn is slim given the fail rates of startups. It is also cruel as it feeds the over-investment that perpetuates overwork and sustains the holistic hold these companies have over their employees. Isaac (2019: 5, original emphasis) describes this dynamic: for tech workers, the "anxiety, stress, and crushing schedule of twelve-plus-hour days was all going to be worth it. They were all going to get paid, *big time.*" Sometimes, the relationship between overwork and stock options is made overt. Former Facebook employee Katherine Losse draws a direct relationship between the immersion in work that this normalized and the promise of future gain.

> We didn't have a nonwork life: Life was work and work was life. We did this because we expected that we would be rewarded accordingly – any short-term losses, such as the option to date casually and devote energy to nonwork pastimes, would be more than compensated by long-term gains in the form of stock options that we hoped would one day be worth millions of dollars. (Losse 2012: 74)

In digital media industries, hope is a management tool.

Wendy Liu summarizes her own experience of cruel optimism within the exhausting working practices of Silicon Valley's startup culture. She rejected a secure job offer at Google in favor of founding her own startup and the freedom, agency, and meaning that were promised to follow working for oneself on self-defined projects. Subscribing to an exhortation by PayPal co-founder and VC Peter Thiel, she wanted not only to have agency in her own life but to leave a mark on the world. The pursuit of this goal led to a culture of overwork, and the investment of time and energy it demanded created an inertia that perpetuated this cycle and ensured commitment to projects in which she had long ago lost faith.

> The truth was, I was afraid to work less because it would make my life feel meaningless. I had wholeheartedly absorbed the belief that work should be the center of my life, and yet the work I had found myself doing was nowhere near fulfilling. If this had been my real job, a 9–5 with OKRs and performance reviews, I would quit it in an instant. The work was a slog, the use cases were trivial, and the customers annoyed me. But I had come too far to quit, so instead I accelerated forward. (Liu 2020: 93)

Despite the autonomy and agency she was granted and experienced in her work, the organization of work through the prism of hope and meaning organized Liu's labor into routines and temporalities that she clearly did not own or control. As a startup founder, Liu is also her own manager, which means the discipline and control being exerted is not emanating from an employer but is immanent within the culture of digital capitalism and Silicon Valley.

Liu's experience is arguably not that of the average digital laborer doing microwork for an online platform or creating content in the hope of securing an audience. Nevertheless, the valorization of autonomy, the jarring relationship of that vision with the reality of day-to-day digital labor, and the cruel optimism that drives this investment that she articulates is a dynamic that widely animates digital labor. The following chapter will pick up the thread of how the entrepreneurial mindset of the Silicon Valley startup founder imbued with this cruel optimism is a widespread aspiration. It will also explore how this is a figure sticky with libidinal energies and positive affects which are integral to understanding not only what digital labor is but how it manages its workers so effectively.

4

Alienation: The Romance of Entrepreneurialism

In 2017, Microsoft released an advertisement for their hp Spectre x360 tablet (Genuine 2017). Featuring blogger, podcaster, and author Emma Gannon, it describes the perfect fit of this technology for the lives of millennials. The ad begins with Gannon narrating: "They say that the millennial generation will have more than five jobs in their lifetime." Shifting to close-up, she then adds, "I think that's really exciting." In a blog post about this appearance, Gannon wrote how happy she was that Microsoft was showcasing her story about "being a multi-hyphenate twenty-something woman (aka 'slashie')." She points out that she is not alone in this type of career, with many other people of her generation similarly pursuing complex, non-linear professional paths and being involved in multiple simultaneous endeavors that together make "One Big Career." For Gannon, this is considered an empowering proposition. She concludes, "I might not have One Job but that's okay. I have multiple skills, multiple income streams, fingers in pies and many strings to my bow. Turns out I've never felt more stable or powerful since being a slashie."

What is most intriguing to me about Gannon's discourse is that it contains no aspiration to stable and secure work; her current precarious state is not presented merely as a hopeful stepping-stone as described in other forms of under-compensated, creative digital labor (Duffy 2017; Kuehn and Corrigan 2013). Rather, it is an end in itself. Moreover, it is to be celebrated.

This valorization of the fractured career paths of the digital economy in Gannon's narrative chimed with presentations by other young people at the ILO-run Future of Work conference that I'd attended earlier that year. At this event, the same suggestion about the freedom or agency that comes from piecemeal gig work was on display. Given the discussion in the previous chapters about the mostly negative consequences of such stable instability, this seems counterintuitive. It certainly puzzled me every time I encountered the Microsoft ad. How, I wondered, has precarity, insecurity, overwork, and lifelong labor instability become an ideal? What makes this resonate? How have we been sold the neoliberal Kool-Aid of precarity?

But my instinctive, critical response may be asking the wrong questions. Perhaps celebrating entrepreneurial, precarious work contexts is not Kool-Aid at all. Certainly, many workers find opportunities and higher incomes in the gig economy than would otherwise be available in their local contexts. This has been documented in platform work, particularly within developing economies (Anwar and Graham 2020; Kashyap and Bhatia 2018; Wood et al. 2019). As Huws (2019: 150) notes, for a New York-, London-, or Sydney-based graphic designer working for a platform may comprise a reduced, untenable set of conditions but "could open up marvellous opportunities for another designer in Kiev, or Hanoi, or Dhaka." But there is more in the casting of digital labor as "good work" than its ability to offer better incomes. Despite the precarious conditions with which it is associated, Gannon's story tells us that digital labor is understood and experienced as actively desirable by many workers. How then do we reconcile this framework with the litany of horrors outlined in the previous chapters?

This chapter is focused on these questions. It casts a critical eye over the libidinal drives that animate digital labor but without dismissing the reality of its pleasures and desirability. Following ideas from SRT, it doesn't assume that workers are a fixed subjectivity but that they are constantly in the process of being produced and reproduced as workers by their material and cultural environments. Using this framework, this chapter explores some of the conceptual frameworks associated with precarity in digital labor, the entrepreneurial, "slashie" subjects who valorize it, and the agency that lies therein. Rather than looking at the nature of this work per se, it examines the cultural formations into which digital labor is embedded, focusing in particular on the discursive environment that makes these material conditions sensible. By drawing on the ideas of Luc Boltanski, Laurent Thévenot, and Eve Chiapello on capitalism's justificatory regimes and considering the pervasive role of Romantic thought in the cultures of hustle that pervade digital labor, it also reframes orthodox Marxist assumptions about the inherent alienation of work under capitalism.

(Dis-)Alienation and digital labor

One of the great promises of the post-Fordist labor environment was improved conditions in the workplace and for work to become more meaningful. As we saw in the last chapter, the newly emerging creative and conceptually rich work common in the digital media industries has been depicted as doing away with the emotional and creative constraints imposed upon industrialized workers. It has been associated with upending the soulless, stultifying, repetitive processes of the industrial factory, and replacing the bland bureaucratic hoop jumping of the assembly lines and cubicles of the Fordist-era firm. The petty life and frustrated self-expression of the everyday worker, epitomized in Sloan Wilson's (2005 [1955]) "man in the grey flannel suit," was said to be transformed by the flattened hierarchies and dynamic and flexible career paths associated with digital labor and by the demands for innovation and creative thinking within all kinds of work. As Eran Fisher (2010) notes, the exemplar model for post-Fordist corporations, work arrangements, and the technologies that support them is the network. In this model, workers become reconceptualized as nodes among a peer group of competing nodes rather than cogs in a machine. This rearticulation around the metaphor of the network changes, he says, the very nature of work by opening up space for creative expression. By blurring rigid definitions of when and how work happens, networks allow "the reintegration of play, joy, and passion into the reproduction of society. These novelties allow workers to bring their personal, lifeworld qualities of creativity and deep personal engagement to bear on their work activities, and re-eroticize the disenchanted world of work" (2010: 238). In doing so, the network model "does away with the bureaucratic, gray, stifling organization" (2010: 238).

What is also striking about the narratives associated with post-Fordism is the shift in how work mediated by technologies is viewed.

> During the Fordist phase of capitalism, technology discourse extolled the capacity of technology to enhance social goals of security, stability, and equality by mitigating the *exploitative* nature of capitalism. In contrast, during the contemporary post-Fordist phase of capitalism, technology discourse extols the capacity of technology to enhance individual goals of personal empowerment, authenticity, and creativity by mitigating the *alienating* nature of capitalism. (Fisher 2010: 234)

Rather than a mechanism of crushing corporate control, technologically shaped, networked work in post-Fordism was to become a site for self-realization and creative and personal agency. It was to become dis-alienated.

In orthodox Marxism, alienation is one of the great tragedies inflicted upon the worker by the imposition of capitalist labor relations. In the *Economic and Philosophic Manuscripts* (2013), Marx defines four key forms of this dispossession. Under the wage relation and the forms of labor organization associated with it, workers become alienated from the products of their labor as it is their employer who decides the nature and ultimate fate of what they produce. Most importantly, the worker is no longer able to use the products of their labor to sustain themselves and instead becomes reliant on the purchasing of commodities for survival. Under capitalism, the fruits of a worker's labor – embodiments of their living energies – become instead detached objects in the world. Their own laboring energy thus "becomes an object, assumes an *external* existence" that "stands opposed" to the worker "as an autonomous power" (Marx 2013: 83, original emphasis). This is the alienation from the products of labor.

Workers are also alienated from their own work activity as they are not able to decide when and how they work or use their activity to achieve their own ends. Waged labor converts worker's physical or intellectual capacity – their embodied labor-power – into the abstracted concept of labor-time which is then sold to an employer. After this conversion, decisions about the directions and goal of that activity are removed from the worker. This often includes the specific processes, steps, and gestures of that work, as we saw in the previous chapter. The worker's labor thus becomes both objectified in the abstract form of time and removed from its context of meaning. Their working body and self no longer belong to the worker but to someone else, and their work is performed not to address self-determined needs or for self-realization but solely to earn an income to consume the products of other people's labor.

The third form of alienation that Marx describes is that from "species-being," that is, alienation from the essence of humanity. He argues that as work ceases to be a free, conscious activity and instead becomes solely a means to generate income to purchase the commodities needed to survive, it becomes stripped of the higher purposes that differentiate human labor from the activity of animals. When work becomes solely about enabling consumption for survival, productive activity is no longer fulfilling its function of creating a meaningful life. As the activities that define the human species are turned into merely the means for existence, the worker becomes alienated from their own body, nature, their mental capacities and, through that, humanity itself; the worker under capitalism becomes less than human.

The consequence of this alienation from "species-being" is the final form of alienation, which is from other people. Because of their mutual alienation from meaningful selfhood, each individual worker is thus unable to connect meaningfully with every other worker and so is unable to build a collective good and through that a vibrant, equitable society. For humans to be emancipated and to realize their collective species-being, Marx contends, workers must reject the capitalist system and its alienating qualities. Human activity must be dis-alienated – or re-enchanted – returned to a state where it is located within and gives meaning to human essence and higher goals.

To dis-alienate work, then, is to give workers agency within their laboring life, control over what they do, investment in the products they make, the capacity to work with others to achieve common goals, and, most importantly, for those goals to be an expression of self, creativity, passion, and ambition. As I and others have pointed out elsewhere (Fromm 2013; Jarrett 2016b), the alienation thesis and its emphasis on human essences and species-being may be dismissed as the musings of a young Marx in thrall to Hegel. Nevertheless, the alienation thesis has significant purchase even within the scientific materialism of his later works such as *Capital* (Fromm 2013; Wartenberg 1982). In particular, it has a long resonance within studies of digital cultures and digital labor in which the liberatory potential attributed to the internet has long focused on the possibilities for re-enchanting media production and consumption (Andrejevic 2009). When the digital intersects with the post-Fordist reorganization of the economy around flexibility, de-hierarchization, and individual empowerment, the potential for re-enchantment of work seems realizable.

Digital labor is thus deeply connected to the potential for dis-alienation, even if it does not actually achieve this reality.

As described in the previous chapter, having the semblance of autonomy and agency at work is an important attractor for various kinds of digital employment. Additionally, "doing what you love" – or what has profound personal or social impact and thus engages species-being – is also a promise threaded through all its forms (Duffy 2017; Liu 2004; Neff et al. 2005; Ross 2009; Tokumitsu 2014). Certainly, affect and autonomous self-expression drive the user-generated content and data-generating environments of social media, not least because such work is formally uncontracted, has no real connection to financial compensation, and is often experienced as fun rather than work. Creating content for profit online is also associated with self-actualization and doing "good work," particularly given its association with creativity and self-expression; the increasing use of the phrase "creator culture" as a blanket term for describing this activity speaks of this framing (Cunningham and Craig 2021). To cite a specific example, Instagram's (n.d.) recruitment of potential unpaid user laborers – and thus also influencers and other commercial content creators who may use the platform – describes this work as "Bringing you closer to the people and things you love." After establishing the social good of this digital labor, it then describes the agency and self-determination that its workers can experience, saying that the site allows a potential Instagrammer to "express yourself in new ways with the latest Instagram features" and "connect with more people, build influence, and create compelling content that is distinctly yours."

In creative, elite occupations, such as game design, programming, web design, or graphic artistry, the relationship to dis-alienated labor is also clear. Having the products of your labor be (ideally) a realization of individual creativity or something that creates a social good is an alluring privilege, regardless of whether this work is formally freelance or contained within a relatively stable corporate environment. In its recruitment pages, Facebook (Facebook n.d.) overtly asserts this logic, enticing potential employees with the promise of doing the "most meaningful work of their career." Similarly, online payment systems company Stripe (n.d.) recruits workers by referring to the social good of putting "the global economy within everyone's reach while doing the most important work of your career."

But the pull of dis-alienated labor is also felt in the less privileged context of the platform economy and in the work of more marginal workers. Along with the ideals of autonomy described in the previous chapter, platform labor is often sold using appeals to its affective and cultural value. Ola drivers, for instance, are recruited not only with the lure of making money and securing a future but also in order to "earn respect" (Ola n.d.). Rosenblat (2018) describes the mobilization of "millennial glamour" in the promotion of work for platforms such as Uber and Fiverr. Drawing on myths of technological exceptionalism and sharing, which positions the industry in terms of a social good, work is presented as chasing dreams of self-determination. She describes one ad asking the negatively inflected question: "How much did you make for your boss today?" (2018: 35), linking platform work with independence. Uber, she notes, promotes itself as "a pathway to the middle class for anyone who wanted to drive" (2018: 25) that can be accessed via the mechanism of entrepreneurship with references to independence, freedom, and being your own boss.

There is also often a mix of instrumental and affective motivations in the logics of workers who take on these roles. Rosenblat's study cites the importance of flexibility over their working lives as well as making social connections as a motivation for both full-time drivers and those for whom it is a hobby. Similarly, "control, autonomy, and self-efficacy" was recognized as an important aspect of the work of Brazilian platform drivers studied by Marcia C. Vaclavik and Liana H. Pithan (2018). For workers in Gray and Suri's (2019) study, doing the "ghost work" of digital microwork platforms was considered a desirable alternative to low-end service work but also valued in its own right. It was considered attractive for how it fit around workers' other life commitments, giving "some semblance of control over their time, work environment, and what they took on and valued as 'meaningful' work" (2019: 96). Some of their research subjects also describe taking on work specifically for self-improvement or for self-determination, in particular being one's own boss.

Even in contexts where the organization and control of the labor process most overtly alienate workers, the promise of dis-alienated work plays out as an unrealized and, by this absence, animating force in how this work is experienced. This is certainly the underlying narrative arc of Heike Geissler's (2018) *Seasonal Associate* in which she describes her work as a temporary contractor in an Amazon fulfillment center. The book documents some of the intense labor management systems and the punishing rules imposed on workers. However, the central concern of Geissler's narrative is how such work lacked meaning and was stripped of dignity. Even when it is not realized, dis-alienated digital labor remains an aspirational ideal.

Adam Arvidsson (2019) argues that seeking this kind of fulfillment in work, and in particular seeking work that produces social change, is a key driver within what he refers to as "industrious capitalism." He contends that meaningful work has become the existential solution to the instabilities generated by the neoliberal assault on labor security. Dis-alienated labor is the positive face of the kinds of labor-intensive, small-scale, petty commodity production we see in digital media such as platform work, freelance creative production, and tech startups. In these contexts, work and its products remain under the apparent autonomous control of the worker and can be invested with the use-values and meaning specific to that worker's needs and desires – or those of their society, family, or community. While work and incomes may be insecure and so require sustained and constant effort, it can also be experienced as personally rewarding, socially meaningful, and/or produce quality goods in which the worker is invested.

While the hustle that typifies this kind of work is often associated with millennials, Arvidsson instead describes a longer history. He locates it in the advanced pre-capitalist economies of medieval and early modern Europe, India, the Islamic Empire, and Ming and Qing China, which were marked by small-scale, labor-intensive production, a mix of markets and communitarian organizations such as guilds, and slow innovation rooted in tradition. In particular, though, he sees it in the pre-industrial modern phase of capitalism where industriousness and hard work, often without clear goals, was celebrated. Hustle is "a mentality of making do and adapting to what is at hand. It is informal, entrepreneurial, street-level *bricolage*" (2019: 41, original emphasis). He likens this to Weber's famous Protestants toiling to create change with only a vague idea of where they were heading. But, he says, this dynamic never really went away throughout the goal-oriented period of nation-building, industrial modernity. Something of its kind, he says, has

> always been part of the modern experience for ordinary people. Even in the organized societies of industrial modernity, many operated outside of regulated labour markets or secure careers. . . . This industrious economy – small-scale, flexible and semi-formal – has remained more prevalent in some places, like India or Southern Italy, but it was never entirely eradicated even in the highly organized societies of Northern Europe or the US. (Arvidsson 2019: 4–5)

What is novel, though, is that the marginalized communities and workers who have been pushed out of traditional labor and life patterns through global capitalism and into entrepreneurial hustle are "increasingly joined by middle-class university graduates, who historically used to prefer stable employment to the vagaries of entrepreneurship" (2019: 5).

This shifting of industriousness from the margins is an effect both of capitalist restructuring that has rendered the stability of a job for life untenable, but also of the cultural politics of the global North that reject "bullshit jobs" (Graeber 2018) and which increasingly values work that creates change, either personal or social.

Digital entrepreneurs

The figure that personifies this industriousness and the promise of dis-alienation is the entrepreneur. The idea of enterprise, as it is mobilized by capitalism, is inflected with ideas of freedom, invention and free will (Berardi 2009; Lorusso 2019). The entrepreneur is the self-made, creative, autonomous, disruptive, change-maker of Arvidsson's description. They are the antithesis of the alienated "wage slave" or Braverman's industrial workers, described in the last chapter, who sell their labor-time for eight hours a day to an employer who controls their actions and cares little for their hopes and dreams in order to produce generic products in which they have no investment. Instead, the entrepreneur invests in their work and embraces risk; is the one brave enough to venture out of the "iron cage" of waged labor and fling themselves wholly into the dangerous currents of capitalism. They are independent, self-reliant, and innovative, able to adapt themselves, their labor, and their products to changing circumstances as a matter of necessity. They are also driven, their passion for what they do manifesting in perseverance and intensive work with non-financial motives that often provide as much motivation as financial gain (Weiss 2017). Entrepreneurialism, as Imre Szeman (2015) says, is a "sticky idea" that sutures together ideals and aspirations about good work and wealth creation with the realities of precarious employment, but in a way that renders this work desirable and exciting. It emerges as a logical extension of society where self-worth is bound into market logics, rather than purely social or cultural dynamics, and embodies the dynamics that sustain both the economy and the human subject. As Szeman (2015: 473) adds, "Entrepreneurship exists in the twenty-first century as a commonsense way of navigating the inevitable, irreproachable, and apparently unchangeable reality of global capitalism."

The idealized, aspirational figure of the entrepreneur is at the core of digital labor and its dis-alienating tendencies. We see entrepreneurialism in the networking engaged in by freelance web designers or game developers, discussed in chapter 2, who invest their social lives in generating potential work contacts. We see it in the unpaid "hope labor" (Duffy 2017; Kuehn and Corrigan 2013) of building glamorous and idealized online profiles to provide a positive character reference for any future employer who may search for your name. It also undergirds the platform economy as workers transform talents and skills, such as knowledge of languages, design, fashion, or coding, and personal assets, such as cars or bicycles, into revenue sources to maximize income. This is also a context where being your own boss – "the ultimate expression of freedom in the labour process" (Purcell and Brook 2020: 7) – is centralized. Maximizing the value of your assets (see chapter 5), including your time and subjectivity, is the essence of entrepreneurial activity.

Silicon Valley startup culture provides the emblematic model of entrepreneurialism where dynamism and disruption are highly valued, along with an openness to taking chances. Its widely publicized, mythic tales of successful self-starting, bootstrapped, risk-taking innovators serve to reinforce the value of this mode of being. These success stories mobilize the myth of dis-alienated labor with the heroic startup founder pursuing control of their labor and committed to work with personal meaning – even though once VCs and other investors intervene, this can be far from the actuality (Cockayne 2016; Pein 2018). Silicon Valley and its entrepreneurial workforce function as an imaginary that articulates a normative model for enterprise development which has been adopted by individuals and nation-states far beyond its US geographic and cultural location. For instance, in many African nations, the fostering of digital entrepreneurship has been tied to development and state economic planning (Friederici, Wahome, and Graham 2020; Ndemo and Weiss 2017). This often involves the absorption and then inflection of Silicon Valley's economic and cultural models even if, as Friederici and co-authors' (2020) sober analysis of digital industries across sub-Saharan Africa reminds us, the local context makes the scaling up associated with Silicon Valley much more challenging. Still, the norms of Silicon Valley remain "a set of aspirations for changing old ways" (2020: 215) and a lens through which many African digital laborers inflect their work and goals.

Similarly, China's Rural Revitalization program, which is intended to grow the economy and deal with the problems of internal migration to cities, imagines a countryside "filled with peasants starting e-commerce businesses, small-scale manufacturing, new data centers, and young entrepreneurial workers returning to their rural homes" (Wang 2020: 22). This economic scheme has relied on some success in translating entrepreneurialism into Chinese culture; a Chinese venture capitalist interviewed by Xiaowei Wang describes an increasing tolerance of risk and failure facilitating the kinds of disruptive innovation associated with Silicon Valley. The Rural Revitalization program, the government's Internet+ agenda and its Mass Entrepreneurship and Innovation strategy have dovetailed to create what Jian Lin and Jeroen de Kloet (2019; Craig et al. 2021; Li, Tan, and Yang 2020; Xia 2018) describe as "unlikely" creative workers and cultural entrepreneurs across rural China. In their investigation of technology industries in China's countryside, Wang describes entering the small rural village of Sanqiao. Across the recently completed hospital building is a sign featuring a government exhortation: "being lazy is a disgrace, being self-reliant leads to strength." In this sign, Wang sees the echo of a set of American values emphasizing hard work and bootstrapping. They add, "Hustle has come to Sanqiao" (Wang 2020: 48).

The Global Entrepreneurship Monitor (GEM) 2019 report (published in 2020), which examined 50 countries with diverse income levels, reveals significant entrepreneurial activity and evidence that this mode of industry has grown over the 19 years the organization has been collecting data. The report identified "hives" of early-stage entrepreneurial activity ranging from 4% of adults in Italy and Pakistan to over 35% in Chile and Ecuador. The report also identified diverse motivations for engaging in entrepreneurialism. For some, the lure of a quick buck was important, but they also found substantial and growing evidence of purposeful entrepreneurship associated with social change, with women more likely to be driven by this latter motivation. The GEM data clearly indicate that while there are global differences in its penetration, entrepreneurialism is not a niche or uniquely American activity. Moreover, its impact extends beyond digital work into all kinds of labor so that the qualities attributed to Silicon Valley's white male elite workers are considered necessary for all kinds of workers and industries, from retailers and restaurateurs to scavengers and bootleggers (Szeman 2015).

In some ways, this is a peculiar turn of events. The entrepreneur was once associated negatively with taking on unnecessary risk and was a minor figure within capitalism – effectively, the exception that proved the rule about the social value and centrality of fixed wage labor. More recently, though, this character has come to permeate the social imaginary as a model of how to be and do, and not only in business. Nikolas Rose (1998) locates the figure of the entrepreneur within the politics of "enterprise" which emerged in neoliberal politics, particularly in Thatcher's Britain. As this agenda rolled out, economic and social well-being was increasingly viewed as fostered best by the actions of individuals, businesses, and organizations striving to maximize their self-interest, rather than being organized centrally by the state. This focused attention on the individual "enterprising" activities and choices of autonomous entities such as corporations and citizens. Rose says, "Enterprise here designates an array of rules for the conduct of one's everyday existence: energy, initiative, ambition, calculation, and personal responsibility. The enterprising self will make an enterprise of its life, seek to maximize its own human capital, project itself a future, and seek to shape itself in order to become that which it wishes to be" (Rose 1998: 154).

As espoused in Thatcherite ideology, "enterprise culture" was not merely about restructuring selfhood in terms of individualistic wealth creation but also about instilling self-discipline. Rose argues that the ethics of enterprise – "competitiveness, strength, vigor, boldness, outwardness and the urge to succeed" (1998: 157) – worked in tandem with the expanding salience of popular psychology and its therapeutic relationship to Self to make people individually responsible for the scope of their experience. Citizens in Thatcher's Britain were encouraged to become entrepreneurs of the self, working constantly on their subjectivity to enhance the capacity to maximize their assets. Drawing on a conservative, liberal morality, the ideal entrepreneur was charged with exercising their freedom and autonomy, but also with taking sole responsibility for their life's trajectory. This responsibilization became absolute in the context of liberalism's stated (although not actualized) disavowal of state intervention and the rejection of social causes for inequality exemplified in Thatcher's famous reissuing of Bentham's dictum, "There's no such thing as society. There are individual men and women and there are families." Within this framework, the entrepreneur emerges not as a victim of economic circumstances but as an active agent with a moral imperative to seek a good life. Moreover, they need to do this independently and through their own initiative.

To be entrepreneurial is thus a holistic project – a point we will discuss further in chapter 5 – and one that provides a range of affective experiences. One of the highlighted digital laborers in the Global Entrepreneurship Monitor (GEM) report articulates the saturating demands and rewards of entrepreneurial work:

> It's more than just creating a successful business and earning money. It is a lifestyle, full of joy, risk, sadness and often times loneliness. But there is always light at the end of a dark tunnel. We are here to make big changes and create new and fair jobs. However, to do this normally means we have to fail first then recover and start over to be the disruptive entrepreneur. (Global Entrepreneurship Monitor 2020: 35)

False consciousness or the spirit of capitalism?

It would be tempting to dismiss entrepreneurial rhetoric and this worker's narrative as merely examples of false consciousness – the misconception of the true realities of working conditions. It may also be tempting to consider it a comforting delusion that merely makes a virtue out of the necessity for entrepreneurial activity that has been caused by the breakdown of secure labor alternatives. It might also be understood as a "hoax" perpetrated by capitalism upon workers (Morgan and Nelligan 2018). However, this approach would, at worst, presuppose a certain stupidity on behalf of the entrepreneurial digital laborers described in this book and, given the widespread salience of this mode of being, all of society. At best, it assumes that people are somehow unaware of the difficult reality of their lived experience as precarious digital laborers. This is not borne out in the studies explored here. Workers are usually fully cognizant of the iniquities of their working lives. More importantly for the purposes of the analysis in this chapter, an approach predicated on determining the actuality of the promises made by entrepreneurialism does not necessarily get us to the questions of why and how this model of labor has become acceptable. It doesn't allow us to figure out just how amenable entrepreneurial subjects have been produced and reproduced. These questions don't ask whether entrepreneurialism truly offers the rewards it promises or whether it actually constitutes a dis-alienated work environment. I am more interested in how it came to be understood as such: not its actuality, but its conditions of possibility.

To understand how digital labor can be sold and accepted as "good work," the analysis by Boltanski, Thévenot, and Chiapello of the justificatory regimes – or spirits – that drive any given articulation of capitalist accumulation provides a useful lens. By "spirit of capitalism," Boltanski and Chiapello (2005a: 8, original emphasis) mean *"the ideology that justifies engagement in capitalism."* This spirit is what legitimates people's adherence to what is an essentially absurd system in which wage earners are asked to lose "ownership of the fruits of their labour and the possibility of pursuing a working life free of subordination" (2005a: 7). They argue that capitalism's survival is based on the internalization of duress, which in turn relies on "a number of shared representations – capable of guiding action – and justifications, which present it as an acceptable and even desirable order of things: the only possible order, or the best of all possible orders" (2005a: 10). The dominant shared representations about "good work" are "the spirit" of that time that inspires industry, labor, management, and ultimately, capitalist subjects. These spirits are "dialectically enacted as ways of acting ... and inculcated as ways of being or identities" (Chiapello and Fairclough 2002: 188). By internalizing this spirit, actors ranging from corporations to individual workers become bound by the legitimate, legal, and "fair" practices it enshrines and are provided with aspirational goals.

This spirit, however, is not merely a "simple adornment or 'superstructure'" but is "central to the process of capitalistic accumulation that it serves because it applies constraints to this process" (Boltanski and Chiapello 2005b: 163). Boltanski and Chiapello contend that the "amorality" of capitalism requires that it have enemies – people who oppose it. By responding to criticisms voiced by these opponents, capitalism generates "the moral foundations that it lacks, and [which] enable it to incorporate justice-enhancing mechanisms whose relevancy it would not otherwise have to acknowledge" (2005b: 163). Criticisms thus provide the impetus for changes to an underlying spirit and, in doing so, are what enables capitalism to be experienced as an acceptable or "fair" system for the general population. This also means that what is defined as the acceptable mode of accumulation alters over time. Consequently, observing the animating logics of capitalism at a given moment offers insight into what is defined – and likely experienced – as "good work" during that period. These models are not mutually exclusive and multiple forms may exist at the same time. Nevertheless, there is typically a dominant spirit that most accords with the socio-technical conditions of that period.

Each spirit is marked by a unique "grammar" that is used to specify objects, practices, and ways of being that are justified or legitimated in that discourse. The idea of a grammar can be taken almost literally, with key terms and concepts organized differently between the different spirits. To offer a short summary (see Boltanski and Chiapello 2005b: 168 for a full list), the grammar of each regime specifies what constitutes appropriate or "great" behavior; defines the objects, people, and relations between them that are considered important and which become indexed to greatness; and is a format of activity which links greatness to some kind of sacrifice. Each spirit is based upon a different "equivalency principle," which nominates a standard from which actions are assessed and valued. The "greatness" of an individual is attributed in terms of this standard. It is the description of this figure that interests us in trying to understand the valorization of the entrepreneur in digital labor.

In their analysis of management literature outlining moral practice in business between the 1960s and 1990, Boltanski and Thévenot (2006 [1991]) identified six dominant justificatory regimes, each of which describes different versions of legitimate capitalist practice:

1 The Inspired Spirit
2 The Domestic Spirit
3 The Spirit of Fame
4 The Civic Spirit
5 The Market Spirit
6 The Industrial Spirit

It is not possible to explore all of these spirits in any detail, but to identify the great individual within two of the above regimes shows something of how each regime creates a different ideal laboring subject. In the Domestic Spirit, for instance, the great person is one who relies on "their hierarchical position in a chain of personal interdependencies" (Chiapello and Fairclough 2002: 190). Work here is organized through regimes of subordination based on models of nuclear domesticity centered in the patriarchal figure of the father. This patriarch becomes the great figure "to whom respect and allegiance are due, and who in turn grants protection and support" (Chiapello and Fairclough 2002: 190). This can be contrasted with the standard by which "greatness" is attributed in the Market Spirit. In this instance, the "great" person resembles more the cliché of the capitalist trader. This figure "makes a fortune for him- or herself by offering highly coveted goods in a competitive marketplace – and who knows when to seize the right opportunities" (Chiapello and Fairclough 2002: 190–1).

Later in the 1990s, Boltanski and Chiapello identified the emergence of a new and increasingly dominant value system in commerce literature. During this period, they argue, the dominant justificatory logic became the Projective Spirit, and it is here that we find the naturalized home of the digital laborer. Within this regime, the network is the harmonious figure of natural order, so the dignity of persons is involved in the creation of connections. Just action is thus associated with facilitating those connections. These connections are the key relationship between actors and are based on communication, trust, and adjusting to/coordinating with others. Key agents are mediators who use new technologies, information relations, alliances, projects, and relationships of trust in the process of developing networked relations. The goal here is activity in itself rather than, as would have been the case in the Market Spirit, profit. This is a logic exemplified in Silicon Valley economics where actually generating profits often takes a back seat to a technology, platform, or company's level of activity and position within the network of similar firms.

This regime has been linked to the rise of digital labor, with a few scholars focusing on the ways the precarity, freelancing and short-term contracts, soft control, and the mobility of digital labor in its self-employed forms map onto the contours of, and are legitimated by, the projective regime (for instance, Fisher 2010; Hearn 2008; Karatzogianni and Matthews 2020; Morgan and Nelligan 2018; Rosenblat and Stark 2016). Few, though, have focused on what the wide social embedding of this regime means for subjectivity and the reproduction of the laboring self. But it is here we find the ideal, entrepreneurial digital laborer.

The great person in the projective regime is one who is engaged, mobile, and flexible, while autonomy, enthusiasm, and adaptability – particularly in relation to others – are also highly prized characteristics. These are precisely the qualities personified by the industrious, hustling digital worker. The "little person," on the other hand, becomes unemployable for they are unadaptable and rigid and rooted to the security that does not accord with the flexible labor and economic conditions of the networked world. This behavior brings about the closure of the network, benefiting only a small number of people and so is considered unfair. Just behavior of a "great person," therefore, lies in extending the network, redistributing information, and facilitating contacts, particularly of the "little people" who are yet to embrace networks and flexibility. The cost of achieving this status, though, is the sacrifice of anything that impedes flexibility and availability such as attachments to the local and security of roots. This encourages the absorption of risk which, as Gina Neff (2012) points out, is a feature of precarious, contract work but is also central to the dynamics of entrepreneurialism. Precarity is the cost of being great in contemporary capitalism. Greatness in this regime also involves the renunciation of authority that comes from institutional hierarchical status – each worker is only as valid as their competence within each project – leading to the instability of these careers. The ability to move between projects – to juggle multiple career paths, multiple gigs, multiple responsibilities – is thus the key test of success within this regime. Rejection or exclusion are its key sanctions, manifesting as failure to get the next gig, while renewed calls for participation – the next contract or project – are key rewards.

In this justificatory regime, good work becomes positively associated with hustle, industriousness, and entrepreneurialism: to be precarious and a risk taker becomes a virtuous state as it articulates the mobility and adaptability of the ideal subject. But I would add to this regime the impetus for work to be meaningful. Good work also becomes about doing dis-alienated activity that allows for self-expression and self-realization as embodied in the craving for autonomy and social change that Arvidsson identifies. The "great person" in this regime is a creative entrepreneur. This paves the way for the legitimacy and desirability of the kinds of unstable, exploitative conditions we see in digital labor. The widespread inculcation and acceptance of this ideal subjectivity is what allows digital laborers such as Emma Gannon to not only accept but desire their insecure work conditions.

Artistic critique

What particularly interests me is that this regime emerged in response to what Boltanski and his colleagues describe as the "artistic critique" of capitalism that was developed in academic and popular analyses of labor since the 1950s. This critique focuses on problems of authenticity and alienation in the work of industrial capital rather than the distribution of resources (Boltanski and Chiapello 2005a: 419–82). These evaluations – even in their popular form – were often articulated from an underlying or explicit Marxist premise. They ranged from condemnation of workplace hierarchies and organizational fixity to the debased nature of mass-produced consumer goods and the subjective oppression associated with bureaucratic, micromanaged labor. The capitalism this critique depicts is the hollowed-out and controlled spaces we see occupied by Braverman's (1998 [1974]; see also ch. 3 above) de-skilled worker, C. Wright Mills' (1951) white-collar worker who produces nothing and is forced into cheerful compliance, and in which William H. Whyte's (2002 [1956]) "organization man" is resident. We also see echoes of Theodor Adorno and Max Horkheimer (1992) and Herbert Marcuse's (1991 [1964]) commentaries on the subsumptive, instrumental rationalities of popular capitalist culture. At its core, we see in the artistic critiques of the middle of the twentieth century the influence of early Marx's insistence on the centrality of alienation from species-being as the key detrimental impact of capitalist labor relations. The projective regime of capitalism and its ideal, industrious entrepreneurial worker embody the rejection of this principle and so become, effectively, the solution to the vagaries of capitalist exploitation, even while furthering that system.

What's important to underscore is that the artistic critique was not only an academic exercise by sociologists and Marxist theorists. The 1960s' and 1970s' countercultures materially modeled many of the positions of these critical thinkers in railing against "the man" and the stultifying effects of conventional work and cultural practices associated with Fordist-era norms (Frayssé 2015). Relatedly, struggle against draining and unrewarding labor conditions, particularly in low-level service work, was an important element of union organizing during this period, and various studies from the 1970s document growing job dissatisfaction centered on the qualities of labor (Braverman 1998 [1974]: 21–7). The dream of dis-alienated work also has a material basis in lived experience and intensely felt dreams of the good life. In her study of contemporary creative work, Angela McRobbie neatly describes this logic: "From the point of view of the young black British woman from a working-class background who has graduated in media studies, the element of struggle to work in film and television is articulated through an often family-based narrative of somehow not doing the menial and repetitive jobs that her mother had to do" (2016: 38–9).

The echoes of this critique across society exemplify the ways the spirit that animates a particular epoch of capitalism extends beyond the confines of management practices or factory floors. Rather, it permeates through a range of arenas from consumption to education to personal identity; it penetrates all the realms of life where laboring subjects are produced and reproduced. And if the critique figures throughout the social fabric, then similar widespread purchase is given to the spirit that models its solution and proposes the figure of the entrepreneur as a solution to the "bad work" of industrial capitalism.

While the nuance and critical politics of many critiques of alienated labor may have been lost in translation, their absorption into popular culture and business models is important for understanding the desirability of digital labor. The influence of the artistic critique and the response to it has provided the conditions of possibility – as well as the conditions of desirability – for the idealized laboring subjectivity that identifies alienated work as anathema but only in the sense of how it alienates the worker from their species-being. This leaves in place other forms of alienation and embeds an exploitative regime based on instability and risk. These are overlooked, though, in a regime where capitalism becomes justified if it enables work that facilitates self-realization and meaning. Because it addresses a critique of capitalism, the dubious and troubling structural position of the precariously employed digital laborer achieves legitimacy and mystique. Perfectly attuned to the projective capitalist spirit in which it operates, the digital laborer becomes an ideal subjectivity for capital and worker alike. This does beg the cheeky question, however: with the artistic critique's roots in Marxism, are precarious digital laborers, in fact, Marx's children?

The romance of precarity

A crucial additional ingredient of the artistic critique is its Romantic qualities that further link the rise of the entrepreneurial, hustler subjectivity of digital labor to much wider social and cultural trends (Thrift 2001). In a fascinating analysis mapped onto Weber's *Protestant Ethic*, Colin Campbell (1987) argues that the nature of consumption, particularly as represented in advertising, is essentially Romantic in that it taps into the hopes and dreams of consumers. However, he argues that we should not understand this as solely meaning that the Romantic aspirations of individuals are colonized and exploited in the service of consumer society, but rather that the reverse relationship also exists; that the Romantic element of western culture can be understood as crucial in the development of modern consumer culture.

Campbell seeks to explain the "puzzle of modern consumerism," that is, how, given the dominance of the Protestant ethic identified by Weber, the antithetical practice of consumption based on ever-changing modes of fashion could arise. This mystery, he says, does not concern the particular choice of products nor the subconscious desires which influence these consumer decisions. It is about the question of "insatiability" in consumption – the persistent want for new goods and new variety – which cannot be explained by rational utility. A truly rational consumer, driven by the *satisfaction* of needs, would not give up the gratification of habitual consumption for the risk associated with untried products. Thus, Campbell contends, a non-rational or hedonistic impulse is behind modern consumption. This drive, he says, is concerned with "valuing the experiences pleasure can bring" (1987: 69) and thus involves attempts to "squeeze as much of the quality of pleasure as one can from all those sensations which one actually experiences during the course of the process of living" (1987: 69). As this does not accord with the Protestant ethic described by Weber, Campbell concludes that there must be another cultural development which created and justified this type of behavior. It is here that he points to the influence of Romanticism – along with its affiliate and precursor, Sentimentalism – and their conceptualization of the self "which stressed a person's uniqueness or peculiarity" rather than the features shared with all humanity (1987: 182).

Romanticism is characterized by a primary emphasis on creativity, which presupposes God as a supernatural force present in the natural world but also present within every individual as "a unique and personalized spirit: that of his [sic] 'genius'" (1987: 182). In accordance with this focus on individual creativity, "imagination became the most significant and prized of personal qualities" (1987: 193), and, given the Romantic claim that imagination is the realm of beauty, its exercise is accompanied by pleasure. In this ethic, though, imagination and the experience of pleasure became considered commensurate and also moral. The obligation to their own genius felt by the Romantic can thus be found in creative actions, which included externalized modes of self-expression such as that enabled by consumption activity. In doing so, Romanticism provides "a philosophy which legitimates the search for pleasure as good in itself and not merely of value because it restores the individual to an optimum efficiency" (1987: 201). Consumption – as a source and expression of pleasure and imagination – becomes a mechanism to experience or, more actively, to cultivate a righteous self. Passion, enjoyment, and self-actualization through material activity become virtues in Romanticism, driving desires for new and novel consumption activities as part of subjective expression.

I suggest, though, that today it is not only in consumerism that we see the effect of a Romantic ethos. The obligation to their genius felt by the Romantics is commensurate with the obligation of the digital laborer, and indeed all of us, to "do what we love." Codified in business self-help books and in the projective spirit that animates capitalism, the true goal of work is to self-actualize – to engage with species-being in all you do. The Romantic spirit is what allows entrepreneurial work to function as a "calling" which, as Berg, Grant, and Johnson (2010) define it, is an occupation a person feels compelled to pursue, is enjoyable and meaningful, and a central part of their identity. By its nature, entrepreneurialism is passionate work, a form of "hedonic well-being" that is "the privilege of the few infused with a divine spirit that leads them to pursue work they feel is conducive to a happy and self-fulfilled life" (Styhre 2019: 91). In a secular world – or at least one inextricably shaped by neoliberal individualism and consumer culture and where the market is looked to for solutions to social, cultural, and individual problems – the tendency for self-actualization to be centered on work is increased. It becomes one more avenue in which to pursue the Romantic ideal.

Arvidsson ties the industrious dynamic he outlines with the puritanical Protestant ethic as described by Weber. Hard work in this doctrine serves to grant life meaning. It offers "a sense of purpose and something to believe in" (2019: 55). Inflected by American Protestantism which centralizes the market rather than society as the arbiter of value and definitions of what is meaningful, he contends that Weber's Protestant ethic is still driving the current capitalist mode. I suggest, though, that this doesn't adequately capture the impetus – nor the virtue – associated with the creativity, pleasure, and dis-alienation that is part of entrepreneurial industriousness and digital hustle. If you are not doing what you love passionately, you are not doing it right. Yet perhaps there is a marrying of the two ethics. If, as Campbell suggests, we see the puritanical Protestant work ethic operating in tandem with the Romantic impulses that had hitherto been aligned to consumption, the existence of a cultural logic which valorizes puritanical hard work in the service of Romantic creative, self-realization makes a great deal of sense.

This marrying seems even more relevant when we understand the Romantic subject of consumption is also an entrepreneurial subject, particularly in the way it is defined by Rose (1998, 1999). Both figures are choosing, self-directed and creative subjects. The Romantic and the neoliberal self-steering subject that Rose describes share the same ethical relationship to the self, involving continual labor to maximize and express the truth of that being. Central to both are the self-interrogation and confessional practices which emerge from a "logic of personhood, organized around the key concepts of conscience, consciousness, feeling and sentiment" (Abercrombie, Hill, and Turner 1986: 48). They share a sense of autonomy and individuality along with a quest for external manifestations of inner being (lifestyle or work style). They are also both animated by the imperative to "be creative" through which the self is given form and which works both as a source of pleasure and discipline (McRobbie 2016). The extension of this lifestyling through work and leisure is the plain upon which we find the digital laborer and their celebration of the self-actualization that comes from piecing together a career through constant hustle and disruptive innovation. The digital laborer is seeking to maximize their life through free choice – Gannon's apparently voluntary decision to "own the fact" of her precarity – but one in which Romantic ideals of selfhood and creative expression permeate.

The art of hacking

In its popular interpretation, the figure this critique embodies is the artist and their rejection of regimentation, domination, and principles of profit (Boltanski and Chiapello 2005a: 38). For Mills (1951: 126), writing in the 1950s, the "independent artist and intellectual" was one of the few "equipped to resist and to fight the stereotyping and consequent death of genuinely lively things" and so beat the flattening effects of corporate and state bureaucratization. But more than this, McRobbie (2001, 2016) has noted that the artist is the paradigmatic model for contemporary labor relations. This is not only because of the increasing importance of culture and cultural production in the shift to a service-driven economy. It is also because of the artist's historically precarious and irregular relationship to income, their often-antagonistic relationship to market logics which justifies those irregularities (but which increasingly embraces commercialism), and the discipline imposed by the drive to self-actualize through productive activity. They are typically self-employed and comfortable with moving from project to project over their working lives, as well as juggling multiple, simultaneous gigs. Self-directed and autonomous, they embody creative, flexible thinking and doing. They are also involved in romanticized, "cool" work that is associated with self-expression, freedom, and, most importantly, passion. Moreover, in exhortations for creativity today, the term is often not used in the sense that we would associate with the arts, but is used to mean dynamic, flexible, and innovative responses to local conditions. Through this discursive shift, the Romantic, creative artist can serve as the archetype of the industrious entrepreneur.

The relationship between artistic, creative production and digital labor is often made overt in digital labor work environments. In their 2015 exposé of working conditions in a Seattle Amazon corporate office, journalists Jodi Kantor and David Streitfeld describe a company environment of overwork, brutal competition between staff, long hours, and constant surveillance and monitoring by the corporation and peers alike. They described annual culls of staff and constructive dismissal of staff members suffering ill health. And yet, these workers were willing to accept these conditions for the opportunities such work gave for creative expression and self-realization. "However, more than 100 current and former Amazonians – members of the leadership team, human resources executives, marketers, retail specialists and engineers who worked on projects from the Kindle to grocery delivery to the recent mobile phone launch – described how they tried to reconcile the sometimes-punishing aspects of their workplace with what many called its thrilling power to create" (Kantor and Streitfeld 2015).

Like artists, these Amazon workers are "doing what they love," an impetus that may well be the trap attributed to it in a variety of studies (Duffy and Hund 2015; Gill and Pratt 2008; Thrift 2005; Tokumitsu 2014). Nevertheless, it is still an opportunity to experience (relatively) dis-alienated, creative, self-actualizing labor and so is legitimated as good work within the dominant regime.

Elite digital labor workplaces often overtly enact a Romantic response to the artistic critique. Fred Turner (2009: 88) describes how the 1960s countercultural resistance to bad work is a feature of Silicon Valley. Engineering at Google, he says, is reframed as "artistic" and "creative", a feature of the company's culture exemplified in the almost compulsory attendance at the Burning Man festival. Similarly, Jamie Woodcock describes how game company Atari was able to channel the 1960s countercultural "refusal of work" into its company agenda by incorporating fun and passion into its models of labor: "Atari promised 'play as work' as an alternative to the restrictive conditions of an industrial or office-based Fordism" (Woodcock 2019: 23). In his study of the rise and fall of web services company Razorfish, Andrew Ross also notes that, "Capitalism was a dirty word for most of the industry employees . . . capitalism was something practiced by other, larger companies, especially those that exhibited rule-ridden bureaucracies, bottom-line thinking, bland employee cultures, and conservative business strategies. By contrast, companies that were small, fast-moving, innovative, entre-preneurial, brand active, and socially aware escaped all such scorn" (Ross 2003: 48). The fostering of creativity and self-expression at Razorfish offered employees absolution from the perceived sins of laboring under capitalism.

The challenge to capitalism-as-usual offered by digital labor is exemplified in the hacker credo – move fast and break things. This mythic concept is a core part of the GAFAM/BAT and startup imaginary. The capacity to disrupt is, as former Facebook employee Katherine Losse (2012: 38) puts it, "a source of power and profit for tech companies," but the concept of hacking is valued for more than the strictly economic or technical advantage it may accrue. It is an animating dynamic within the occupational identities of tech workers and, at the very least, is articulated in corporate mythology. The heroic, renegade figure of the hacker animates workplace cultures, even if the bulk of the company is, in reality, commercially friendly corporate leaders or dependable, standard programmers (Losse 2012). For instance, the word "HACK" is embedded in the central courtyard of Facebook's Menlo Park campus and until 2014 "move fast and break things" was the company motto. That most workers are waged employees does not detract from the potency of this mythology, its ability to attract people into the industry, and to sustain them once they are ensconced.

The Romantic figure of the transgressive hacker manifests today in the mythical figure of the startup founder: the quintessential entrepreneur. The founder is considered a "sacred figure" in Silicon Valley, with starting a business seen as "the highest form of human achievement" (Tarnoff and Weigel 2020: 12). Isaac directly locates the source of this mythology in the dis-alienating dreams of 1960s counterculture. "Founder culture – or more accurately, founder *workshop* – emerged as bedrock faith in Silicon Valley from several strains of quasi-religious philosophy. Sixties-era San Francisco embraced a sexual, chemical, hippie-led revolution inspired by dreams of liberated consciousness and utopian social structures. This anti-establishment counterculture mixed well with emerging ideas about the efficiency of individual greed and the gospel of creative destruction" (Isaac 2019: 75).

Tied to the disruptive mystique of the hacker, startup founders become "the philosopher kings, the rugged individualists who would save society from bureaucratic, unfair, and outmoded systems" (Isaac 2019: 75). More often than not, founders do not actually experience creative autonomy or achieve the god-like status ascribed to them, ending up effectively working for investors until they are retrenched from their own companies (Cockayne 2016; Pein 2018: 75). Nevertheless, the Romantic mythology of these creative, entrepreneurial, "great men" – the gendered term is used consciously – personify the allure and promise of digital labor. These myths are not merely media constructions but are part and parcel of Silicon Valley's modes of working. From the impish, everyman figure of Jack Ma to the aloof, technophilic character of Larry Page, to the single-minded visionary status of Mark Zuckerberg, the personalities of tech company founders form part of the entrepreneurial mythology. As these Romantic, hacking, entrepreneurial figures have come to embody the definition of "good work," not only have digital labor's exploitative practices been normalized, they have also been reified so that alternative ways of achieving the same ends are no longer thinkable.

Beyond the Valley

It is also notable that, like the cheap labor discussed in chapter 2, entrepreneurial hustle has long been part of the experience of marginalized workers. To return to a point made earlier, entrepreneurialism has long been on the margins of industrial capitalism, a necessary and cautionary other to the safety and security offered by the jobs for life of the industrial compact. Associated with the "messy bazaar economies, dirty street vendors, inefficient artisan workshops, and the infamous labour-intensive wet-rice agriculture that, until the 1960s, appeared to condemn those practising it to eternal underdevelopment" (Arvidsson 2019: 41), the racialized nature of this mode of work is made clear. That the Romantic impetus of capitalism's new spirit has rendered this form of working – with all its precarity and unfair distribution of labor – desirable and something to aspire to speaks of the adaptability of capitalism and its capacity to absorb critique.

Arguably, though, the aspirational figure of the Silicon Valley founder that exemplifies the new spirit of hustle only resonates within the elite technology sectors and in the already economically privileged parts of the world. And, certainly, the goal to become the kind of technology startup founder who achieves stratospheric economic success is not necessarily viable outside of specific socio-technical, cultural, political, and economic contexts. However, the ability of the global North and in particular Silicon Valley to establish the economic and cultural imaginary – to provide supposedly universal models of "good work" – remains apparent, and oftentimes troubling. Who exactly benefits the most from the celebration of precarious, entrepreneurial, high-risk work? This is a question that will be picked up again in the conclusion of this book.

That said, there is significant consistency in the way the romanticism of the creative entrepreneurial subject is articulated in a wide range of digital labor contexts. It often resides alongside the more prosaic imperative to earn an income in contexts where secure employment options are limited, where digital labor can be relatively lucrative, and where, at the very least, it provides an additional revenue source. In the middle-class Australian woman selling her craftwares via Etsy, who values work that can fit around her family-care responsibilities, we see the privileging of autonomy and agency (Luckman 2018). In the rural Chinese short-video makers monetizing their content on Kuaishou, we see the impulse for creative expression (Lin and de Kloet 2019). In the low-level games tester who finds fun in their work, we see the impetus to do what you love (Bulut 2015). Promoted on the TaskRabbit (n.d.) company website, we see workers not only doing what they love but engaging in heroic social change, "all while saving the day for someone in [their] city."

These more marginalized digital laborers may not consciously aspire to become a tech startup founder or even have as a goal the economic and social status of these figures. Nevertheless, the Romantic figure of the Silicon Valley startup founder exemplifies the narrative that animates this work and which is validated in a variety of global cultural contexts. That the promises made about such work may never be actualized is irrelevant to its ability to justify and mystify that labor. That we are striving toward dis-alienation is all that is required. Emma Gannon's positive embrace of precarity in the narrative that opens this chapter now makes sense. Tied to the possibility of self-realization and species-being, this is appealing work despite, or perhaps because of, its association with risk and instability.

And so, if we are to respond to the question of how people have come to embrace digital labor despite its precarity, the answer is simple: it is because it *is* desirable and pleasurable work that is socially validated and from which both psychic and monetary rewards can be derived. It is, conceptually, good work.

5

Commodification: Affective Attachment and Inalienable Assets

Former Disney star and singer Bella Thorne caused quite a stir in 2020 when she launched an OnlyFans page. OnlyFans is a social media platform where users subscribe to a creator's site and pay fees to gain access to images, videos, and other content. Since its launch in 2016, the site had become popular among musicians and fitness experts, but particularly among sex workers. As one of the few sites enabling direct monetary exchange with clients, particularly in the context of the FOSTA-SESTA laws which have been closing off other revenue or promotional sources, OnlyFans had become a vital part of the social media ecosystem for this group of digital laborers. For Thorne, the move onto the platform was very lucrative; selling exclusive content through the site, she made over US$2 million in less than a week.

OnlyFans' sex worker community, however, did not appreciate Thorne's success. They feared that her presence and the apparent ease with which she raised money would create a false impression about the difficult labor involved in managing an OnlyFans account. By bringing the site into the mainstream and identifying it as a place to make a quick buck, sex workers argued that Thorne's story and the growing influx of celebrities to the platform was increasing competition and thereby reducing their earnings. That these celebrities were able to benefit from the platform's dynamics which had been honed and built by sex workers without facing the stigmatization they routinely encounter was particularly galling. More materially, Thorne's decision to advertise nudes for US$200 but then only supply lingerie shots – and the ensuing demand for refunds from her subscribers – was alleged to be behind OnlyFans' introduction of a US$50 cap on content fees and US$100 on tips, as well as its change from a weekly to a monthly distribution of revenues. The changes caused by Bella Thorne's experiment with digital labor meant not only reduced opportunities for sex workers but also delayed receipt of their wages which was devastating for those using the site as a vital source of income (Noor 2020). The trend of celebrities setting up on OnlyFans was described as gentrification (Are and Paasonen 2021; Dickson 2020), with sex workers being edged out of the platform and increasingly marginalized in promotional materials.

But Bella Thorne's foray into the realm of online sex work also tapped into a much longer, more deep-seated controversy: the legitimacy of commodifying inalienable aspects of self and relationships in commercial venues. Slut-shaming, the continued demonization of sex work, and the dismissal of reality celebrities such as Kim Kardashian all speak to an ongoing disquiet with selling bodies, subjectivities, and affect. There is, as Viviana Zelizer (2005, 2011) reminds us, ongoing and continual negotiations in any society or culture about what constitutes a legitimate commercialization of intimacy. This debate hinges on the drawing and redrawing of distinctions between legitimate commodities and illegitimate commodities as social and cultural norms change. For anti-sex work activists such as Julie Bindel (2020), though, OnlyFans crosses the current line of acceptability. In her argument, it can only be seen as a site of illegitimate work because "being treated as a commodity for consumption takes its toll."

It is here that the critique of OnlyFans draws on – or at least connects with – the Marxist critique of alienation described in the previous chapter. Underpinning the concept of species-being is the idea that aspects of self are only able to allow human flourishing when they are in an inalienable form. Our realization of our species-being is what differentiates us from animals and allows our labor to fulfill us and be a manifestation of life as a free, conscious activity. To market your body, identity, or image for financial gain is to commodify that embodied subjectivity and thus alienate it from you. In Marxist thinking, commodification is the process by which objects with use-value – an ability to satisfy unique human needs and higher purposes – become dominated by exchange-value – what they can realize in the marketplace, based on abstracted calculations. This process strips the objects of their richer, culturally embedded meaning; through commodification, meaningful artefacts and practices develop "a new objectivity, a new substantiality . . . which destroys their original and authentic substantiality" (Lukács 1971: 92). In transformation into a commodity, an object or subject becomes reified – thing-like – and thus passive and static. Read through this framework, to commodify your self or, as in Thorne's case, your embodied sexuality is to transform one of the more intimate and generally considered inalienable aspects of human existence into a reified object suitable for exchange. It renders the core of your being into something that can, effectively, be removed from your control, sold, and consumed outside of its context. In the process, you become alienated from your species-being, undermining your intrinsic dignity. This assumption underpins the general disquiet in mainstream reports of Thorne's entrepreneurialism, even when the specific logic remains unstated or even unrecognized.

Work for OnlyFans may be a particularly loaded example of alienation but, from the outset, digital labor has been associated with extensive commodification of subjectivity and the incursion of economic thinking into the lifeworld of workers. Led by Michael Hardt and Antonio Negri's (2000, 2005, 2009) use of autonomist Marxist thought to describe contemporary capitalism, immaterial labor in its digital forms has long been associated with the extension of commercial logics throughout all of society (Fuchs 2008, 2009; Jarrett

2016a). Encapsulated in Mario Tronti's (1973) concept of the social factory, Hardt and Negri argued that the centralizing of knowledge, sociability, and affect in work reorganizes the inalienable dimensions of self into the logics of industrial capitalism. Aspects of life once considered outside commercial exchange – and only meaningful in that context – were not only being captured, measured, and valued within the economy but were reconfigured into a reflection of capital in that process. In contemporary capitalism, subjectivity itself becomes productive as life is "put to work" (Morini and Fumagalli 2010). This marked the shift from, in Marx's terms, the formal subsumption of life, in which life-processes are incorporated into capital, to a context of real subsumption, in which those life-processes are fundamentally altered to reflect capitalist dynamics.

As I have argued elsewhere (Jarrett 2017, 2018), it is important not to claim any novelty for this condition of commodification and subsumption as porous boundaries between work and non-work have long been a feature of life for many workers. Nevertheless, it is still useful to recognize some of the ways digital labor occupations have expanded work into the lifeworlds of their workers. This is both in the form of extending value-producing activity into ostensible leisure time, but also by articulating and mobilizing inalienable aspects of self, such as subjectivity and passion. Through the pincer movement of these mechanisms, opportunities for exploitation are extended but also workers' subjectivities become refashioned into economically valuable forms. Chapter 2 has already described some of the ways extending work into unpaid time enables exploitation, so this chapter will primarily focus on how digital laborers' subjectivities are holistically absorbed into the digital economy. It will also consider, though, how this dynamic is gendered, mapping onto longer trends of feminization in capitalist economics. Through that lens, it will go on to consider whether "commodification" is the right concept for understanding the subsumptive dynamics of digital labor. Using insights from Michel Feher (2018), it will suggest understanding the processes of self-exploitation associated with digital labor as instances of assetization rather than commodification. At first glance, the distinction between these terms might seem to be merely splitting hairs, but the difference between commodities and assets is vital for understanding the complex dynamics of digital labor.

Counting human capital

In creative and knowledge industries, it is not uncommon for employers to claim ownership of more than a worker's physical outputs. The amorphous nature of immaterial labor – that involving knowledge, creativity, affect, interpersonal dynamics – means it is difficult to isolate value-creating activity from that which is leisure or formally "not work." Especially in the elite creative occupations of digital labor, but also in any entrepreneurial setting, what a worker does that adds value is difficult to contain within officially designated office hours. Creative, innovative, work-related ideas can occur at any time during the day – while walking the dog, in the shower, or while doomscrolling Twitter on the bus. The passion that drives entrepreneurialism can also be a deeply held affect that permeates a person's sense of self. Work that is reliant on the knowledge of workers depends on "expressive and cooperative capacities that cannot be taught, on a vivacity in the deployment of knowledge that is part of the culture of everyday life" (Gorz 2010: 9). It is this embedding in human energies that encourages employers to extend to digital labor the kinds of independence and autonomy that we discussed in chapter 3. But it is also this dynamic which draws the whole of life into capitalist logics and into economic calculation.

These life energies of a company's workforce are expressed in the accounting fictions of "human capital" or "intellectual capital" that inform a company's share price. The concept of human capital began as a means for understanding and calculating the increase in income associated with educational attainment. It was primarily used as a measure of the return on investment – the impact on future earnings – of schooling and skills development (Feher 2009). However, it increasingly became divested from its significance to the individual worker and framed instead as a form of value-adding to corporations. In particular, as the economic center swung increasingly to knowledge-intensive and service industries over the latter half of the twentieth century, the accumulation and deployment of human capital began increasingly to be viewed as a company's competitive advantage. The "enterprise value" or total capital of a firm is defined by its tangible assets, such as its material infrastructure and financial state, calculated in concert with the intangibilities of "intellectual capital." This is comprised of human capital – "skills, personality traits, attributes, and competencies of employees" (Abhayawansa and Abeysekera 2008: 51–2); relational capital – customer-supplier and other external relationships; and structural intellectual capital, such as intellectual property and copyright (Todericiu and Stănit 2015). Notably, both the latter forms of intellectual capital are, arguably, materializations of the labor of workers and products of the deployment of their human capital. Over the latter part of the twentieth century, human capital became something a company invested in with a view to future growth and retaining competitive advantage: "the sine qua non condition for the development and success of all organizations" (Todericiu and Stănit 2015: 677).

Accordingly, corporate human resources departments began to shift toward enhancing this form of capital through staff development, hiring, and retention practices with a view to long-term competitive advantage. But it was also about the more immediate concern of share price which may be associated with the perceived value of the workforce. Human capital – as the central element of intellectual capital – is subject to quantification within the accounting of firms

(Abhayawansa and Abeysekera 2008), and financial statements, IPO prospectus, and business reports should, ideally, contain data on the intellectual capital of a firm. This is particularly the case for digital media companies, many of which, as noted in the *Harvard Business Review*, "have no physical products and have no inventory to report" (Govindarajan, Rajgopal, and Srivastava 2018) and so rely substantially on the perceived value of their workforces' abilities. The difficulties in accurately quantifying this kind of human capital explains some of the apparently illogical valuations of companies that are yet to turn a material profit; it is, in part, a measure of the potential housed in their embodied workforce. Standard accounting practices do not and cannot apply.

Digital human capital

Unpaid user labor is perhaps the most obvious example of human capital being directly enrolled in corporate accounting. As already noted, whether they are actively providing content or passively generating data, what users do is central to the economics of a good deal of the digital media sector. They are thus a central part of the human capital that determine the viability and value of many platforms, apps, or sites. This is a holistic contribution for, as already noted, the opportunities to gather data on users are 100 percent of online time (Fuchs 2014a: 115). This effect is amplified by the mobility of digital media platforms as smartphones and smart homes extend their reach into all aspects of life. A digital laborer can be generating data with commercial value while on the toilet, in the doctor's waiting room, or when asking Alexa to play music while baking cakes using ingredients taken from a smart fridge that records their consumption. They generate data while catching up on news via Facebook or a commercial news provider's website, playing Candy Crush to stave off boredom, sharing memes and reaction gifs with friends on Twitter, and while organizing hookups through dating apps.

Not only then is the potential for data capture and thus digital labor present across a range of scenarios, it also enters into the realm of leisure and other intimate and personal areas of life central to the creation, expression, and maintenance of subjectivity. All these intimate aspects of a user's life are potentially capitalized on by a platform as they are measured and quantified and transformed into a commodity which has an exchange-value.

User activity is also integral to the share prices of digital media companies. Adam Arvidsson and Elanor Colleoni (2012) argue that users' key contribution is not data at all but their affective investment in the platform, site, or app that they are using. They note that many digital media companies are not successful because they are generating profit through advertising revenue or the sale of commodities. Rather, their corporate worth is generated entirely in the share market where market valuations can diverge wildly from the actual profits generated by advertising revenue and user data. Twitter, for instance has notoriously struggled to turn an actual profit and has been flatlining user growth for some time. Nevertheless, in early 2021, Twitter Inc. had a market capitalization of US$57 billion and a share price showing steady growth of 22 percent per year over the previous five years (*Simply Wall St* 2021). Where users and their labor are involved in this valuation is in the creation and maintenance of "brand value," which is the set of associations users bring to a platform, company, or its products. A successful brand is one that is loved and deeply embedded in the lives of users, stimulating continued and returned consumption of its products or, in this case, continued and sustained use of the technology. In the share market, brand value can be used to explain the "discrepancy between market and book value" (Arvidsson and Colleoni 2012: 141).

Like human capital, brand value is another accounting fiction which is predicated on assessing, measuring, and valuing ineffable and inalienable dimensions of human activity. It is also a product of labor. When first outlining the importance of "immaterial labor" to the economy, Hardt and Negri (2000) link its emergence to the growing importance of industries associated with symbol manipulation in the post-industrial economy. Maurizio Lazzarato also articulates this idea and ties immaterial labor more overtly to that which produces the meaning of a commodity, "in other words, the kinds of activities involved in defining and fixing cultural and artistic standards, fashions, tastes, consumer norms, and, more strategically, public opinion" (1996: 133). Creating brand value is thus a form of labor undertaken by users. Often, brand value is tied less to the platform than to the interpersonal relationships or affective intensities that are activated or sustained through it. Nevertheless, the pull of these dimensions of the lifeworld brings about the kind of consumer lock-in and commitment to continued use that constitutes effective brand loyalty and thus brand value. For instance, despite being a highly critical and trained internet researcher, my continued use of Facebook is tied to the rich affective connections that I sustain there, especially with my family who all reside in Australia which is very far from my current home in Ireland. As this is where my personal connections are, Facebook has locked me in as a customer and has achieved a kind of platform dependency. Consequently, my interactions with the site may not be about the site per se but they nevertheless generate data that can be monetized *and* contribute to the growth of the company's brand value and subsequent share price.

The exploitation of digital laborers' affective investment in a platform is not only a feature of unpaid user activity. As described in the previous two chapters, passion for "cool work" and "doing what you love" can shape employment in elite occupations as well as in the less compensated, less valorized forms of platform work. It is worth returning to this idea in the context of this chapter. Associated with both platform and formal work, entrepreneurialism involves psychic investment

(Scharff 2016). As Silvio Lorusso (2019: 18) describes, its spirit "invades the realm of character, making good humor, optimism and cordiality a competitive advantage to cultivate." In a study of the San Francisco tech startup sector, Daniel Cockayne (2016) describes the affective attachment to entrepreneurial forms of work in the digital laborers he studies. In particular, he notes their investment in the "powerful and productive fantasy" of achieving personal satisfaction through work, but specifically self-directed work. Satisfaction, he says, is "an ambivalent though productive feeling of anxiety or pleasure located directly in their productive capacities, compelling the entrepreneur to partake in a circuitous repetition of production, which is also a repetition of affect" (Cockayne 2016: 461). Passion was also identified as important to these workers, encouraging doubling down on hard work when goals were not achieved in order to secure a return on their libidinal investment in the company and its products. These affects align with Arvidsson's description of the importance of "meaningful work" within industrious capitalism discussed previously. Overlaid onto the risks, hard work, and challenges of entrepreneurialism is the promise of satisfying and meaningful labor – "heroic individualism, a fulfillment of the promise of liberal sovereignty" (Cockayne 2016: 462) – and it is a belief in that ideal that secures ongoing enrollment in such work.

Notably it is not a particular company or platform that is vying to secure investment in its brand through this widespread and diffuse discursive framework. It is alignment with entrepreneurialism itself – a generalized economic imaginary grounded in the demands of neoliberal, post-industrial capitalism. What this means, though, is that a deep-seated affective investment in being entrepreneurial that may lie at the core of a worker's sense of self becomes another asset belonging to a company. It is what secures that worker's commitment to the firm and thus the retention of their human capital. It means, though, the enrollment of that worker's subjectivity in contemporary capitalist logics as desire and affect – some of the most intimate, inalienable aspects of subjectivity – becomes economic.

Affect and immersion

Affective investments in entrepreneurial work can also be strategically implemented by particular companies. Work in the elite digital media companies and startups is renowned for its immersive qualities. Tech workers are expected to show their dedication to their craft by working extremely long hours: a feature of the hacker mythology in which absolute dedication to the hack is valued. This immersion isn't only about how much time is spent at work. It is also about a deep investment in workplace cultural norms, penetrating deep into the psyche of the worker and manifesting externally in action and self-presentation. Silicon Valley entrepreneur and former Facebook employee Antonio García Martínez (2016) describes the key trait of being a successful startup founder as sheer bloody-mindedness manifesting as an ability to cope with "endless amounts of shit" and having the "ability to monomaniacally and obsessively focus on one thing and one thing only, at the expense of everything else in life" (2016: 164–5). Later, he describes the importance of researching anyone he was due to meet through their social media and LinkedIn accounts. He recommends wariness about any who appear as if they have maintained some kind of work–life balance:

> Total commitment, like unconditional love, is the only type that matters. The bike-riding, date-night-going types will never give everything to a company or an idea, and are nothing more than complacent bourgeois, whatever trappings of the "disruptive innovator" they may sport . . . The ones who could pass for a homeless person, though, are the startup kamikazes who will give everything for the entrepreneurial cause, and are stopped only by death or jail. (García Martinez 2016: 179)

This commitment to work is also bolstered by the offsetting of wages into stock options that creates a "sincere attachment" of the worker to the success and share price of the enterprise (Feher 2018: 80).

An association of digital media companies with cults is an intriguing feature of memoirs and observations of Silicon Valley and startups, with "drinking the Kool-Aid," a phrase widely used within the industry itself to describe workers being absorbed into organizational beliefs and behaviors. Alibaba employees are described as "disciples" (Clark 2016: 28) and appraised according to the "Six Vein Spirit Sword" that encapsulates the company's values: putting the customer first, teamwork, embracing changing, integrity, passion, and commitment. Emily Chang (2019: 32–4) documents the cult-like immersion of new employees at 1990s software superstar company Trilogy, a process designed to create a patriotic devotion to the company that encouraged its "hard work, hard play" dynamic. At Uber, early employees' performance reviews included their level of "super-pumpedness" – their ability to do whatever it takes (Isaac 2019: 13). Marketing software company HubSpot's cultural code, articulated into a 128-slide Powerpoint deck by co-founder Dharmesh Shah, depicts a corporate environment "where the needs of the individual become secondary to the needs of the group . . . and where people don't worry about work–life balance because their work *is* their life" (Lyons 2016: 52). To be "Hubspotty", and thus to succeed in the company, is described on the careers page (Hubspot n.d.) as requiring HEART – an acrostic standing for being humble, effective, adaptable, remarkable, and transparent. It is not enough to be skilled at your role; your whole subjectivity needs to be calibrated to the workplace culture. In a context where interpersonal relationships and company fit can determine both hiring and firing (see chapter 3), such calibrations take on a powerful urgency.

These cultural dynamics also become self-perpetuating. The more time is spent at work or engaging in compulsory sociality (Gregg 2010) with work colleagues, the more inculcated someone becomes into the sector or the company's credo. Describing the boyish, fraternity behaviors witnessed during her career as a customer-support manager at Facebook, Losse (2012) notes that these gendered dynamics were heightened due to the complete immersion of employees in corporate culture.

> Bringing employees together, in the life-as-work-and-work-as-life culture of late 2000s Silicon Valley, was a core business mission of any startup. It wasn't enough to work there, you had to devote as much of your life to it as possible. At Facebook, being a startup devoted to virtual socializing, we couldn't just work all the time ... We needed to entertain each other. (Losse 2012: 30)

In the hothouse environment of Silicon Valley, there becomes no outside-of-work for other identities to form and be affirmed. This dynamic is also evident in the story of former Google employee Doug Edwards, who describes the work–life balance challenge he faced as a middle-aged father when compared to his younger, unattached colleagues. "They had no local friends, no attachments, no relatives, and often no TVs to distract them. They had Google" (Edwards 2011: 85). The "cocoon of essential services" and "intelligent companionship," he says, were all used so workers could resist the "allure of some idyllic 'real life'" (2011: 85).

As already described, the cool workplaces of Silicon Valley not only serve to increase exploitation by extending the working day and function as a mechanism for managing work time, they also play a part in building the company's brand value for employees. Stabile (2008) argues that the perk-laden workplace Google provided its employees helped set their staff apart from other, less autonomous, less creative workers. The provisions of gyms, food, massage therapists, and laundry facilities are, she says, partly about morale. They cultivate and sustain the human capital of the company by adding affective layers that support the entrepreneurial or hacker mystique it demands. These measures, along with generous salaries and stock options, are designed to "make work obsession both easier to indulge in and more enjoyable" (Chang 2019: 209). They also, as technology journalist Emily Chang points out, lead not to work–life balance but to work–life blending or integration. It is not merely that life is absorbed into work but also that work becomes life.

In this dual action, the immersive nature of tech work extends deeply into spheres of life traditionally considered outside of commercial logics. The social and sex lives of elite Silicon Valley workers are imbued with the cultural dynamics of the work culture and are also sites for economically valuable activity. Losse (2012) notes the difficulties of socializing beyond Facebook, both through a lack of free time but also the risk of letting slip sensitive product information to tech workers from rival companies. It was easier, she said, to stay inside the social bubble and to pursue relationships only with other Facebook employees. In *Brotopia* (2019), Chang documents the array of sex parties and non-monogamous relationships that have become part of the industry. Transgressions of bourgeois heteronormativity are considered an extension of the disruptive nature of the industry, cast as hacking social norms. She quotes one anonymous tech company founder saying that what produced the dynamic sexuality of the sector "is the same progressiveness and open-mindedness that allowed us to be creative and disruptive about ideas" (Chang 2019: 185). Business and deals are also discussed at these parties, which also become sites for career advancement or damage (a particular risk for women, gay men, and people of color who, despite the permissiveness of tech culture, still encounter sexual double standards).

Perhaps the most striking example of the incorporation of the whole of life into work, though, is the 2014 decision by Facebook and Apple – followed swiftly by Google, Intel, Spotify, and Salesforce – to subsidize female employees to freeze their eggs so they could defer parenthood until later in their careers and continue to produce for the company in the immediate term. Large tech firms may also support IVF treatment, sperm banking, or support adoption and surrogacy measures. Led by then Facebook COO Sheryl Sandberg, such programs literally put the essence of life into a corporate logic.

This all-encompassing work environment comes with many problems, not least its retrenchment of inequalities. The dominance of a masculine drinking culture in Silicon Valley is striking. Drinks in the workplace, at parties, bars, strip clubs, and in hot tubs feature prominently in the memoirs of tech workers. It is in these environments that the all-important workplace culture that allows startups to move quickly (chapter 2) is iterated and reiterated, where workplace allegiances are bolstered, where status within the group is cemented, where trade deals are greased, and so where career advancement is fostered. Women engineers in particular note the importance of engaging in this and other aspects of brogrammer culture in order to secure status as "one of the boys" and thus be accorded respect in the workplace. They also, unfortunately, report these scenes as those where the always smoldering embers of workplace sexual harassment would flare into life, sometimes into sexual assault (Chang 2019; Losse 2012; Wiener 2020). For women of color, these spaces are even more fraught as the power dynamics of such environments demand silence on a number of levels in order not to disrupt the dominant culture (Chang 2019: 126–7).

The degendering (Wajcman 2010) of women tech workers by their becoming "one of the boys" can begin early. An instructive example of this process is provided by former software engineer and startup founder Wendy Liu, who documents her growing interest and skills with technology as a teenager. Having accidentally passed as male through her long-standing online handle, she considered outing herself in order to stop deceiving others in the open-source communities in which she was involved and to support others on the bulletin boards who were openly female. She resisted doing so, however, for in her experience "being openly female on the Internet seemed like a magnet for being mocked, or hit on, or both" (Liu 2020: 16). In response to the extra scrutiny, derision, and sexualization she saw inflicted on female-identifying programmers, she chose instead to degender herself. "I carefully studied all the apparently incorrect ways for women to behave to ensure that I would model only the correct ones. The conclusion I had internalised was that feminine traits were inferior" (2020: 16). In Liu's story, we see some of the most intimate and privately held aspects of self – gender identity and expression – being modified and reshaped by the demands of digital labor.

Digital makeovers

Refashioning your subjectivity in line with corporate goals and norms seems extreme, although certainly it is understandable. But such reconfiguring is a feature across other forms of digital labor. Users and their interpersonal relationships are, arguably, disciplined by the affordances of social media platforms in ways that reconfigure identities, events, and connections. Ensuring legibility to the visual, semantic, and algorithmic structures of a platform ensures visibility to those for whom our messages are intended. As we have already noted multiple times, such attention to platform norms is often associated with influencers, as their income is tied to their findability on platforms as well as their maintenance of an "authentic" persona to which fans can relate (Abidin 2017; Banet-Weiser 2012; Kanai 2019). In reality, however, all social media users regularly reconstitute their interactions with the site – and thus with each other – to align with the dictates established by a platform's affordances. Creating an aesthetically pleasing, "Insta-worthy" setting so that you can share a personal moment (Leaver, Highfield, and Abidin 2020), categorizing your sexual preferences and personal description through the narrow definitions set by a hookup app (Mowlabocus 2010), or presenting an abrasive, cynical persona on a subreddit to secure upvotes (Massanari 2015) all suggest the influence of social media platform norms within identity presentation and interpersonal relationships. Our self is remade through the economics of liking, the visual language of social media, and the socio-technical logics of platform architecture. Moreover, as Coté and Pybus (2007; see also Jarrett 2008) argued about the now defunct MySpace, the affective intensities of the connections forged through social media platforms encourage further engagement, entangling users in the commodity – and entrepreneurial – logics of the digital media economy with increasing intensity. This is how users generate brand value, but it also has the function of shaping and reshaping subjectivity in the terms set by digital capital. We become better digital laborers the more we contribute to these sites.

This disciplining is also a feature of paid digital labor. Alessandro Gandini (2016) describes the contemporary workplace as a "reputation economy" and how the mobilization of a person's reputation works as a disciplining mechanism, rewarding alignment with commercial goals and punishing those who lose "reputational capital." The accounting and recording of personal activity on searchable platforms such as Facebook or Twitter, alongside the more professionally oriented sites such as LinkedIn, make a user's subjectivity publicly visible and tangible. It is common for potential employers to search a job applicant's name and determine their suitability based on what they find (Paasonen et al. 2019). Inappropriate social media posts have cost workers their jobs. There is thus a premium placed on having a "clean," or positive, representation of your self in social media.

But this dynamic of preemptive reputation management extends into the construction of identity itself. Studies of job advertisements for game industry community managers and social media marketers show the importance placed on performing appropriate affects, such as passion and being kind-hearted or fun. Manifesting these affects is not only essential to the role but to securing employment in the first instance (Duffy and Schwartz 2018; Kerr and Kelleher 2015). Alice Marwick (2013) documents the importance of self-branding for workers in the San Francisco technology sector she researched from 2006 to 2010. One of the features she notes in the profiles built up in both online and offline contexts was that a particular "authenticity" was required. This was not about revealing a "true" self but about constantly performing an "edited self" that reflected the ideals of the audience, in this case an "entrepreneurial, knowledgeable, positive, and self-motivated" persona (Marwick 2013: 194). However, with the porous borders between work and life that exist in the tech industry, digital laborers must always be "on" – must be continually and consistently performing this identity – encouraging continued alignment with desirable, dynamic, entrepreneurial qualities. Effective self-branding thus requires constant self-surveillance and emotional and psychic regulation.

In platform work, the disciplining mechanisms of reputation management are more overt. They typically take the form of customer ratings of workers – and sometimes workers' ratings of clients. As already discussed in chapter 3, platforms use these assessments to evaluate and manage their workforce and often act on them unilaterally and opaquely in determining the quality of a digital laborer's work and thus the continuity – or not – of their employment. But ratings are also disciplinary at the level of subjectivity. When customers' ratings can directly determine your employment status, the incentive to reconfigure your presentation of self in line with their expectations is powerful. This often means doing more than a good job or more than managing the subjectivity directly enrolled in work. Platforms such as UrbanSitter, SitterCity, and Care.com actively encourage potential employers to search online for more information about their potential employees. The profiles of careworkers who are "verified" through links to their personal social media accounts are also made more visible by such platforms ranking them higher or through visual codes such as stars and ticks. The result is that "careworkers' broader online identities are enrolled into the hiring process" (Ticona and Mateescu 2018: 4396), leading to wide-ranging, active impression management, including social media curation by these workers. These platforms say out loud the unspoken impetus to ensure your entire self aligns with the platform's agenda.

Platform laborers are also asked to perform various additional kinds of emotional labor (Hochschild 2003 [1983]), regulating and maintaining their emotional states as part of their labor contribution. Ride-sharing drivers often go to great lengths to present a professional and friendly demeanor to their passengers – or at least one that is ratings worthy. A clean car and a safe trip are often supplemented with the provision of bottles of water or sweets, acting as tour guide, or by providing polite and engaging repartee – or remaining in silence if that is preferred by the passenger. Other platform workers calibrate their self-brands to assumptions about audience or client expectations. Monika Sengul-Jones (2017; see also Baym 2018; Duffy and Hund 2015; Scolere, Pruchniewska, and Duffy 2018; Ticona and Mateescu 2018) describes the considered and calibrated presentation of self in the platform profiles created by freelance writers. In the struggle to secure and sustain a clientele in a competitive environment, profile creation requires as much close attention to displays of femininity and racial identity as it does to professional credentials. Proactively preempting the sexism and racism that manifests in customer feedback is integral to the work of these digital laborers, both in doing the "body work" of maintaining a desirable profile and in how they engage with clients while completing writing projects. This manifests not least in the form of a disciplining self-narrative focused on doing better in keeping their profile relevant and appropriate to the assumed desires of potential clients. When used as a labor management system, customer ratings and judgments directly enroll affective and embodied states into everyday work and the value-generating mechanisms of the platform. Through such mechanisms, emotional labor thus becomes "a fully recognized and mandatory component" (Gandini 2019: 1047) of the work environment.

A useful – if not extreme – example of this dynamic can be found in the work of Airbnb hosts. Stella Pennell's (2019, 2021) studies of New Zealand hosts found a complex array of accommodations being made for guests that reshaped and repurposed hosts' lives for the sake of commercial gain. Not only were their houses redesigned, redecorated, or renovated to make way for visitors, their lives, interpersonal relationships, and affects were also reconfigured. Pennell describes hosts using alternative entrances, actively suppressing noise such as phone calls, televisions, and conversation, and avoiding family visits – especially those involving children – to reduce the impact on guests. She cites one host who had given over the only bathroom in the house to platform users. While she has paying visitors, she uses a camping toilet in the garage and only undertakes bathing with a washcloth over the sink. This disavowal of their presence in their own home, Pennell notes, causes physical and psychic discomfort for some hosts. Just as impactful was the requirement for emotional labor, with hosts needing to provide a friendly, cheerful service, modulated to the particular demands of the guest, regardless of their own emotional states. On Airbnb, the quality of the host – or the host's qualities – may be as important as the quality of the accommodation.

Pennell also describes how Airbnb actively exerts a soft form of biopower to control their host's behavior to maximize capital extraction. Supplementing the ways in which algorithms determine visibility and customer ratings reward and punish certain behaviors, the platform also provides more qualitative disciplining tools that describe appropriate hosting and home decor standards. Some of these resources are articulated by the platform itself in "how-to" guides. Other aspects emerge within moderated community forums where appropriate regulations of affect within a range of scenarios are described and shared between hosts. In either venue, hosts are offered guidance on becoming a "hospitality entrepreneur" as well as how to represent that identity in profiles and in dealings with guests. The use of such disciplinary communication – or nudges taking the form of alerts, instructional guides, or inspirational stories – is common within the platform economy. They are used quite mechanically to encourage workers to, for instance, start a shift due to an increase in demand in the area, to flag a dip in ratings, or to encourage a review of profile information. But they may also be used more indirectly to model and encourage workers to adopt more customer- and therefore corporate-friendly dispositions and comportments.

Such calibrations of self by Airbnb hosts, influencers, or Uber drivers may not be permanent or, like the air stewards in Hochschild's (2003 [1983]) famous study of emotional labor, worn like a mask and (potentially) removed at will. There may also be a fraught relationship between a worker and the identity they perform in the workplace so demands for subjective alignment may be a site of struggle (Adkins and Lury 1999; Brook 2013; Purcell and Brook 2020). Nevertheless, the widespread calls for these accommodations clearly demonstrate how more than physical dynamics are at stake in digital work, and that there is much more than formally defined, formally compensated, formally contracted labor activities involved in digital media economics. The human capital that the platform economy attempts to draw upon is more than the physical or even the intellectual capabilities of the worker. It is also the diffuse and intimate aspects of self that are brought into the economic logics of the digital media industries. It is, therefore, not only Bella Thorne and the various sex workers on OnlyFans who are entangling intimate and embodied aspects of their subjectivity within their workplace environments. This suggests that all digital laborers are hopelessly commodified and suffering utter alienation of their species-being. However, is this really the case? Are things as grim as this holistic capture of the working subject would suggest? Is digital labor really nothing but a process of commodification?

Feminized human capital

Thus far, we have been discussing human capital or the subjective elements of labor as part of the value of a company and something firms (supposedly) invest in to sustain their market position and share valuations. However, in neoliberal societies, human capital is also something workers are encouraged to build and actively seek to develop in lifelong learning programs or via a wide array of business self-help literature. It is also a feature of the political discourse of the "information" or "knowledge economy" that emerged in the 1990s where "highly skilled knowledge workers and other representatives of the creative class could monetize their educational assets in the same way as investors leveraged their capital assets" (Adkins, Cooper, and Konings 2020: 45). Workers have long been encouraged to work on themselves in order to maximize their potential and, from that, their incomes or career success. But today a worker's human capital is understood not only as their educational level but as a holistic calculation of their subjective value. As Feher (2009: 26) puts it: "my human capital is me, a set of skills and capabilities that is modified by all that affects me and all that I effect." Investment in your human capital thus extends beyond formal education or skills training to include enhancing a range of other subjective aspects such as innate dispositions, physical or psychological capabilities, or inherited traits, as well as managing or maximizing the impact of any life event on those qualities.

Functioning effectively as human capital demands the kinds of self-reflection associated with "reflexive modernity," which sociologists such as Giddens, Bauman, Beck, and Lash describe as the nature of the post-Fordist environment (L. Adkins 2001, 2002). Reflexive modernity refers both to an increasing capacity of individuals to critique social conditions and to an expanded demand by social institutions for self-reflexivity and attendant self-monitoring. To develop and sustain the value of your human capital is an example of such self-reflection and is an underlying assumption in the digital media environment. Google (Google n.d.), for instance, emphasizes the importance of self-reflexivity and self-knowledge for their (potential) workforce. On their Careers page, they provide a handy guide to the various steps of their hiring process, the first of which is "self-reflection." The site offers a "visualization exercise" comprised of a set of questions to the potential applicant about their work history and experiences which they are asked to answer and then "sit with." The goal of this reflection is to generate a picture of their future career. This exercise, the site says, is proposed because, "Your skills, interests, and goals are the result of your life, your experiences, your triumphs, and your failures. If we hire you based on your skills, we'll get a skilled employee. If we hire you based on your skills, and your enduring passions, and your distinct experiences and perspectives, we'll get a Googler. That's what we want" (Google n.d.). All of this leads to an application process where the applicant is asked to focus on "jobs that delight" them, rather than submit a range of applications.

Reflexive modernity places a premium on attention to and regulation of bodily comportment, emotion, and identity performance in the workplace. In many labor environments, there has also been an increased importance placed on a "stylized presentation of self" (L. Adkins 2001: 674; McDowell and Court 1994), such as is achieved in self-branding both online and off. This is related to the rise of service-focused occupations as a component of the economy but can also be connected to the importance of human capital to a company's profits and to the individual employee's career prospects. Constant monitoring of behavior and feelings by employers and customers, but also by the workers themselves, is used to sustain and regulate the accumulation and appropriate deployment of this capital.

Such constant self-reflexivity, though, is gendered, reflecting historically feminized aesthetic and cultural behavior (L. Adkins 2001; Adkins and Lury 1999; Gray 2003). Various kinds of self-knowledge, self-regulation, and self-discipline reflect the narcissistic aesthetics of femininity and feminized consumer culture (Gray 2003; Gill and Scharff 2011). In contexts where human capital is valued, this means that "performances of femininity – for all workers – constitute workplace resources" (L. Adkins 2001: 669). This has been argued to encourage greater gender fluidity in both male and female workers but also taps into wider trends of the "feminization" of economic life. This process describes the mechanisms by which typically feminized qualities, such as caring, sociability, entrepreneurialism, flexibility, and adaptability, have become prized worker attributes, but also as employment settings increasingly reflect the part-time, fractured, and unstable conditions traditionally associated with women's careers (McDowell 1991; Mies, Bennholdt-Thomsen, and von Werlhof 1988; Morini 2007).

Drawing on the provocative work of French author collective Tiqqun (2012), Mareile Pfannebecker and J. A. Smith refer to the centralizing of aesthetic reflexivity as the "Young Girlification" of work. They say:

> Exploitation is not new . . . What has changed over the centuries is the extent to which the demand to perform individual desirability, via technologies of global distribution and communication, has spread from the economic margin to the centre even as it entrenches socioeconomic difference: Young Girlification can account for the similarities between

CEOs and webcammers in their performance of a certain kind of total availability within the same protocols of self-commodification. (Pfannebecker and Smith 2020: 88–9).

Tiqqun's argument – and Pfannebecker and Smith's mobilization of it – is based on the premise that the nominalized "Young Girl" is in a state of becoming but one that is fundamentally, and to her detriment, shaped by the commodity and consumer imperatives of contemporary culture. Tiqqun describes her as the "anthropological concentrate of reification" with "every experience drawn back incessantly into the pre-existing representation she has made for herself" (Tiqqun 2012: 41–2). There is nothing in her life "even in the deepest zones of her intimacy, that escapes the gaze and the codification of the Spectacle" (2012: 48). She "produces herself daily . . . via the maniacal reproduction of the dominant ethos" (2012: 58). In applying this description of the "Young Girl" to working practices, Pfannebecker and Smith are lamenting the commodity logics that animate contemporary selfhood and labor.

From a feminist – and indeed cultural studies – perspective, the patronizing dismissal of the meaningful agency of "Young Girls" by Tiqqun is deeply problematic. Its denigration of traditionally feminized practices of consumption and adornment, as well as its failure to recognize the ways subaltern power can legitimately be articulated, warrants its rejection. Nevertheless, the correlation between the conditions of "Young Girlhood" and contemporary capitalist dynamics is valuable. What Tiqqun describe, perhaps inadvertently, is a non-binary mode of existence and one that is replete with residual use-values and inalienable agency. They depict the "Young Girl" as a commodity but one that actively chooses commodification and does so knowing well her value. She does exert agency, even though it is couched within the transactional terms set by the dominant society. Even in their denigrating construction of her, she is not a passive victim. The contradictions that the "Young Girl" exists within – both object and subject; both active and passive; both observed and watchful; both joyful and involved in meaningless banality – offer a way of understanding the absorption of life into labor that moves us beyond the alienation and commodification thesis. The figure of the "Young Girl" offers us not an either/or distinction between commodity logics and authentic, dignified life but articulates a both/and scenario where commodification and its productive logics coexist with authentic selfhood and its reproductive dynamics.

I have argued elsewhere in relation to unpaid user labor (Fuchs and Sevignani 2013; Jarrett 2016a) – as has a wide literature on sex work, such as Bernstein (2010), Chapkis (1997), and Sanders (2012 [2005]) to name just a few – that it is too reductive to claim that the exploitation of aspects of self grounded in meaningful social, intimate, affective, and psychic dispositions only ever results in the end of their use-value outside of capitalism. While an exchange between users on a social media platform may well be abstracted and expropriated for use in the calculative economics of that platform, it is not only that. That exchange remains a valuable and meaningful interaction replete with use-values and non-instrumental significance even while it serves that other purpose for capital. It has both exchange-value and use-value at the same time. Consequently, the products of this exchange never reach the kind of fungibility or fetish qualities that make them commodities or, at least, make them *merely* commodities. They retain their connection and embedding in their utility and meaning for the users and so continue to resonate in the bodies and affective registers of the humans involved. They remain, at least partially, inalienable.

I suggest that the same is true of the commodification of self and affect that occurs through the exploitation and management of digital laborers of all kinds. A digital laborer may construct an embodied self, informed by capitalist rationality – and one that may be replete with what Karen Gregory and Jathan Sadowski (2021) call "perverse virtues" that work against their interests – but this does not necessarily mean that this self is entirely alienated from them. This remains their lived self, and the exchanges they have with others in that guise are meaningful interpersonal interactions even while ultimately put in service of capitalist exchange. Similarly, a "brogrammer" at a GAFAM company may perform aggressively geeky masculine competencies as part of his alignment with workplace norms and rituals to secure career success. This does not mean, though, that this economically valuable subjectivity is not available to him as a meaningful subject position. The logics of commodification which involve the complete domination of exchange-value that produces absolute alienation does not really capture the persistence of the ineffable and inalienable in evidence in digital labor. It doesn't quite capture the both/and dynamic of reflexive modernity and its particular modes for drawing subjectivity into exploitative contexts. The metaphor of the commodity – of the object that is sold in a marketplace – seems increasingly inappropriate to describe the types of incorporation of worker subjectivity into capital that we see in digital labor. So how then do we understand the enrollment of workers' human capital in the digital media industries?

Assetization vs commodification

Haunting this discussion of commodification is the specter of the stock market and the financialization of the economy that underpin the growth and status of the digital media industries as described in chapter 1. This is the context where financial institutions and their logics of share prices and abstract monetary calculations have come to dominate the economy and, through that, have become an important shaper of values across society. Little of what we have discussed in relation to brand value, human capital, and the incorporation of subjectivity makes sense unless it is placed in a context where material outputs and fungible monetary assets no longer determine the worth of a company. Financialization is the logic that animates the startup sector where a company's actual or potential share price is more important than its realization of actual profits. The embedding of stock options in salaries centralizes this logic within the elite arms of this industry. But this rationality extends beyond this sector into all of society as indebtedness – often through investment in education – and share portfolios – instead of state pensions and safety nets – but, most importantly, the logics of human capital become pervasive (Adkins et al. 2020). It is also the essence of neoliberal entrepreneurialism which is focused on treating your life as a business, seeking to maximize profit through strategic deployment of your resources (Feher 2018: 13).

In financialized capitalism, prosperity is always speculative and wagered on the future. It is based on "the continuously rated value" of a person's assets, rather than on maximizing of income or direct profitability (Adkins et al. 2020; Feher 2018). These assets include material objects such as the family home, but also the immaterial, embodied subjectivity of the worker – their human capital. When considered in relation to work, financialization shifts the idea of labor-power from a commodity sold to employers in the form of labor-time to it being conceived of as an asset held by the worker which can be leveraged in a marketplace to gain investment by creditors. The ideal digital laborer's self is thus crafted and recrafted with a view to actual or potential investors – or stakeholders (Feher 2018: 63) – whether they be the GAFAM/BAT companies who may hire them, a venture capitalist who may fund them, an audience member who may follow them, a brand who may partner with them, or a customer who may give them a good rating. Through this, they are, as Feher (2009: 30–1) points out, viewed as producers, "as entrepreneurs of themselves or, more precisely, as investors in themselves, as human capital that wishes to appreciate and to value itself and thus allocate it skills accordingly." Workers become both investor and investee in their laboring subjectivity. Additionally, with the path dependency created by platform infrastructures and the offsetting of salaries into shares, they may at the same time also be considered stakeholders – if not actual shareholders – in the platforms or companies for which they work. They may be invested in a corporation or a platform's success as the realization of their own human capital may depend upon it. In this way, workers become more actively engaged with capitalist logics than the free laborer selling their labor-power described by Marx. Through this process, the worker becomes not commodified, but "assetized."

The asset is very different to the commodity. The commodity is associated with heavy industry and the production of tangible goods for consumption by others. The asset, however, is immaterial, light, and mobile, but also – by virtue of its imaginary and plastic character – tied to the actions, desires, and potentials of its stakeholders, including the laborers themselves. Unlike the commodity, an asset is alive and unfixed, retaining its subjective qualities, and so it refuses total objectification even when it is being subject to abstract valuations. A worker who is marketing their own assets is not selling their labor-power to a platform to do with as it wills but opening those assets to a valuation by the marketplace. This value, however, cannot be entirely produced or captured by the enterprise that exploits it; the value of that asset is merely tapped into and channeled (Gorz 2010) and remains in important ways bound to the subjectivity of the worker.

Additionally, the subjectivity that is incorporated into the economic calculations of capital is – to use the language of economics – often a non-rivalrous good which means consumption by one person does not preclude its consumption by another or, in this case, require it to lose its substantive meaning or value to the supplier. As already noted, a game developer's knowledge of code, a TikToker's "relatable" (Kanai 2019) personality, or a graphic designer's aesthetic sensibility are not removed from them in its application to a thorny glitch, in the creation of promotional content, or a website redesign. More materially, Didi drivers, Deliveroo riders, and Airbnb hosts are not packaging up and transferring full ownership of their cars, bikes, or houses to a customer or a platform as would be expected of a commodity exchange. These assets are still, no matter how constrained, formally available to the digital laborer for their own use. Obviously, there is wear and tear both of material things and human subjects in this use. There are costs of this incorporation into economic logics, and I may be overstating the non-rivalrous nature of the personal subjects and objects drawn upon in the contemporary workplace, but this does not mean that these assets ever fully change ownership through their commercial exchanges. As Elizabeth Bernstein's (2010) book on sex work states, when you buy embodied subjectivity in the marketplace, it is only ever temporarily yours.

Moreover, the assetized worker doesn't sell their labor-power in its generalized form but seeks investors for it in terms of its specific, subjective character. Consequently, the assetized subject's labor-power keeps at least one foot in the inalienable at all times as that is the source of its value. Conceived in this way, the assetized worker – or the "Young Girl" – manifests a subjectivity crafted for the logics of neoliberal capitalism and in relation to expected investors but also in ways that ensures it remains meaningful to that worker. It is both inside capitalism and outside its logics simultaneously. This is a position with a greater sense of agency than that attributed to the worker alienated by the commodification of their labor-power. This agency may not be that associated with the unalienated worker or the class collective aspired to in orthodox Marxist critique, but it remains a form of inalienable embeddedness and source of resistance. This means that while digital labor may happen in the context of the social factory and involve the exploitation of the subjectivities of workers, it is possible to move beyond the entirely negative estimations of that practice while still critiquing its economic role. Understanding the incorporation of subjectivity into capitalism as "assetization," rather than commodification, allows room for dis-alienated, meaningful life to manifest, even within the social factory.

The assetization of Bella Thorne

The shift away from understanding digital labor through the lens of commodification advocated in this book makes sense because the mechanisms through which capitalism extracts value from workers has changed. As Adkins and colleagues (2020) argue, Marx's foregrounding of commodification was tied to his critique of a particular kind of exploitation associated with waged labor. In the digital economy, where self-exploitation, self-employment (both legitimate and bogus), and entrepreneurial industriousness abound, this model is not always fit for purpose.

The critical concept of commodification does remain relevant, though. Not all workers experience the same impetus or opportunities to assetize their subjectivity and embodiment as digital laborers, and not all digital laborers experience this dynamic to the same extent. Commodification of labor-power arguably remains a means for understanding a good deal of gig work, despite the formal context of self-employment in which many workers labor. Many of these workers, as well as a large number of workers in the global economy, continue to labor in ways that do not enroll all of their lives or are more readily separable from other aspects of the human condition. Additionally, there is an uneven distribution in how much control over their assets a worker has in their labor context. For digital laborers in low-paid and marginalized occupations in the digital media industries, such as Google Book's invisible workforce of book scanners (Wen 2014), it may be more correct to describe their exploitation as a commodification of their labor-power by an employer rather than a strategic leveraging of assets by a worker. And as Adkins et al. (2020: 72) argue, the divide between assetized and commodified workers is, in fact, an important emerging source of inequality.

Nevertheless, the framework of assetization means we can reassess Bella Thorne's use of OnlyFans described at the start of this chapter. In posting images to be viewed by subscribers, she was not reifying herself as an object to be consumed and discarded by her followers. At all times and in important ways, the embodied self captured in those images and made available behind the site's paywalls remains under her control and definition. Rather than commodify these dimensions of her self, she instead leveraged her assets – her normatively attractive body, her (hetero)sexuality, her mastery of social media and sexual visual codes, her pre-existing fan base, her understanding of her own brand – in order to generate revenue. Her sexuality may have been performed with a view to potential investors' desires and demands, ranging from the fans who might subscribe to the feed to art house film directors who might offer a breakthrough part outside the Disney Studio framework. But that does not make it any less *her* sexuality, intricately tied to her sense of self, her ambitions, her affective intensities, her desires. It is a living, adapting, growing embodied subjectivity rather than a fixed and reified object on a shelf. For some, setting up an OnlyFans page may still be considered an unfortunate or distasteful mode of generating revenue and one that may seem to indicate the mechanics of misogyny, providing further evidence or cause of the psychic harms caused by hetero-patriarchal capitalism. This position, however, suggests a naive, false consciousness by Thorne, as well as assuming the commodity logic that something inalienable was taken from her as her followers consumed her image. Conceived as a process of assetization, though, her work for OnlyFans can – and I suggest should – be considered a canny and very knowing mobilization of a valuable asset over which Bella Thorne retains possession and which is full of rich and agential affects and substance. While it may remain unfortunate that this subjective agency is shaped by hetero-patriarchal capitalism and so succeeds primarily in replicating its logic, it is, nevertheless, a meaningful form of agency.

It is not only digital laborers who experience assetization as a driving force. The feminization of the workplace, the human capital model of subjectivity, and the particular mechanisms for incorporating subjectivity into corporate logics documented in this chapter are widespread phenomena within post-Fordist, neoliberal capitalism. Indeed, Feher (2009) argues that there has been a widespread shift from workers understanding themselves as the "free laborers" of Marx's reckoning who sell their labor-power to instead seeing themselves in terms of human capital. Embodied in the "Young Girl," as Pfannebecker and Smith (2020) describe her, the assetized worker articulates a generalizable tendency within contemporary capital. This makes further discussion of assetization necessary.

Understanding digital labor through this lens is also useful because, in recognizing the persistence of the inalienable, it acknowledges the agency of a great variety of workers whose subjectivity is integral to their exploitation. Inherent to the mechanics of assetization is a capacity that, even when it is severely attenuated by economic logics, has the potential to recognize and articulate challenges to exploitation and to advocate for better working conditions. Under the commodification thesis, this would normally not be possible for those whose labor-power extends into their subjectivity because the processes of commodification would entirely subsume these workers into economic logics (Lukács 1971). In eschewing the logic of the commodity – the dead object handed about in marketplaces – in favor of the dynamic ongoing processes of assetization, a renewed vigor is potentially brought to the struggle for better work. It is to articulations of that struggle that we turn next.

6

Struggle: The Workers United(ish)

Documented throughout this book has been a litany of appalling practices and experiences. From wage theft to unsafe work environments to invasive surveillance and micromanagement to gender and age discrimination, digital labor has been associated with a range of undesirable and sometimes brutal industrial practices. The positive affects associated with the ostensibly good work of entrepreneurialism and workplace autonomy have been described as meaningful, but illusory when the material conditions of that work are taken into account. At worst, they are used as a veneer to mask the weakened employment status of many digital laborers and the precarity and insecurity experienced by all. Digital labor, it would seem, is a hellscape of exploitative and cruel practices.

A materialist understanding of history, though, tells us that at the heart of capitalism is a dialectical opposition between classes – the struggle between the proletarian and the capitalist over the socioeconomic and political conditions of their existence. While ranging across the spectrum of social formations, this antagonism is particularly pronounced in the struggle between labor and management over the conditions of work and its exploitation for profit. The freedom a laborer must know to be able to sell their labor-power is in conflict with the need to control and corral that agency in the service of an employer, creating a fundamental tension at the heart of the capitalist system. Workplace antagonisms – and the responses to them by workers and employer alike – emerge from this conflict and are a key driver of change in social, economic, and labor relations. When work contexts become untenable, agitation by workers challenge and sometimes reorder that work in ways that, ideally, create more dignity and equality in the workplace. This then establishes another set of conditions that an employer exploits or degrades, creating another set of antagonisms. The cycles of conflict continue in this way, reshaping work, industries, and people's lives as they go.

What this dialectic emphasizes, though, is that the undesirable conditions we have been describing as core features of digital labor are neither blindly accepted nor able to be imposed unilaterally. There is always the possibility for opposition, resistance, and progressive change. Worker struggles are forever producing new terrain for autonomy and security, as well as new avenues for exploitation and control as employers respond to those challenges. Moreover, in the constantly developing world of digital technologies, new tools for and spaces of resistance are emerging, along with different models for articulating work rights and collective action. Understanding digital labor, then, requires understanding these dynamics.

It is impossible for this chapter, or even this book, to cover the nuance of every type of labor struggle as it manifests in every industry or in every jurisdiction. Instead, this chapter will draw on a series of examples intended to illustrate some of the forms this struggle is taking across the various digital labor environments we have been considering in this book. This context has been described as posing significant challenges for traditional forms of organized collective resistance such as labor unions. The competitive, individualized, and distributed nature of the digital workforce is often claimed to be too averse or difficult to marshal into collective action. Despite these assumptions, digital workers are increasingly organizing and pushing back against the power of employers. Accordingly, this chapter will first explore the challenges that digital labor is assumed to pose to labor organization but then examine some of the forms that are nevertheless emerging among its workers. It will explore formal, strategic action and organization processes, such as that seen at Deliveroo (Cant 2020), in new media journalism (Cohen and de Peuter 2020), and in the games industry (Bulut 2020; Woodcock 2019, 2021a). It will also, though, pay particular attention to forms of resistance that occur outside of traditional trade union structures and formats. It will consider the importance and value of less structurally coherent, often temporary, tactical responses to the organization and exploitation of their work by a range of digital laborers. Through this exploration, we will build a picture of digital laborers' struggle in all its varied forms.

The death of labor organization

The contexts of digital labor have been described as diminishing, if not destroying, the potential for labor organization in three main ways: the distributed workforce; the individualizing nature of the labor; and the desirability of entrepreneurialism. It is these material and cultural qualities of the work – and how they interact – which have allegedly brought about the death of traditional, collective labor organization. Each of these features impacts differently in different sectors of the digital labor trilogy that we are discussing here and those differences are important to acknowledge. But it is assumed generally that these qualities reduce opportunities for developing solidarity within a workforce – a sense of shared interest and purpose that leads to collective action – as well as complicating the capacity to organize and mobilize that solidarity to achieve meaningful outcomes.

Problems of the distributed workforce are particularly notable in the platform economy, particularly in crowd or microwork settings where workers – as well as customers and employers – may quite literally be scattered across the world. Unlike the Fordist industrial factory, laborers are not gathered on the same shop floor and so are unable to recognize that they share a common experience of exploitation and poor conditions. The bonds of solidarity and camaraderie that underpin co-present working and the potential for an organic sense of the collective to emerge are, it is said, not available in the distributed digital workplace. This also reduces the opportunities for the kinds of union recruitment activities and consciousness-raising discussions that may take place during formal work time or break periods. Simply not being in the same room together can diminish the potential for workers to activate, organize, and mobilize collectively.

The distributed workplace is also linked to the individualizing nature of digital labor – workers operating in isolation are prone to understanding their work in individual terms. Being employed through a series of contracts or projects, as is the case for freelancers, many game developers, and some programmers, can also make it difficult for any worker to recognize or invest in relationships within any one workplace. Additionally, when the experience of others in the same situation is not visible, hidden by the personalized messaging of the app or the generalized promise of individual success, it can be difficult to recognize a shared experience. But the failure to foster solidarity is caused by more than the inability to recognize or value the existence of colleagues and comrades. It is also about the highly competitive environment that divides workers' interests. Chapter 3 documented the deep levels of competition for elite positions within the GAFAM/BAT companies and the often brutal politics involved in maintaining these posts. Similarly, freelance creative workers are always competing with each other for the next gig, as are platform workers in the struggle to secure jobs or clients. What all this competition does is pit workers against each other, individualizing their struggle for adequate incomes and reducing the bonds of solidarity.

Both of these dynamics are captured in the exploration of ride-sharing explored by Kafui Attoh, Katie Wells, and Declan Cullen (2019). In their study of Uber drivers in

Washington DC, they describe a labor process that produced the isolation and alienation from other workers that undermined collective action. Most of the forty people interviewed for their study had never met any of the other drivers who were their co-workers, and the few who had managed such encounters had not engaged in meaningful interactions. Attoh and his team suggest that this is not surprising, given the "zero-sum competition for passengers" (2019: 1015) which, coupled with gamified rewards for responding first to an emerging surge, creates tensions between co-workers. Drivers seeking gain through the personalized reward system of the platform became individualized in their work; isolated from others, they could not see their shared experience with other drivers. Additionally, the anonymity provided by the app also facilitated "scab" workers, creating yet another barrier to the kinds of solidarity associated with traditional labor organization. Some of the drivers in their study suggested that such atomization of the workforce by Uber was intentional and allowed Uber to "inoculate itself from attempts by drivers to unionize, 'create lawsuits,' or demand that they be recognized as employees" (2019: 1018). Whatever the case, in Attoh and colleagues' estimation, the distributed nature of the workforce and the intense competition of the work acted against the possibility of meaningful collectivism.

There are also other, more cultural, and personal reasons for the difficulty in organizing digital workers. The promise of "being your own boss" that animates digital labor, the relative degree of entrepreneurial autonomy experienced by many workers, and the aspirations of class mobility that have become bound up with such work obscure the nature of struggle – who are you organizing against when you, ostensibly, determine the time and nature of your work? Who do you resist when you are your own boss? In small firms, of the kind commonly found within the freelance creative economy and in startups, close relationships with employers can also make challenging management more fraught (Woodcock 2021a; see also ch. 3 above). Other difficulties affect more marginalized workers. For some workers, particularly in the global South, the opportunities provided by digital labor may, in fact, be experienced as relatively good work, providing greater earnings and opportunities for advancement than other low-end service jobs (Anwar and Graham 2020; Kashyap and Bhatia 2018; Wood et al. 2019). It may also be the only work available, so incentives to challenge the associated employment conditions may be low. No matter how exploitative, digital labor may be the least worst option.

In entrepreneurial and creative environments, it can also be difficult for workers to see the point of trade unions which are often associated with the stultified, heavy, blue-collar labor of the Fordist factory and considered to have little relevance to the professional identities of the agential, creative, white collar – or no-collar (Ross 2003) – workers of the digital economy. In elite digital creative environments, the apparent irrelevance of unionization has been aided by "a heady mix of techno-libertarianism and free market credo" (Cohen and de Peuter 2020: 15) working in concert with the holistic absorption into competitive workplace cultures. The autonomous hacker ethic that animates workers in elite digital media companies, startups, and the games industry also fosters individualized responses or work-arounds, rather than encouraging collective, structural change. This all occurs within a work environment defined as a "neutral, meritocracy-based creative profession rather than concrete work defined by politics" (Bulut 2020: 167).

Wendy Liu's memoir provides insight into the thought processes about unionization within the technology sector with its competitive meritocratic principles, immersive working environment, and commitment to breaking norms.

> This new world of technology, with its quirky founders and work that wasn't really work, transcended the archaic legal framework mandated by the government. It wasn't like I planned to sue my employer; surely that was the province

of the weak, those inclined to play the victim because they knew they couldn't win otherwise. I, on the other hand, would always be loyal, and I would always be valuable. (Liu 2020: 38)

Unions, she says, seemed like something that interested miners or factory workers and, it is implied, those stuck in the repetitive drone life of the stodgy traditional corporation. Unions were for interchangeable cogs in a corporate machine and not for those with the superior intelligence, creativity, and entrepreneurial energy to adapt to and flourish within the neoliberal landscape of Silicon Valley. With unions and collective organization incompatible with the self-directed and adaptable figure of the digital labor entrepreneur, to struggle against exploitation could only be seen as the action of a loser who had failed to realize their own potential. With all this stacked against it, the future for digital labor collectivism – and digital laborers' struggle against exploitation – seems very bleak.

The digital shop floor

However – and with all due apologies to an already misquoted Mark Twain – reports of the death of labor organization and collectivism have been greatly exaggerated. Digital laborers of various kinds are increasingly organizing – and increasingly achieving success in their demands for improved pay and conditions. Despite the assumptions of a fragmented workforce, for some forms of "geographically tethered" digital labor (Woodcock and Graham 2020), there are many opportunities for the types of collective meetings that facilitate solidarity and work organization. Callum Cant (2020) describes how the gathering of UK Deliveroo riders while waiting for orders provided space outside of management control for conversation about work practices. He describes how, as incomes and conditions deteriorated due to an influx of new riders generating competition for jobs, these conversations began to develop into impromptu rallies. This led to calls for industrial action as well as the impetus for a more formal organizing of the workforce under the umbrella of the Independent Workers Union of Great Britain (discussed more on p. 185). On the back of these initially informal gatherings, a strike of Deliveroo riders was called in the Brighton area for February 2017 and Deliveroo was issued with a series of demands: (1) a pay rise to £5 per drop; (2) a freeze on hiring; and (3) no victimization of union members. Despite attempts by Deliveroo management to derail the collective movement through arranging one-on-one meetings with riders, the workers continued their action. These workers eventually won the concession of a hiring freeze which, in turn, resolved some of the concerns about wages. Unfortunately, high staff turnover, a reiteration of the app which enabled better organization of work schedules for riders, and a decline in the number of workers gathering at Jubilee Square resulted in reduced activism and membership over time. Nevertheless, the type of struggle they articulated has been replicated by platform workers who share space across the globe.

For workers who do not share a geographic space or time, as well as for those who do, online forums are important spaces of collectivism. Worker-organized Facebook, WeChat, or WhatsApp groups and purpose-built forums or apps have taken on the role once played by the shop floor, providing avenues for workers to gather outside of the direct control of management to voice concerns about their work experience (Bryson, Gomez, and Willman 2010). This covers the spectrum from sharing helpful work practices to identifying risky jobs to union recruitment. These "digital watercoolers" (Woodcock 2021b: 2) allow workers "to share experiences, provide pay and tax advice and even advice on how to 'perform' labour" (Purcell and Brook 2020: 11). In the opaque environments of workplaces, these forums also provide spaces "where hegemonies are enacted, debated and contested, indirectly through competitive, but fraternal 'games', and directly through heated exchanges on the nature of the work and the relationship . . . to platform managers" (Purcell and Brook 2020: 11).

Online communication is also identified as central to the forms of collective struggle of digital freelancers found across the South-East Asian and sub-Saharan African countries explored by Alex J. Wood, Vili Lehdonvirta, and Mark Graham (2018). Their survey found that 58% of their respondents communicated with other workers weekly, predominantly through social media. Similarly, in a wide survey of Mechanical Turk microworkers, Ming Yin et al. (2016) suggest that almost 59% of all workers use online forums to communicate with other workers, with an additional 10% using one-on-one technologies such as phone calls, email, text messages, and video chat. Wood and colleagues (2018) also found that the demand for such interconnection increased as workers became more invested in the job. Such communication may be informal and focused initially on gaining prosaic knowledge about the work, but online communication nevertheless offers spaces for mutual support between workers. This, in turn, allows for the identification of common cause, to surface specific issues of concern, and to begin recruitment into more formal solidarity activities, including attempts to influence wages by sharing price norms.

Yin et al. (2016: 1293) also found a "rich network topology" of communication between workers. Not only is there a complex interconnection and discussion between workers, a great variety of platforms are also being used. Forums were distributed across a number of subreddits, discussion boards (MTurkGrind, TurkerNation, and MTurkForum), a range of Facebook groups, and a small number of workers were on a now defunct, purpose-built website CloudMeBaby. Some communications are one-on-one. Others facilitate community development. Building such forums is common across forms of digital labor. Workers have built a range of applications and sites that enable collective engagement and collective action and facilitate worker protections. Online sex workers, for instance, use sites such as the webcam model forum AmberCutie to offer support and guidance, and to share links to resources (Hardy and Barbagallo 2021). They also build on long-standing practices learned from street-level sex work and sites such as UglyMugs.org to aggregate "bad date lists," flagging clients who may not pay fairly or could be physically dangerous. The Turkopticon (n.d.) plug-in similarly draws on crowdsourced ratings to allow MTurkers to screen clients for bad behavior and underpayment. As the website notes, the app helps people "watch out for each other – because nobody else seems to be." Like the discussion with a colleague in the staff canteen about how to handle a difficult manager or how to most effectively minimize workload, these sites provide spaces for workers to gain some control over their work. Rather than being absent from the digital labor workplace, free spaces for workers to congregate, to share reports of injustice, and to work together to create better labor conditions are, in fact, proliferating.

Collective action

There is also a rich topology of actions being taken by digital laborers with the help of these forums. These range from various kinds of strike actions about pay and conditions that echo labor struggles of the past to campaigns for diversity and equality in the workplace happening through less confronting mechanisms. These actions are taking place on the streets, online, in court rooms, and in the polling booth as law and legislation are increasingly drawn into the mediation of digital labor.

Some of the more spectacular versions of these actions have been taking place within the ride-sharing and delivery platform work sectors (Woodcock 2021b). The last few years have seen growing dissatisfaction among these digital laborers which has spilled over into industrial unrest and strike actions across the globe, including an international strike of Uber drivers in May 2019. Industrial actions ranging from strikes, to demonstrations, to walkouts/logoffs, to legal challenges have taken place from Ireland to China to Argentina. One study of only platform food-delivery workers identified 527 incidents of labor unrest between January 2017 and May 2020 across 36 countries (Trapmann et al. 2020). Many of these actions were short-lived and involved relatively few actors, but a still significant number were of a larger scale and duration. Importantly, many of these actions involved coordination between workers using different platforms or working for different companies and in different locations. The report's authors argue that the key power these workers articulated in these actions was the power of association: the power of the collective.

A valuable example is the long-running dispute about income and conditions between drivers and the Ola and Uber ride-sharing platforms in India which has regularly spilled over into coordinated strike action. Between 2016 and 2018, there were fifteen major driver strikes in the country (Ray 2019). *Peoples Dispatch* (2019) reported that one rally in July 2019 involved tens of thousands of drivers in New Delhi, Kolkata, and Mumbai who gathered in public squares, taking thousands of cars off the road and crippling the lives of many middle-class urban commuters. The drivers' complaints have focused on matters relating to income – in particular, increasing fuel prices that have not been matched by increases in fare prices, an overall reduction in incentive payments, and the loss of fares that has accompanied increased competition as the platforms continue to recruit new drivers. Drivers report earnings falling by conservative estimates of 30–45 percent from three or four years prior. Yet, like so many platform drivers, they were still required to service debts for cars purchased when assurances of much higher earnings were given (Ray 2019; Surie 2018). Drivers were also concerned about safety and were agitating for the companies to provide medical insurance and the right to claim for accident costs. Notably, as the number of these strikes has increased, they have become increasingly well organized and increasingly been coordinated through driver trade organizations and unions. Some of this collective action, though, has been informal and involved direct communication between non-unionized workers via networks established in previous workplaces or from drivers manually collecting contact numbers when encountering other drivers at depots (Yadav 2017).

Another key site of struggle for platform workers has been centered on the legal definition of their employment status, with many asserting that their self-employed status is bogus and seeking reclassification as employees. Such cases hinge on the differences between subordinated work and independent or autonomous labor, the former characteristic being an indicator of employee status and the latter of self-employment. Among other dimensions of work practices, the tests of such status focus on the degree of integration into the company, the distribution of risk (as employees must not share the risks of the employer), the genuine reality of self-employment, and, importantly, the degree of control over everyday work practices experienced by the worker (Doherty and Franca 2020a).

Such demands to be recognized as employees have a long history in digital media industries. A notable early instance was the unpaid America Online (AOL) community moderators who, having experienced a change in conditions of their freely supplied and passionately driven volunteer contribution to the site's communities, began to develop a sense of their activity as a form of labor (Postigo 2003, 2009). With this growing consciousness of their exploitation, and as the benefits attached to their work diminished, these volunteers began organizing against AOL, including some discussion of strike action. One community moderator, Erol Trobee, took a lawsuit against the company in 1996 after being let go from the volunteer program. While only asking for about US$600 to compensate for the free usage hours he had banked in compensation for this work, he nevertheless asserted that by AOL's own definition he was acting as an employee. AOL was forced to settle this suit and this, in part, led to further restructuring of the volunteer program that added to the weakened conditions for other AOL community moderators. In 1999, another group of ex-volunteers filed a class-action lawsuit against AOL, also contending that they were employees of the company. They argued that AOL was in breach of US Fair Labor Standards by failing to provide a minimum wage. AOL finally settled the case in 2009, reportedly for US$15 million (Grove, Malone, and Dillion 2001).

More recently, as on-demand platform mediated work has become more common, such claims have increased in number but with varying degrees of success. Successful cases claiming employee status by ride-sharing drivers and delivery workers have been made in Switzerland, France, Spain, Australia, and China – to name merely a few. Some of these cases have been taken by individuals – albeit with clear implications for their colleagues – but others by labor organizations. In 2016, UK trade union GMB began its landmark case against Uber, successfully securing the relabelling of drivers as employees. Despite three challenges to the ruling by the platform, in 2021 the UK Supreme Court confirmed that the designation of UK Uber drivers as employees stands. In other jurisdictions – such as Brazil and Italy – similar cases have failed, and, in still others, initially successful cases have been overturned on appeal – such as has happened in South Africa. In at least one instance, the outcome was reversed. An initial ruling against recognition of a Glovo rider as an employee was later overturned by the Spanish Supreme Court.

The employment status of platform workers has also become a matter for legislators. In California in 2020, Proposition 22 was passed with 58.6 percent of the vote, granting on-demand companies such as Uber, Lyft, and

DoorDash an exemption from Assembly Bill 5 that had previously extended employee rights to gig workers. In France, though, legislation from 2016 grants platform workers a range of rights associated with employees, such as work-related accident insurance, continued training, and the right to join a trade union. As these examples indicate, the employment status of platform workers remains a complicated and highly contested terrain but one in which labor struggle – both individual and collective – is taking on a vital form.

Other collective struggles by digital laborers have been centered less on the elemental issues of income and labor security and instead have been focused on changing conditions, and in particular challenging inequalities in the workplace. In 2020, a group of Facebook content moderators successfully settled for US$52 million compensation for the post-traumatic stress developed through their work (Newton 2020). Across a range of locations, 20,000 Google/Alphabet workers also staged a mass walkout in 2018. Some of their demands were focused on traditional labor concerns – an end to forced arbitration and a commitment to end pay inequality. But the rest – as well as the impetus for addressing fairness in incomes – were focused on questions of diversity and equity within the workplace. They demanded a report into sexual harassment, a more inclusive reporting process for sexual misconduct, and increased status and voice within the company for the chief of diversity. One of the organizers, marketing manager Claire Stapleton, described the initial plan as a "day without women" to protest the mishandling of sexual assault allegations against Android designer Andy Rubin (O'Brien 2020). This framing linked this protest firmly to questions of workplace inequality rather than wages or labor security – although these are obviously entangled. Similarly, one of the grievances of the digital journalists whose unionization process is described by Cohen and de Peuter (2020: 7) was about challenging the "homogeneity of the industry," demanding an end to the elitism associated with the internship route into employment within the sector which worked against minorities, as well as pay and career advancement inequalities based on race, gender, and class.

Other forms of collective action and legislative change not directly about pay or employment status have also become a feature of the digital economy. In 2020, a coalition of trade unions, environmental groups, and social justice organizations greeted the news that Amazon had become the first ever trillion-dollar corporation by staging a global boycott of the site on the annual Black Friday sales day, including some walkout strike actions at fulfillment centers. Organized under the #MakeAmazonPay hashtag, the action demanded the corporation share more of this wealth with its workers and with society more generally by increasing its shockingly minimal tax contributions to the countries in which it operates (*Peoples Dispatch* 2020). Amazon workers in various countries also organized strikes and protests against hazardous working conditions during the Covid pandemic, as did a large number of other gig-economy workers across Latin America (Connell 2020). In 2021, California legislators moved to ensure that Amazon staff were no longer required to meet quotas that did not comply with breaks, rest periods, and other occupational health and safety requirements (Wakefield 2021). The range of actions being taken by digital laborers, and those taken by others in support of them, makes the digital economy a key battleground in the contemporary struggle for dignity in the workplace and social equality more generally.

Hacking the master's tools

Against Audre Lorde's dictum, digital workers also often wield the master's tools in their struggle for improved conditions and wages. Cohen and de Peuter (2020) document how online journalists drew strategically on their skills in generating publicity and their already visible communication platforms to provide live and ongoing social media updates about union negotiations with management. In doing so, they bolstered the informational and affective context that supported their success. YouTubers and influencers – as the job title of the latter suggests – have also very successfully mobilized their cultural capital, using their public profiles and their rich networks in pursuit of fair treatment from clients and platforms alike. In these instances, it is notable that the assetized subjective resources that digital media platforms and employers exploit are turned directly against corporate interests in the tug-of-war between control and autonomy, resistance, and recuperation that is at the heart of class conflict.

Other workers quite materially manipulate the master's tool in their struggle for income regularity and equitable conditions. Strategic deployment of multiple devices and applications can facilitate multi-homing – working across multiple platforms simultaneously – and programs, apps, and plug-ins are often used to work around platform systems to find the highest-paying gigs. Julie Yujie Chen's 2017 study of Didi drivers' negotiation of their working life includes a striking image of an array of devices attached to the console of one driver's cab. In conjunction with various bots, these gadgets and the apps in operation on them were used to game the algorithms, enabling the driver to reject ride requests without penalty, to identify the highest fares, and to work across different platforms in the quest for the best-paid work. DoorDash workers used technology differently but to the same end. They not only worked together to increase base wages through their #DeclineNow strategy of collectively rejecting low-paid jobs, they also have used the Drivers Utility Helper – an Android-only application exploiting a back door into older versions of the app – to identify the existence of tips that were hidden from the contemporary interface, putting them in a better position to decide on the viability of certain jobs (Ongweso 2021). Hacks such as these enable platform workers to manage better their time and the pace of their work, as well as secure more certain and higher-paid work.

Digital laborers are also building other mechanisms to prevent wage theft and wage minimization by platforms. After noting some problematic accounting by the platform, UberEats rider Armin Samii, who is also a software engineer, developed a Chrome extension called UberCheats to spot pay discrepancies by calculating the distance between pickup and delivery and assessing whether this matched the price paid by Uber (Marshall 2021). Other workers use the less technical methods of spreadsheets or pen and paper to log miles, mileage, or hours worked, comparing these figures against the amount compensated by the company. The worker-owned Drivers Seat Cooperative (https://www.driversseat.co/) helpfully provides an app to collate this kind of data, allowing ride-sharing and delivery workers to make choices about the kinds of platforms they work for, to manage their routes, or to optimize their earnings.

Another mechanism – and perhaps the end point of this form of resistance – is the wholesale reinvention of the master's tools so that they no longer replicate the injustices built into their original design. Cooperative platforms that copy models from the gig economy but undermine the exploitative, capitalist imperatives encoded into them enable workers to achieve varying degrees of autonomy and agency in their work. In doing so, they also allow them to avoid the alienation, brutal conditions, and chronic undercompensation of other commercial platforms. As Trebor Scholz (2016) describes, cooperative platforms can vary on how substantially they embed workers' rights and communal ideals, but a valuable model is worker-owned cooperatives which not only distribute profits to all registered laborers but also share decision making among employees. This may include contributing to the design of the site and/or involve commitment to other anti-commercial ideals such as open data. Other models might be publicly owned platforms working with citizens – as opposed to employees – to distribute and organize work in civil society, or membership models where profit is shared among the collective of the membership. The Platform Cooperative Consortium (https://platform.coop/) is a useful aggregator and interpreter of various models.

It can be difficult to find successful, long-running cooperative platforms but there are some useful examples that illustrate some of the varied forms they take. Fairmondo (https://www.fairmondo.de/) is an example of an online marketplace – a cooperative version of Amazon or Alibaba. It is not only run through democratic ownership and decision making with fair distribution of dividends to all cooperative members, but it also advocates ethical and fair consumption. Stocksy (https://www.stocksy.com/), on the other hand, is not run on the kind of anti-commercial principles of Fairmondo but is nevertheless designed to challenge the exploitation of workers by similar commercial stock image and video platforms. The agency is artist-owned and tries to minimize the exploitation of the creative work of their curated collection of contributors through more equitable distribution of fees. Described as "fair pay" on the site, 50–75 percent of all license fees from the site's clients are distributed to the artists. Enspiral (https://www.enspiral.com/) is slightly different again and is a collective of entrepreneurs operating a lab to generate innovative commercial ventures via a member-owned charitable company. These ventures range from software development to a web development academy to a creative media company to social enterprises. Not all of these ventures involve digital technologies, but many do, and the collective manages itself through an internally designed digital collaboration platform called Loomio. Members of the collective share decision making and are involved in co-budgeting but may be either contributors or members, with slightly different rights and expectations for each. Despite their many differences, in all of these examples, workers are given some kind of expanded agency within the workplace that runs counter to traditional capitalist imperatives.

Another well-documented and usefully illustrative, but seemingly defunct, example of how such coops might challenge the norms of the sector is the crowdwork platform Daemo. Described as a "crowd built, self-governed crowdsourcing marketplace" (Stanford Crowd Research Collective 2015), Daemo was built by Stanford researchers to enable greater dialogue between workers and requesters. To do so, it provided more transparent ratings mechanisms and also adopted an open-governance model for the platform, with leaders elected from across the pool of workers, requesters, and researchers running the platform. In doing so, it intervened directly by redistributing power within the labor management processes. Another ongoing example – taxi cooperatives in Austin and Denver in the United States – indicates how worker cooperatives can work as part of a broader network of actions. These drivers successfully moved against Uber and Lyft by lobbying for regulations that drove the companies out of the market and then replaced them with a self-built, worker-led alternative platform (Schneider 2016; Willis Garcés 2016).

This success aside, taking on established digital media platforms with the deep pockets of Silicon Valley behind them remains a challenging prospect. Scaling up and reaching a critical mass of users – both as clients and workers – is not an easy task so many cooperative initiatives fail. Additionally, this kind of entrepreneurial activism (Sandoval 2020) often merely replicates capitalist economic frameworks and so fails to radically disrupt capitalism's exploitative dynamics in the way they attest; Lorde's critique that using the master's tools will never bring down the master's house may well hold. Nevertheless, as culminations of workers' struggles to achieve dignity in work and a fair day's pay, cooperative platforms are important models for understanding labor resistance.

Formalizing the struggle

Underpinning some, but not all, of these actions has been the emergence of new trade unions – such as the Union of Platform Workers (UNIDAPP) set up in 2020 by Colombian Rappi delivery workers – or the reconstitution of older organizations to accommodate the specific contractual conditions, experiences, and challenges associated with digital laborers, in particular their supposedly self-employed status. Existing freelance unions are increasingly including gig-economy workers, as are large, existing unions such as 3F in Denmark and IG Metall in Germany – the largest trade union in Europe. A significant and influential example of a union moving to support digital laborers is the Independent Workers Union of Great Britain (IWGB), which was founded in 2012 to provide a collective voice for typically non-unionized and highly marginalized, often migrant, contract workers such as cleaners, security guards, or careworkers. It now includes platform workers under its remit. International alliances and networks are also being built between national organizations such as the International Alliance of App-Based Transport Workers (https://iaatw.org/; Varghese 2020), which has affiliated labor organizations in seventeen countries and on every continent.

While the bulk of visible activity for platform workers has been in ride-sharing and delivery sectors, other types of digital laborers are also looking toward formalizing their struggles. UK Influencers and media creators have begun organizing under the newly formed the Creator Union (https://thecreatorunion.com/) and in the United States under the American Influencer Council (https://www.americaninfluencercouncil.com/). Podcasters at Gimlet Media unionized in 2019 and successfully negotiated their first collective bargaining agreement in 2021 (Clementi 2019), a group of YouTubers formed the YouTubers Union (https://youtubersunion.org/; Niebler and Kern 2020) in

2018, and the IG Meme Union Local 69-420 (Lorenz 2019) was also set up in 2019. While not all these workers' collectives are recognized as unions or are big enough to function as advocates against a large multinational – they typically become affiliated to other established labor organizations to gain heft as the YouTubers Union ultimately did – they nevertheless demonstrate the appetite for formalizing collective action and solidarity building across the whole platform worker infrastructure.

Contrary to expectations about its irrelevance to its cohort of workers, more formal digital media workplaces have also seen the emergence of new unions, branches, or trade associations. Cohen and de Peuter (2020) usefully track the creation of union chapters for digital journalists within Gawker Media from the initial identification of the need for some kind of organization through formal recognition of the union to labor contract negotiation. Gawker is considered one of the first digital media companies to successfully unionize (see the useful timeline at Cultural Workers Organize n.d.) but journalists at Buzzfeed News have also organized, forming the Buzzfeed News Union within the NewsGuild of New York, while HuffingtonPost, the Intercept, and Thrillist unions have allied with the Writers Guild of America, East. Various international unions in the game sector are brought together under the Game Workers Unite (GWU) banner (https://www.gameworkersunite.org/). Members of this group are nested within other, larger unions as formal branches or chapters – GWU Ireland, for instance, is a branch of the Financial Services Union, whereas Game Makers Finland is part of the Union of Professional Engineers in Finland – but they find common purpose in these international coalitions. Similarly, the US-based Tech Workers Coalition (https://techworkerscoalition.org/) works in solidarity with a range of movements and formal trade union chapters to foster unionization within a wide range of digital industries.

An interesting and perhaps unexpected new union in the tech sector is the Alphabet Workers Union (AWU), set up by North American Google/Alphabet workers at the very end of 2020. Affiliated with the Communication Workers of America union, the AWU grew from 230 members to over 700 within a week of its launch (Schiffer 2021a, 2021b). Moreover, Alphabet employees created a global alliance – Alpha Global – comprised of 13 unions representing workers in ten countries. The AWU is designed primarily to "give structure and longevity to activism at Google." At the time of writing, it is an unrecognized "minority union," representing only a small number of the company's 260,000 full-time employees and contractors (Conger 2021). Nevertheless, it is a formalized, collective mechanism by which workers can exert pressure on the company to create better conditions and build solidarity between workers. It also provides mechanisms to bring into dialogue the concerns of Google's elite, full-time programming and engineer workforce and its more marginalized and contracted workers. Its material impact is yet to be seen, but the very existence of a formal organization and the momentum it demonstrates in an industry sector typically considered antithetical to unionization speaks of the growing importance of organized collective action for elite digital laborers.

This increasing formal organization of workers is likely an effect of a maturing industry and a growing professionalization of the sector as states increase regulation and as startup companies scale up or become increasingly bound to investor, shareholder, and other commercial demands. Digital media is now big business, as Cohen and de Peuter succinctly summarize: "Over the past decade or so, digital media has grown from a 'boot-strappy' collection of blogs, independent sites, and small companies into an established, profitable, and expanding sector, comprised of digital-first and legacy media companies alike. Digital outlets have consolidated as giants like Univision, Disney, Viacom, and Comcast acquire or invest in smaller sites" (2020: 13).

The sector increasingly involves large mergers, costly acquisitions, and huge profit margins. This growth, though, makes it even more obvious that profits are not being fairly distributed. This disparity is leading to increased class consciousness, even among creative, white-collar, and entrepreneurial workers whose self-conception, particularly in North America, may not readily align them with traditional concepts of unionization. For instance, it was Spotify's acquisition of the company for US$230 million that encouraged podcasters at Gimlet Media to unionize because it showed the company was no longer the "small, scrappy operation" (Clementi 2019; Jaffe 2021) whose direction they had previously been able to influence. In the newly visible commercial context of their labor, it became clear to these workers that their interests needed protecting.

As part of this process, digital labor companies – and workers – have been increasingly formalizing their processes, moving from relatively ad hoc businesses with organic working communities to more rigidly managed and structured companies (Cunningham and Craig 2019; Gil and Sequera 2020; Hou 2019; Kim 2012; Lei 2021; Nayar 2017; van Driel and Dumitrica 2021; Zhao 2016, 2019). The growth of the digital media sector is marked by the emergence of specialist professionalization ventures and systems, including the rise of intermediaries such as influencer talent agencies and multichannel networks as well as increased investment in creating best-practice guides, policies, and procedures for workers. In this process, some companies have also tightened their grip on workers' labor practices. Interventions such as YouTube's adpocalypse (see chapter 2) or TaskRabbit's shift from a bidding system to fixed fees have solidified previously fluid labor practices and caused increased discontent among workers. In the algorithmically managed platform economy, this unrest is further fueled by the opacity and unilateral imposition of so much decision making. This increases the sense of unfair treatment, particularly for workers who had hitherto felt invested in the company's fortunes and direction or who had been the sources of its original growth.

Ya-Wen Lei (2021) also describes how the failure to accord employee status to platform workers means that when unscrupulous or inequitable practices are experienced, attempts at redress cannot be readily converted into a legal challenge or progressed through existing labor courts and provisions. Consequently, the "injustice frame" that is actualized in these instances is based on abstract moral principles that lend themselves more readily to collective action, protest, and industrial action. Lei also contends that managing workers through algorithms creates a distance between workers and management that works against settling grievances and allows them to escalate. Without human managers, the emotional labor done to secure consent to changes within work conditions is bypassed so that such changes are not normalized and instead are experienced as extraordinary and imposed. It seems that by deferring control to automated systems, many digital platforms may, in fact, be increasing the potential for the kinds of industrial unrest and collective action being described in this chapter.

Nevertheless, challenges remain to the widespread formalization of labor struggle in digital media industries. Particularly in elite occupations, engrained cultural understandings of the irrelevance of unions to the contemporary workplace, the affective attachment to individualized, entrepreneurial activity, and the competitive environments in which many digital laborers work still mitigate against solidarity and unionization. Global economic conditions which make alternative forms of work less desirable, less secure, and less well paid – or indeed mean there is no real alternative to digital labor – also discourage workers from resisting the conditions on offer in the digital economy. Moreover, the existing structures of industrial relations and unions may not be appropriate for digital laborers – especially platform workers – and unions may also be hesitant to work on redefining "employment" to protect the hard-won rights and protections of existing, formally employed members

(Doherty and Franca 2020b; Lenaerts, Kiljoffer, and Akgüç 2018).

Some other difficulties in unionization, but particularly in achieving sustained improvements in conditions, emerge from the unclear employment status of many digital laborers. Summarizing the 2018 Eurofound study of work conditions for platform workers, Michael Doherty and Valentina Franca (2020a) describe how different jurisdictions make unionization and, most importantly, collective bargaining, more or less challenging for workers without formal employee status. In some jurisdictions – Denmark, for instance – self-employed workers are prohibited from joining trade unions, and in still others they can only join specific unions for the self-employed. Additionally, platforms regularly refuse to recognize and negotiate with trade unions on the basis that they do not recognize their staff as employees (Prassl 2018). Doherty and Franca (2020a) also suggest that a further impediment to collective bargaining in the sector may well be anti-trust laws as, depending on the jurisdiction, competition regulations may prohibit the kinds of sectoral-level wage fixing that such workers would demand. Collective bargaining may also be hampered by workers working for the same platform but operating under different kinds of contracts with different rights and provisions in each. Foodora, for instance, has multiple types of contract connected to how many hours a worker wishes to commit. Part-time or occasional workers using digital labor as a supplement to other incomes may have less interest in pursuing regularization or the formalization of conditions than full-time workers, particularly when to do so would work against the flexibility and higher incomes that are often attached to irregular status. These are all challenges that currently face the union movement in the platform economy but may also be echoed in the world of elite work, particularly where full-time, permanent employees toil alongside freelance and contract workers.

Despite extraordinary gains made by the labor movement in digital industries over the last five years, and with the rich spectacles of gig-worker strikes in mind, it is possible to overstate this success. The failure of US Amazon workers to agree to unionization proposals in April 2021 after a long campaign by activists and in light of well-documented workplace indignities is emblematic of the ongoing difficulties in formalizing collective action. Yes, workers are increasingly uniting into collective movements and, yes, they are increasingly mobilizing and formalizing that solidarity, but there is still much to be done at organizational levels to ensure all digital laborers are adequately protected within their workplaces.

Tactical collaborations

I also don't want to argue that the only type of worker struggle that exists, or indeed that matters, takes place in the context of formal organization and trade unions. Everyday workplace practices of support, collaboration, and tactical resistance that defy the individualizing and alienating tendencies of work – as well as directly challenge labor management processes – are just as important in understanding workers' struggle as industrial actions and unionization statistics. If we are seriously trying to understand the nature of digital labor, then we need to also take these interactions seriously. But we must also interpret these actions on their own terms and not merely for their capacity to contribute – or not – to large-scale collective action. Knowing how workers negotiate the contradictions and tensions of their jobs is important for, as Michael Burawoy (1979: 6) reminds us, "organisations do not simply 'persist' . . . they have to be continually produced – that is, reproduced" in all kinds of interactions within a work context. Similarly, SRT tells us that workers are produced as workers through quotidian interactions and antagonisms inside and outside the workplace. Everyday relations with other workers, management representatives, and with formal and informal structures in the workplace are all sites where workers' subjectivities are made, remade, and may be unmade. Understanding struggle in all the moments of its articulation – whether in mass strike action or in sharing snarky memes with co-workers – is thus important for insight into the nature of work.

Digital laborers engage in various kinds of individualized resistant and subversive strategies to navigate the kinds of control systems and exploitation they experience in their workplaces. These may be individual actions, such as workers whose screens or keystrokes are monitored by their employer using a second screen to avoid detection of personal activity while on paid time (Anwar and Graham 2020). Other informal acts of resistance are more collaborative and driven by interpersonal communication. As has already been noted in this chapter, digital laborers have a wide range of mechanisms to communicate with each other outside of management's line of sight. The mutual dependency and shared feelings within such discussions are expressions of worker solidarity for they imply that "group members recognize their general shared condition and purpose, even when their immediate, individual interests are not fully coincident" (Tassinari and Maccarrone 2020: 39). Such expressions may be considered as the basis of collective action, but they are more than merely vehicles for inevitable unionization; the actions that emerge from these informal dialogues are not merely seeds, destined to either become a full-scale movement or fail. They may very well be an end in themselves, part of the active negotiations and reworking of working lives, and so are still legitimate expressions of worker agency. Revealing information about work practices or how to manage the quirks of individual managers, or discussion of pay scales, can all empower workers to take individual action against an employer or a platform. Sharing war stories with a co-worker can also be an important release valve, reducing the sense of isolation experienced by a worker. The "communities of coping" (Korczynski 2003) that these interactions produce can also serve as an important psychic bulwark against the encroachment of management processes and the challenges or inequalities of such work.

Sophie Bishop (2019b, 2020; see also Cotter 2019; Hardy and Barbagallo 2021) describes how YouTubers use "gossip" to understand and map the opaque algorithms that determine their visibility on the platform and thus their incomes. Coming together in ad hoc and intimate communal spaces across a variety of social media systems, the digital laborers in Bishop's study work to support each other but also to develop collective expertise in the workings of YouTube's algorithms, determine strategies for creating content of a type and frequency that align with the platform's logics, and/or to generate other tactics for gaming those protocols. In these small networks, colleagues call upon each other to add reciprocal likes and engagements to posts to increase impact measures and thus visibility. They also work as a lab, using each other to determine the success or otherwise of attempts to increase visibility, with knowledge of successful tactics thus being made available to other members of that group. Similar communal discussions were also used to call out, and attempt to subvert, the racist bias of the platforms. In effect, the interpersonal communication spaces of these workers were a site for both articulating and mobilizing solidarity and for materially challenging the management of their labor by the platform.

Bishop consciously uses the feminized concept of "gossip" to describe this activity, recognizing in it both the intimacy associated with the term but also the importance of gossip as a form of speech for those lacking structural agency or who, like YouTubers, work in contexts of steep information asymmetry. In a workplace, gossip is valuable for its capacity to happen out of the line of sight of managers and thus to build and sustain worker subcultures that may resist the imposition of management control (K. Adkins 2002; Ray

2019; Scott 1990). Gossip is unruly and contains subversive potential. As Erica Laglisse (2014) points out in her study of a women's action group within a Zapatista solidarity collective, gossip can also be a form of direct action, reclaiming for the marginalized "the power to name . . . experiences" and creating opportunities to cooperate outside of otherwise determining hierarchical institutions.

As Bishop's example demonstrates, the communities of coping created by workers' gossip can readily become informally organized into tactical actions pushing back against unfair and exploitative labor processes. Such organization is not the form of "laborism" associated with Fordist trade unions (Standing 2016) but small-scale, temporary acts of collaborative resistance that improve, even if only temporarily, the working conditions and/or incomes of small groups of workers. Such acts feature across the platform economy. Gray and Suri (2019: 122), for instance, describe the "complex and thriving social network" created by microworkers in India and the rich forms of collaboration that emerge from them. They describe workers messaging to inform each other of well-paying jobs, reliable clients, or potential scams; sharing tips on managing particular tasks; raising money to repair co-workers' equipment; and sharing internet connections and devices. They also describe the sharing of tactical workarounds for platform features or common tasks. Sharing or trading accounts or tasks, while not allowed on MTurk, was nevertheless commonly used by workers to retain high reputation scores and to address the difficulties some workers found in setting up accounts because of burdensome or impossible identification requirements set by the platform. While these actions fall very short of transformative industrial action, they are collaborative activities – expressions of worker solidarity – that are successful in improving the working conditions of these digital laborers.

Another useful example of this ambiguous form of labor resistance is the work of platform work influencers in the

Philippines. Here, the work of gossip and building communities of coping has become a specific occupational role. Cheryll Ruth Soriano, Earvin Charles Cabalquinto, and Joy Hannah Panaligan (2021) describe the emergence of a form of influencer who provides advice and guidance to other workers on succeeding in the platform economy. These influencers and the "strategies of survival" (2021: 89) they share have become an important component of the very large platform labor sector in the country. Their role, though, is complex. On the one hand, their aspirational narratives and coaching of potential workers into entrepreneurial attitudes are used to bridge gaps in the organization of the industry by the state and employers. In this form, their work primarily serves to support the platforms that exploit workers and bolster the digital economy. On the other hand, as Soriano and colleagues argue, they are also engaged in the practice of *bayanihan* (helping others in a time of crisis), providing opportunities for digital laborers to create community, find information, and secure the vital material and economic support to sustain themselves within the context of economic precarity.

As with the formally organized actions described above, other informally coordinated actions are less targeted at pay and focus on wider concerns impacting workers. Jeanna Sybert (2021) describes how Tumblr users engaged in widespread contestation of the ban on sexual content unilaterally enacted by the platform in 2018. Hitherto, the site had been valued for its openness to sex- and body-positive content, as well as providing a unique "safe space" for expressions of queer and trans practices (Paasonen et al. 2019; Tiidenberg 2019; Tiidenberg and van der Nagel 2020). For this disparate workforce, the ban was experienced as a violation of their implicit contract with the platform, and the Tumblr user community actively resisted its imposition through a variety of tactics ranging from petitions to non-compliance to a boycott to snarky memes to a campaign to archive threatened content. Never centrally organized, collectivity was nevertheless ensured through the use of hashtags such as #adultban, #censorship, #tumblrprotest, and #femalepresentingnipples which collated users into a wide-ranging, collective voice contesting and challenging the legitimacy of the site's management. While this campaign was ultimately unsuccessful in overturning the ban, "by accumulating mass opposition" these activities "served as direct threats to the owners' decision-making power" (Sybert 2021: 8). They were a form of unpaid worker resistance.

It is also worth noting that the flight from Tumblr of the user community after this ban – which can be read as a refusal of work by digital laborers – arguably did substantial damage to the platform's audience traffic and ultimately its share price. The platform was bought by Yahoo in 2013 for US$1.1 billion and was then acquired by Verizon in 2017 when it purchased all of Yahoo. In 2019, though, Tumblr was bought by web services company Automattic (owner of Wordpress) for allegedly less than US$3 million (Hern 2019). While it is not possible to associate this dramatic decline in value entirely with the loss of users because of the ban, it certainly has played a role. Arguably, then, the type of loosely or uncoordinated actions of the Tumblr user community have been a very successful example of labor struggle. They might also be described as the kind of stakeholder actions argued by Feher (2018) to be an increasingly relevant form of industrial action. By withdrawing their contributions – their labor of content creation, data generation, and their affective investment in the platform's success – these users attacked the financial bottom line of the company. This served as an effective means of redressing the power imbalance between the company and digital laborers.

Seen as a stakeholder action, struggle over Tumblr's sexual content can thus be connected to the actions of Deliveroo workers whose protesting over their rights in 2021 targeted the company's imminent £1.5 billion IPO on the London Stock Exchange. The unease and concerns about regulation raised by the strikes and protests caused an initial drop in valuation in the lead up to the offering. The initial flotation price then dropped 31% in the first minutes, ultimately closing the day down 26% from the initial offering price (Gopinath 2021). The Deliveroo action was organized and strategic, the Tumblr action was not, but both are instances where the battleground moved from labor–employer relations to the arena of investment – those investors in the stock market and those whose investment in sustaining a platform is essential for its survival. In financialized industries, the arena of share price, shareholder, and stakeholder relations is an increasingly important site of struggle (Feher 2018).

Such individualized antagonisms as seen in the Tumblr and influencer actions may not be the ideal version of labor struggle advocated in much Marxist thinking and mobilized throughout the histories of worker struggles. Gaming the system or finding work-arounds to technical controls may ultimately manifest in conservative ways and do little more than suture a worker more comfortably into the rationalities of their workplace. As Burawoy (1979: 80–1) contends, not all instances of resistance are developed against management but can emerge organically from the labor process itself in order to achieve only the "relative satisfaction" of work-related needs. The forms of uncoordinated, gossipy struggle in some digital labor workplaces may thus be lamented because they are not the "right" form. However, these informal struggles may also be more meaningful forms of action than traditionally organized industrial action for workers who, as Feher reminds us, are not the free laborers of Marxism selling their labor-power as a commodity but assetized workers, speculating on the value of their embodied subjective assets in a workplace (see chapter 5). In these latter instances, workers are invested in the future of the company and the platform and so are more likely to align themselves with its needs. The antagonistic relations between the company and workers are thus differently calibrated and so both generate and require different mechanisms of action.

Additionally, for platform workers within a distributed workforce or for those who have individualized entrepreneurial dynamics written deep into their subjectivity, power may not come through association and collectivity, or even be available in that form. Individual actions against the management and exploitation of their labor – or expressions of "entrepreneurial agency" (Barratt, Goods, and Veen 2020) – may thus have a greater salience for digital laborers than they might for other workers (Anwar and Graham 2020). In the context of assetization and a financialized economy, attention to dimensions of gossip and invisible or informal organization is thus of heightened importance. This draws our gaze from the spectacular public strikes by Deliveroo and Ola workers to the intimate, interpersonal relationships of other kinds of digital laborers to see how these may also be powerful tools of struggle.

There is power in the union – and elsewhere

From this discussion, it is clear that digital workers of all kinds are very active in resisting and reshaping how their labor is exploited and the conditions under which they work. It should also be clear that these antagonisms are focused on a diverse range of issues and have various goals. They also appear in various forms, from traditional collective actions, such as strikes, boycotts, protests, and legal challenges, to the more individualized responses of exploiting loopholes in platform or device architecture, meme making, and building knowledge through gossip. In all these instances, digital laborers are articulating their agency and some form of resistance to the impositions placed on them by their employers, even when those employers deny their role as employers. Whether united – or merely united-ish – digital laborers of all kinds are clearly exerting power and reshaping their experience of work.

Workers' agency is still contested, though. Employers are responding to the growing resistance in a variety of ways: refusing to recognize unions; mounting active legal defenses to refute employee status; undertaking cosmetic changes to algorithms; or taking the nuclear option of ending operations in jurisdictions where workers have won significant rights or where the legal and policy environment has been rendered hostile to their interests. In these latter instances, workers' victories are pyrrhic as an often necessary income source – regardless of how inadequate – is lost. Some other gains by digital laborers are also very short-lived or are responded to by employers in ways that ultimately work against workers – for instance, where introducing formalized contracts reduces flexibility and, ultimately, incomes. Legal and policy environments may also remain hostile to both unionization and to establishing and policing the rights of workers in various jurisdictions, rendering it difficult to build and sustain effective resistance.

In all these instances, however, workers will continue to contest the arrangements and exploitation of their labor. They will continue to follow the logic of history in which the struggle of workers and the recuperation of that agency by employers work in tandem to bring about economic, political, and social change in an ever-flowing circuit. The workers' struggles documented here – both large and small – are rewriting the history of the digital media industries and of society more broadly. There is power in the union, and power in individual acts of subversion, and understanding these dynamics is vital for understanding digital labor as it is now and as it will be in the future. As Jamie Woodcock and Callum Cant (2019) put it, we are only at "the end of the beginning" of digital labor organization so there is much more to know, explore, and for which to hope.

7

Conclusion: Digital Labor on the Edge

Writing this book has been quite a challenge. It was produced during a series of national lockdowns during the Covid-19 global pandemic which added all kinds of complications onto already difficult work. The last months of my term as head of department where I was managing the first – and sudden – move off campus and the necessary reorganization of two other projects to deal with lockdown conditions added extra complexities to my workload and soaked up time I would otherwise have spent developing this book. Consequently, the argument on these pages was not clear to me before I began writing, leading to some difficult moments where I became hopelessly entangled in my own ideas, unable to find the pathway through – at least that's what it felt like in the intensity of lockdown isolation. I was privileged, though, to be on research leave for most of 2021, with a stable, secure income, and very comfortable living arrangements. Most importantly, I also did not lose anyone I cared about to the virus; too many people were not so lucky. Nevertheless, the writing of this book, my relationship to it, and presumably aspects of its content are marked by the trials of the Covid pandemic.

But more pertinently, there were also a range of difficulties associated with the subject matter that made this a challenging project. The first of these, as the introduction explains, was the problem of defining the terms of the inquiry: defining what I mean by "digital labor." I finally settled on a quite capacious definition which included unpaid user labor as in the original use of the term; platform workers, which

I expanded out to encompass gig workers and social media creators; and formally employed workers, a term which – at the behest of proposal reviewers – included elite professionals in the tech industry. It also included freelancers and subcontracted workers within the digital media industries, and, perhaps more controversially, employees in the infrastructure arms of the digital media sector such as fulfillment and datacenter workers. This definition created its own challenges as it demanded review of a vast range of studies covering a great variety of workplaces and working practices. It also involved identifying appropriate sources for understanding the nature of work in elite sectors which remains underresearched, hidden behind non-disclosure agreements and corporate secrecy. The research was made much harder by the sheer volume of new publications on digital labor – books and journal articles – as well as the range of emerging news events involving digital workers. The stuffed bookshelves in my home office and the overflowing folders of e-books and journal articles in my various devices and cloud storage hubs are testimony to the scope of the task I set myself in this project.

Beyond these material difficulties, this definition also created the challenge of how to identify commonalities across such a diverse range of occupations, contractual relationships, and workforces with their incredibly divergent challenges, pleasures, practices, economics, processes, and cultural norms. As I began researching and writing this book in August 2020, I was not sure what I would find to connect these disparate forms of work and use to typify the nature of digital labor. I went into this project knowing that I would be able to describe their nature but unsure whether there would be any common threads to allow any conclusion to be drawn about this thing called digital labor.

As the writing progressed, though, an important – and unexpected – theme did emerge that connected Google programmers with *zhubos*, Deliveroo riders, and tweeters.

This was the structural similarities or tendencies toward the kinds of work historically associated with the margins of the economy. Although differently articulated in each sector, this association with the fringes emerged as a persistent framework for understanding the socioeconomic and cultural underpinnings of labor in the digital media industries, as well as linking them to wider global economic trends. To conclude the overview provided by this book, then, this chapter will pull harder on this thread and attempt to weave from it a story about the wider politics of digital labor. This short chapter is thus more speculative than many of the others, drawing less on empirical studies and more on theoretical frameworks. It will also ask more questions than it can answer. What it does do, though, is telescope out from digital labor itself to consider the wider economic context and through that provide insight into the nature of contemporary capitalism.

Of centers and margins

Across the chapters in this book, various links are made between the nature of digital labor – or the ways this work has been constructed – and socioeconomic dynamics associated with workers, citizens, and actors either excluded from or pushed to the edges of the economy. In chapter 2, the discussion of exploitation described the various kinds of income instability experienced by all digital laborers as examples of "cheap labor." Drawn from the work of Pham (2015) on Asian style bloggers, this concept describes work that is undervalued and insecure and workers who are disposable and marginalized. In this chapter, I associate the chronic under-compensation, the vulnerability of incomes, and insecurity of jobs themselves with pressures from algorithms, policy changes, corporate restructuring, or audience tastes. But I also argue that this precarity indicates a similar form of cheapness in how digital labor is structurally positioned to that described by Pham. In some ways, it was a little preemptive to apply that description at that point. The true sense of the disposability of the digital workforce is made more apparent in chapter 3, where the informality of the sector at contractual and organizational levels is described as fraying the bonds of care for workers. Even elite, formal workers in apparently secure employment in GAFAM/BAT companies are described as experiencing role and job insecurity which, while very different to the way these insecurities are experienced by platform workers, demonstrate a similar relocation of risk and a laissez-faire approach to the material and psychic security of the workforce. This situation is of no great novelty to workers on the margins, but that these conditions can also be tracked in well-compensated, elite forms of white-collar work is more surprising.

Some of this dynamic is also picked up in chapter 4 in which the entrepreneurial logics of digital labor are explored. The valorization and romanticization of the spirit of entrepreneurialism is the core theme of this chapter, which draws direct parallels between this kind of glamorized "good work" and labor on the margins of the economy. Arvidsson's very valuable discussion of "industrious capitalism" associates this risky mode of working with activity until recently considered illegitimate and an economic edge case. He understands "hustle" as integral to those pushed out of the benefits and security of the structured formal economy, such as migrants, undocumented workers, racial and ethnic minority groups, and others in the lowest socioeconomic strata. As already noted, he also associates such work with pre-capitalist economies and then, in turn, draws a link to racialized – but specifically Asian – labor by likening hustle to "street-level bricolage," "messy bazaars," and "labour-intensive wet-rice agriculture" (Arvidsson 2019: 41). Despite, he says, being denigrated in this orientalist view as an impediment to industrial modernity, such work nevertheless persisted in the peripheries of the economy but as a devalued and aberrant form. Entrepreneurial hustle has been the work of the other, defining what good capitalism is by defining the limits of acceptability. It is thus associated with "edge populations" of capitalism – those with "occasional entry to insecure waged work and participating in consumer markets shaped by those productive forces, yet unable to gain recognition or secure entry to the terms of capitalist citizenship in that location" (Bhattacharyya 2018: 26). Today, though, this work is promoted and idealized throughout society as a form of dis-alienated and, therefore, desirable labor; a model of good work to which we should aspire. Through this valorization of entrepreneurialism, such racialized forms of labor activity have now been placed at the center of the economy. It is not only cheap labor but also outsider economic logics that have come to drive the digital society.

Digital labor is also associated with work that is marginalized due to its gendering. In the chapter focusing on commodification, a parallel was also drawn between the holistic demands of digital labor and the "Young Girlification" of the economy as self-reflexivity and self-fashioning have become integrated as sources of value. The absorption of the whole of the self demanded by digital labor's social factory manifests in a variety of ways – from the cultish adherence to corporate ethos in elite tech work, to the reliance on interpersonal networks to secure freelance contracts, to the selective curation of self-presentation designed to generate positive ratings by clients in platform work, to the reshaping of sociality by social media. All these activities are about enrolling more than physical outputs. They are about, as Berardi (2009) suggests, putting the "soul" of the worker to work. But the aestheticization and narcissistic reflexivity that accompanies this kind of work is, Lisa Adkins (2001, 2002) argues, traditionally feminized activity happening outside of the formal economy. Self-making has historically been unrecognized as work or as having a relationship with value creation. Considered part of reproductive activity and so associated with private spaces and domestic work, it is "women's work" and its centrality within digital labor suggests a particularly feminized field of labor. This gendering and the focus on the interpersonal are also why feminized dynamics such as "gossip" become increasingly important in struggles by workers as discussed in chapter 6.

The connections between gendered forms of work and digital labor are also deeper than this. In *The Digital Housewife* (Jarrett 2016a), I argue for the similarity between the structural position of unpaid user labor and that of the traditionally conceived "housewife" because of the way their labor produces use-values that persist as use-values within the capitalist production value chain. In chapter 5, I have described the same dynamic where workers' subjectivities may be produced for, but are not entirely subsumed into, exchange in the marketplace. The assetized worker leveraging their embodied subjectivity within the marketplace has a feminized history. Cheap labor, with its racialization, also has a gendered quality. As noted in chapter 2 and by Pham (2015), Asian labor has historically been feminized, partly because of a locus within feminized industries, but also because of the feminization of the Asian worker. The cheapness of digital labor – its disposability and instability – also reflects what Mies and colleagues (1988) refer to as the "housewifization" of labor in the global economy. They contend that the contemporary economy is no longer dominated by the figure of the proletariat. Rather, it is the figure of the housewife and the principles of undercompensated and fragmented labor that she represents that stands at the center of the labor imaginary. This, they argue, is not only because of the increasing presence of women in the paid labor force but because the structural conditions that have typically followed women's work have come to dominate labor relations in the global neoliberal economy (see also Morini 2007; van Doorn 2017). Digital labor as it is described here is cheap Asian labor, is fringe economics, is women's work.

Entangled throughout the book, then, are three core descriptions of digital labor that argue its resemblance to work on the margins. In digital labor, however, these forms of work have shifted from the periphery or exterior of the formal economy to become core; they have made their way from the margins to the center. This movement is not unique to the digital media industries. Rather, it is a tendency across all sectors. The cheapening of labor, not least because that concept is another way of framing precarity, is central to contemporary capitalism. To be exploited by capital has always been about being made disposable and undervalued but this dynamic has arguably been re-intensified since the breakdown of the industrial compact of the twentieth century (Standing 2016). In the race to the bottom that typifies contemporary labor dynamics across the globe, digital laborers are not necessarily leading the charge. Workers in unregulated mines, outsourced factories, and informal domestic service are some of the workers at the vanguard of the dynamics we see in digital labor. So are many migrant workers, slave laborers, and people across the global South whose racialized hyper-exploitation is integral to the generation of surplus value at a transnational level. Nevertheless, digital laborers still embody and, given the increasing centrality of digital media industries in the economy, arguably exemplify this tendency toward imposing increasingly marginal labor conditions on workers.

This is also not a novel argument – although the route taken to reach this conclusion may well be a unique path. Well-established links between precarity and the conditions of some forms of digital labor – and the global precariat and digital laborers – have already informed the understanding of exploitation that starts this book's analysis. The key difference is that I argue that this trend also impacts white-collar workers in the digital media industries. For many of the elite digital laborers in this study, the experience of marginal labor conditions is contrary to the promises made by capitalism. Throughout the course of the twentieth century, elite, white-collar professionals (and many blue-collar workers) were promised secure, if not lifelong, employment with consistently rising living standards and consumption levels. This was always a racialized privilege, found predominantly in the global North and available primarily to white workers, and was articulated differently and secured through varying mechanisms in different places. It also may never have been quite delivered in the form it was promised. Nevertheless, it is the narrative that secured consent to the consumer and industrial capitalist complex of the twentieth century. Today, though, the secure, industrial contract of Fordism looks more like an exception rather than the rule of capitalism, particularly as work becomes reorganized in proto- or pre-capitalist industrious forms associated with the edges of the Fordist complex (Neilson and Rossiter 2008).

The questions that follow

But this shift in the centrifugal forces of the economy that we see in digital labor as it serves as an exemplar of global trends, raises troubling questions for how we understand labor exploitation more generally. What does it mean when what we have hitherto understood as marginalized work is performed by the most privileged of white male workers? What does it mean when cheap labor gains in social prestige? And what does that do to those in groups long allocated to cheapened work? Does the historically cheap worker become cheaper, pushed further into penury? Where is there for these workers to go?

The tendency in capitalism that digital labor exemplifies expands the center further into the margins. What is central to the formal economy thus becomes more marginal and the margins become even thinner and less sustainable. In this process, the distribution of privilege is not reallocated. Dividing people by race, gender, sexuality, or ability is fundamental to the mechanisms of capitalism (Bhattacharyya 2018;

Dalla Costa and James 1975; Davis 1983; Robinson 2021 [1983]; van Doorn 2017). The accumulation of surplus still leans heavily on a division of labor that devalues some work by casting it as not-work or lesser-work. This division thus defines an unemployed or underemployed population. It also has a racializing logic, with different kinds of work (and their attendant valuations) becoming attached (either by design or effect) to particular bodies and social groups. The less valued, recognized, and compensated forms of work have typically followed the most othered bodies. In this way, capitalism produces difference, allocating people into outsider status and into roles and functions it has already marked as less valuable, even excluding some from the mainstream economy. It does this so it can create competition between workers that diminishes solidarity, maintain a reserve army to suppress wages, and continue to extract maximum surplus value by exploiting more intensely those pushed to the edges and who, therefore, have little agency. These mechanisms remain integral to the capitalist mode of accumulation, so the recalibration of the qualities associated with valuable work suggests merely a reconstitution of the values that define the periphery and the center, but not a change in the populations located in each sphere. The gendering and racialization of labor may be unsettled by the dynamics we see in digital media, but this is not the same as them being dismantled (Bhattacharyya 2018: 168–9).

This raises further questions though. As the center of value creation shifts to work with formal properties until recently associated with marginalized workers, what other entanglements, mechanisms, dynamics are mobilized to continue the oppression of those groups? By what mechanisms is the racialized and gendered division of labor being maintained in contemporary capitalism? What I am really asking is: what does the whitening of cheap, industrious labor that digital labor embodies do to those who have historically worked in this way? This is worthy of more investigation.

The shifts that digital labor exemplifies also upset long-standing means of stratifying and classifying labor, particularly those articulated in Marxist thought. This is first flagged – but not fully explored – in the first chapters of the book where I touch upon the contractual relationships of the three larger subgroups of workers that I place under the digital labor umbrella. From the users contracted to contribute data and content by consumer licenses rather than labor contracts, to the (bogus) self-employment of platform workers and freelance subcontractors in the formal economy, and to the deferral of wages into stock options for elite workers, digital labor shows a tendency toward self-exploitation. Workers, including those at the bottom of the income scale, are increasingly not – or not always – waged workers in the sense that this idea has been understood throughout the twentieth century.

This has implications for how we understand their exploitation that I have only begun to consider in these pages. Workers under all three forms of digital labor have a peculiar class position when viewed using traditional Marxist lenses. The standard definition of the working class in Marxist thought is that they are employed in productive activity by capital, but without owning the means of production and so must sell their labor-power to survive (Marx and Engels 2012 [1888]). This means they are (typically) waged workers. It is the shared experience of the social relations encoded into the exploitative dynamics of waged work that forms the basis of the class struggle and class identities we typically understand. In digital labor environments, however, the conditions of direct employment associated with the working class are more likely to be the experience of elite digital workers such as game developers or programmers, particularly if we read the salary as hourly-waged labor that is merely not described as such. The proletariat, though, typically has no economic independence or agency within their occupational activities. This is a privilege, however, that often is held by the waged workers of Silicon Valley, suggesting they are not, in fact, in this class. A lack of autonomy, nonetheless, does describe the conditions of platform workers' labor who are micromanaged by algorithms and company dictates. However, these workers are also formally self-employed – not formally waged workers – and so, technically, control their own labor and own (some of) the means of production associated with their work. Like freelance creative workers running their own small or micro-businesses, platform workers are thus, formally, part of the petty bourgeoisie or the lower-middle classes. They are not the working class. But this seems counterintuitive. Workers earning small, precarious incomes from intensely managed labor such as Deliveroo riders are more likely candidates to belong to the class we associate with repression than a well-compensated creative designer at EA Games or a Google brogrammer. Yet, by orthodox, formal understandings of class, the reverse would be true.

This may be a gross simplification of how scholars after Marx and Engels have come to understand the nature of class and to differentiate between the bourgeoisie and the proletariat. Nevertheless, problems of class composition are important to consider for, as the 2015 ILO report on the changing nature of work suggests, full-time permanent work is in decline across the globe – and was already proportionally small in places – with increasing numbers of unemployed and self-employed workers. Digital labor is thus at the leading edge of this growing trend away from waged work which, in turn, challenges the ways we have traditionally understood class location to be delineated (Tsing 2009). What qualities, then, actually differentiate classes in the current form of capitalism? How do we critique work and workers in capitalism without a cogent understanding of the class structures contemporary capitalism mobilizes? The problems of this structural relationship to capital also add another, very important, complication. How do we understand the experience of vulnerable workers when the labor theory of value – tied to contracted, waged work – no longer seems the most useful tool for grasping their exploitation?

Digital labor, it seems, is not playing by the old analytical rules. As an exemplary form of labor practices in contemporary capitalism, this also suggests that capitalism as a whole is also playing the game differently. Sure, wealth is still accruing to the wealthiest and the whitest and the system is fundamentally based on the exploitation of hierarchical differences. The basic principles of this mode of accumulation remain, but there has been an adaptation affecting the dynamics of labor exploitation and thus the dynamics of the social relations they enact. It is here that frameworks such as Feher's assetization – discussed in chapter 5 – or Arvidsson's concept of industrious capitalism – discussed in chapter 4 – become useful. They give us ways into a critique of capitalism that draws on Marxism but inflects it for the contemporary age and its reconstituted economic strata. Such extensions to the critical toolkit are, I think, vital. Marx's critique of capitalism remains a superb framework for understanding industrial capitalism, and the key analytical categories his analysis offers remain valuable tools for cracking open the dynamics of any mode of accumulation. But Marx is not – and should not – be wielded like a blunt object. Marx's economic thinking needs to breathe and be extended and adapted to reflect contemporary circumstances. To do this we need what Bhattacharyya calls – in a delightful turn of phrase – "quirky Marxists" (2018: 38) to show us different ways of approaching the political economy of labor. Most importantly, as the entangled threads that have emerged from this analysis of digital labor clearly tell us, we need scholars who understand the racial, gendered, and sexed dimensions of capitalism to recognize better the precursors, contemporary resonances, and futures of both digital labor and the wider capitalist tendency.

Digital labor and beyond

Recently, Alessandro Gandini (2021) reminded me that in writing this book I have breached my own argument that what is needed in studies of digital labor is research that focuses on its specific qualities, rather than generalizations. This is an argument I made while describing how the social conditions that produced the detention of women in the Magdalene Laundry system in Ireland was profoundly entwined with the economic, and how this challenges normative assumptions about the novelty of the entanglement of the cultural and the economic in digital media's social factory (Jarrett 2018). A tome like this one that tries to map commonalities across the very broad – and vague – concept of "digital labor" stands in complete contradiction to that dictate. It seems this book is very much a case of do as I say, not as I do.

I do still hold with the demand to develop more specific insights. All digital labor and digital laborers are unique in their manifestations and have geographical, temporal, technological, and embodied particularities that require identification, exploration, and critique. Differences in the political economy of a place, the historical context, the gender, sex, age of the worker, or the type of platform, for instance, all matter in how digital labor manifests. It remains vital that the specific qualities of different forms be mapped and that generalizations of the kind I have made throughout this book be used sparingly. This applies to this conclusion where I have made broad, sweeping claims about transformations in capitalism which may not reflect historical conditions outside of my global North understanding of its dynamics. As Bhattacharyya (2018: 8, original emphasis; see also Tsing 2009) reminds us, there is "No such thing as *the* capitalist state. No arrangement of workers that is replicated everywhere. No necessary similarity in the pattern of concessions that workers may win." Global capitalism is highly variegated. The one consistency is the will to accumulate, so how this happens in all its specificity is work that will – and should – be ongoing. More is to be done on the particular dynamics of particular manifestations of particular forms of digital labor.

However, my real point in the article cited by Gandini was to avoid simplistic claims of novelty attached to work involving digital technologies which has too often led to the dismissal of knowledge about precursor varieties of labor. Having researched the internet since the 1990s, I have too often seen the analytical wheel being reinvented as new technologies, platforms, or practices emerge. This often means the neglect of scholars and perspectives already marginalized in the academy or the ideas of these researchers being reproduced without acknowledgment. More importantly, failure to place an emerging form of labor – or a digital technology or cultural practice – into a longer lineage means it is often impossible to see the continuities, extensions, reorganizations, or ruptures in the historic oppressions that it articulates. These are important to map. I advocate for avoiding blanket claims of the novelty of the digital but instead for a focus on identifying how what we see in emerging forms of work reconfigure and/or rearticulate existing socioeconomic structures. Even though I have taken digital labor as a monolithic entity as the object of study in this book, I have nevertheless been trying to locate it within wider geographical, cultural, and historical contexts and been actively thinking through its links to long-standing exclusions and inequalities. The work of this conclusion has been to make clearer some of those connections and their implications for how we understand both digital labor and the contemporary capitalist system.

And so I hope what I have done in this book by looking at digital labor as a singular form of work has been more valuable than merely providing an introductory overview of the field – although I certainly hope it has been useful in that, too. Approaching the topic at a general level has allowed the identification of trends in the organization of work, mechanisms of exploitation, workers' resistance, and class composition, the pertinence or extent of which can be tested in future studies of specific digital labor formations. It has also provided some insight into the workings of contemporary capitalism and how it may be articulating not a new but a recalibrated organization of labor. It has also indicated that perhaps we need more – to return to Bhattacharyya's term – quirky critical approaches if we are to know meaningfully the contemporary articulation of capitalism. Digital labor and digital laborers are valuable test cases for capitalist critique, and this book is only the start of this understanding.

References

Abercrombie, Nicholas, Hill, Stephen, and Turner, Bryan S. 1986. *Sovereign Individuals of Capitalism*. London: Allen & Unwin.

Abhayawansa, Subhash and Abeysekera, Indra. 2008. "An Explanation of Human Capital Disclosure from the Resource-Based Perspective." *Journal of Human Resource Costing and Accounting* 12(1): 51–64.

Abidin, Crystal. 2017. "#familygoals: Family Influencers, Calibrated Amateurism, and Justifying Young Digital Labor." *Social Media + Society* 3(2). https://doi.org/10.1177/2056305117707191

Adkins, Karen C. 2002. "The Real Dirt: Gossip and Feminist Epistemology." *Social Epistemology* 16(3): 215–32.

Adkins, Lisa. 2001. "Cultural Feminization: 'Money, Sex and Power' for Women." *Signs* 26(3): 669–95.

Adkins, Lisa. 2002. *Revisions: Gender and Sexuality in Late Modernity*. Buckingham: Open University Press.

Adkins, Lisa and Lury, Celia. 1999. "The Labour of Identity: Performing Identities, Performing Economies." *Economy and Society* 28(4): 598–614.

Adkins, Lisa, Cooper, Melinda, and Konings, Martijn. 2020. *The Asset Economy*. Cambridge, UK: Polity Press.

Adorno, Theodor and Horkheimer, Max. 1992. *Dialectic of Enlightenment*. London: Verso.

Andrejevic, Mark. 2002. "The Work of Being Watched: Interactive Media and the Exploitation of Self-disclosure." *Critical Studies in Mass Communication* 19(2): 230–48.

Andrejevic, Mark. 2009. "Critical Media Studies 2.0: An Interactive Upgrade." *Interactions: Studies in Communication and Culture* 1(1): 35–51. http://doi.org/10.1386/iscc.1.1.35/1

Anwar, Mohammad Amir and Graham, Mark. 2020. "Hidden Transcripts of the Gig Economy: Labour Agency and the New Art of Resistance among African Gig Workers." *Environment and Planning A: Economy and Space* 52(7): 1269–91.

Are, Carolina. 2020. "How Instagram's Algorithm is Censoring

Women and Vulnerable Users but Helping Online Abusers." *Feminist Media Studies* 20(5): 741–4.
Are, Carolina. 2021. "The Shadowban Cycle: An Autoethnography of Pole Dancing, Nudity and Censorship on Instagram." *Feminist Media Studies*. https://doi.org/10.1080/14680777.2021.1928259
Are, Carolina and Paasonen, Susanna. 2021. "Sex in the Shadows of Celebrity." *Porn Studies*. https://doi.org/10.1080/23268743.2021.1974311
Arvidsson, Adam. 2019. *Changemakers: The Industrious Future of the Digital Economy*. Cambridge, UK: Polity Press.
Arvidsson, Adam and Colleoni, Elanor. 2012. "Value in Informational Capitalism and on the Internet." *The Information Society* 28(3): 135–50.
Attoh, Kafui, Wells, Katie, and Cullen, Declan. 2019. "'We're Building Their Data': Labor, Alienation, and Idiocy in the Smart City." *Society and Space* 37(6): 1007–24.
Ball, Kirstie. 2010. "Workplace Surveillance: An Overview." *Labor History* 51(1): 87–106.
Banet-Weiser, Sarah. 2012. *Authentic™: The Politics of Ambivalence in a Brand Culture*. New York: New York University Press.
Baraniuk, Chris. 2015. "How Algorithms Run Amazon's Warehouses." *BBC Future*, August 18. https://www.bbc.com/future/article/20150818-how-algorithms-run-amazons-warehouses/
Barratt, Tom, Goods, Caleb, and Veen, Alex. 2020. "'I'm My Own Boss . . .': Active Intermediation and 'Entrepreneurial' Worker Agency in the Australian Gig-Economy." *Environment and Planning A: Economy and Space* 52(8): 1643–61.
Baym, Nancy. 2018. *Playing to the Crowd: Musicians, Audiences, and the Intimate Work of Connection*. New York: New York University Press.
BBC News. 2013. "Amazon Workers Face 'Increased Risk of Mental Illness.'" November 25. https://www.bbc.com/news/business-25034598/
Berardi, Franco "Bifo". 2009. *The Soul at Work: From Alienation to Autonomy*. LA: Semiotext(e).
Berg, Janine, Furrer, Marianne, Harmon, Ellie, Rani, Uma, and Silberman, M. Six. 2018. *Digital Labour Platforms and the Future of Work: Towards Decent Work in the Online World*. Geneva: International Labour Organization.
Berg, Justin M., Grant, Adam M., and Johnson, Victoria. 2010. "When Callings are Calling: Crafting Work and Leisure in Pursuit of Unanswered Occupational Callings." *Organization Science* 21(5): 973–94.

Berlant, Lauren. 2011. *Cruel Optimism*. Durham and London: Duke University Press.

Bernstein, Elizabeth. 2010. *Temporarily Yours: Intimacy, Authenticity, and the Commerce of Sex*. Chicago: University of Chicago Press.

Bhattacharya, Tithi. 2017. "Introduction: Mapping Social Reproduction Theory," in Tithi Bhattacharya (ed.), *Social Reproduction Theory: Remapping Class, Recentering Oppression*. London: Pluto Press, pp. 1–20.

Bhattacharyya, Gargi. 2018. *Rethinking Racial Capitalism: Questions of Reproduction and Survival*. London: Rowman and Littlefield.

Bindel, Julie. 2020. "OnlyFans is Sex Work and Pornography – Stop Calling it 'Empowering.'" *Evening Standard*, September 11. https://www.standard.co.uk/comment/comment/onlyfans-sex-work-pornography-empowering-bella-thorne-a4545501.html/

Bishop, Sophie. 2019a. "Vlogging Parlance: Strategic Talking in Beauty Vlogs," in Crystal Abidin and Megan Lindsay Brown (eds), *Microcelebrity Around the Globe: Approaches to Cultures of Internet Fame*. Bingley, UK: Emerald Publishing, pp. 21–32.

Bishop, Sophie. 2019b. "Managing Visibility on YouTube through Algorithmic Gossip." *New Media & Society* 21(11/12): 2589–606.

Bishop, Sophie. 2020. "Algorithmic Experts: Selling Algorithmic Lore on YouTube." *Social Media + Society* 6(1). https://doi.org/10.1177/2056305119897323

Bishop, Sophie. 2021. "Influencer Management Tools: Algorithmic Cultures, Brand Safety, and Bias." *Social Media + Society* 7(1). https://doi.org/10.1177/20563051211003066

Blunt, Danielle, Coombes, Emily, Mullin, Shanelle, and Wolf, Ariel. 2020. *Posting into the Void: A Community Report by Hacking/Hustling*. https://hackinghustling.org/posting-into-the-void-content-moderation/

Bolin, Göran. 2011. *Value and the Media: Cultural Production and Consumption in Digital Markets*. Farnham, Surrey: Ashgate.

Boltanski, Luc and Chiapello, Eve. 2005a. *The New Spirit of Capitalism*. New York: Verso.

Boltanski, Luc and Chiapello, Eve. 2005b. "The New Spirit of Capitalism." *International Journal of Politics, Culture, and Society* 18: 161–88.

Boltanski, Luc and Thévenot, Laurent. 2006 [1991]. *On Justification: Economies of Worth*. Princeton: Princeton University Press.

Bonifacio, Ross, Hair, Lee, and Wohn, Donghee Yvette. 2021. "Beyond Fans: The Relational Labor and Communication Practices of Creators on Patreon." *New Media & Society*. https://doi.org/10.1177/14614448211027961

Braverman, Harry. 1998 [1974]. *Labor and Monopoly Capital: The Degradation of Work in the Twentieth Century*. New York: Monthly Review Press.

Brook, Paul. 2013. "Emotional Labour and the *Living Personality* at Work: Labour Powers, Materialist Subjectivity and the Dialogical Self." *Culture and Organization* 19(4): 332–52.

Bryant, Sean. 2020. "How Many Startups Fail and Why." *Investopedia*, November 9. https://www.investopedia.com/articles/personal-finance/040915/how-many-startups-fail-and-why.asp/

Bryson, Alex, Gomez, Rafael, and Willman, Paul. 2010. "Online Social Networking and Trade Union Membership: What the Facebook Phenomenon Truly Means for Labor Organizers." *Labor History* 51(1): 41–53.

Bucher, Michael and Shannon, Maggie. 2020. "Behind the Scenes of a TikTok Video: Weeks of Work for Seconds of Content." *Wall Street Journal*, November 14. https://www.wsj.com/story/behind-the-scenes-of-a-tiktok-video-weeks-of-work-for-seconds-of-content-b5d70cd0/

Bucher, Taina. 2012. "Want to Be on the Top? Algorithmic Power and the Threat of Invisibility on Facebook." *New Media & Society* 14(7): 1164–80.

Bulut, Ergin. 2015. "Playboring in the Tester Pit: The Convergence of Precarity and the Degradation of Fun in Videogame Testing." *Television & New Media* 16(3): 240–58.

Bulut, Ergin. 2020. *A Precarious Game: The Illusion of Dream Jobs in the Video Game Industry*. Ithaca: Cornell University Press.

Buni, Catherine and Chemaly, Soraya. 2016. "The Secret Rules of the Internet." *The Verge*, April 13. https://www.theverge.com/2016/4/13/11387934/internet-moderator-history-youtube-facebook-reddit-censorship-free-speech/

Burawoy, Michael. 1979. *Manufacturing Consent: Changes in the Labor Process under Monopoly Capitalism*. Chicago and London: University of Chicago Press.

Cadwalladr, Carole. 2013. "My Week as an Amazon Insider." *Guardian*, December 1. https://www.theguardian.com/technology/2013/dec/01/week-amazon-insider-feature-treatment-employees-work/

Calvino, Flavino, Criscuolo, Chiara, and Menon, Carlo. 2015. *Cross-country Evidence on Start-up Dynamics*. OECD Science, Technology and Industry Working Papers. Paris: OECD Publishing. http://dx.doi.org/10.1787/5jrxtkb9mxtb-en/

Campbell, Colin. 1987. *The Romantic Ethic and the Spirit of Modern Consumerism*. Oxford: Blackwell.

Cant, Callum. 2020. *Riding for Deliveroo: Resistance in the New Economy.* Cambridge, UK: Polity Press.

Caplan, Robyn and Gillespie, Tarleton. 2020. "Tiered Governance and Demonetization: The Shifting Terms of Labor and Compensation in the Platform Economy." *Social Media + Society* 6(2). https://doi.org/10.1177/2056305120936636

Caraway, Brett. 2011. "Audience Labor in the New Media Environment: A Marxian Revisiting of the Audience Commodity." *Media, Culture & Society* 33(5): 693–708.

Carman, Ashley. 2020. "Black Influencers are Underpaid, and a New Instagram Account is Proving It." *The Verge*, July 14. https://www.theverge.com/21324116/instagram-influencer-pay-gap-account-expose/

Chang, Emily. 2019. *Brotopia: Breaking up the Boy's Club of Silicon Valley.* New York: Portfolio/Penguin.

Chapkis, Wendy. 1997. *Live Sex Acts: Women Performing Erotic Labour.* New York: Routledge.

Chen, Adrian. 2012. "Inside Facebook's Outsourced Anti-Porn and Gore Brigade, where 'Camel Toes' are More Offensive Than 'Crushed Heads'." *Gawker*, February 16. http://gawker.com/5885714/inside-facebooks-outsourced-anti-porn-and-gore-brigade-where-camel-toes-are-more-offensive-than-crushed-heads/

Chen, Adrian. 2014. "The Laborers Who Keep Dick Pics and Beheadings Out of Your Facebook Feed." *Wired*, October 23. https://www.wired.com/2014/10/content-moderation/

Chen, Adrian. 2015. "When the Internet's Moderators are Anything But." *The New York Times*, July 21. https://www.nytimes.com/2015/07/26/magazine/when-the-internets-moderators-are-anything-but.html/

Chen, Adrian. 2017. "The Human Toll of Protecting the Internet from the Worst of Humanity." *The New Yorker*, January 28. http://www.newyorker.com/tech/elements/the-human-toll-of-protecting-the-internet-from-the-worst-of-humanity/

Chen, Julie Yujie. 2017. "Thrown Under the Bus and Outrunning It! The Logic of Didi and Taxi Drivers' Labour and Activism in the On-Demand Economy." *New Media & Society* 20(8): 2691–711.

Chen, Julie Yujie. 2018. "Technologies of Control, Communication, and Calculation: Taxi Drivers' Labour in the Platform Economy," in Phoebe V. Moore, Martin Upchurch, and Xanthe Whittaker (eds), *Humans and Machines at Work: Monitoring, Surveillance and Automation in Contemporary Capitalism.* Cham, Switzerland: Palgrave Macmillan, pp. 231–52.

Chen, Julie Yujie and Qiu, Jack. 2019. "Digital Utility: Datafication, Regulation, Labor, and DiDi's Platformization of Urban Transport in China." *Chinese Journal of Communication* 12(3): 274–89.

Chen, Julie Yujie and Sun, Ping. 2020. "Temporal Arbitrage, Fragmented Rush, and Opportunistic Behaviors: The Labor Politics of Time in the Platform Economy." *New Media & Society* 22(9): 1561–79.

Chiapello, Eve and Fairclough, Norman. 2002. "Understanding the New Management Ideology: A Transdisciplinary Contribution from Critical Discourse Analysis and New Sociology of Capitalism." *Discourse & Society* 13(2): 185–208.

Chu, Cassini Sai Kwan. 2018. *Compensated Dating: Buying and Selling Sex in Cyberspace*. Singapore: Palgrave Macmillan.

Clark, Duncan. 2016. *Alibaba: The House that Jack Ma Built*. New York: Harper Collins.

Clementi, Alyssa. 2019. "Gimlet Media Becomes First Podcast Company to Unionize." *Mobile Marketing*, March 13. https://mobilemarketingmagazine.com/the-employees-of-podcast-company-gimlet-media-has-become-unionized-#:~:text=Gimlet%20will%20become%20the%20first,of%20Gimlet%27s%2083%2Dperson%20staff/

Cockayne, Daniel. 2016. "Entrepreneurial Affect: Attachment to Work Practice in San Francisco's Digital Media Sector." *Society and Space* 34(3): 456–73.

Cohen, Nicole S. 2012. "Cultural Work as a Site of Struggle: Freelancers and Exploitation." *TripleC: Communication, Capitalism & Critique* 10(2): 141–55. https://doi.org/10.31269/triplec.v10i2.384

Cohen, Nicole S. and de Peuter, Greig. 2020. *New Media Unions: Organizing Digital Journalists*. Abingdon: Routledge.

Conger, Kate. 2021. "Hundreds of Google Workers Unionize, Culminating Years of Activism." *New York Times*, January 4. https://www.nytimes.com/2021/01/04/technology/google-employees-union.html/

Connell, Tula. 2020. "Colombia Gig Economy Workers Wage Country-Wide Protest for Rights." *Solidarity Center*, October 8. https://www.solidaritycenter.org/colombia-gig-economy-workers-wage-country-wide-protest-for-rights/

Corrigan, Thomas F. 2015. "Media and Cultural Industries Internships: A Thematic Review and Digital Labour Parallels." *Triple C: Communication, Capitalism & Critique* 13(2): 336–50.

Coté, Mark and Pybus, Jennifer. 2007. "Learning to Immaterial Labour 2.0: MySpace and Social Networks." *ephemera* 7(1): 88–106.

Cotter, Kelley. 2019. "Playing the Visibility Game: How Digital Influencers and Algorithms Mediate Influence on Instagram." *New Media & Society* 21(4): 895–913.

Craig, David, Lin, Jian, and Cunningham, Stuart. 2021. *Wanghong as Social Media Entertainment in China*. Cham, Switzerland: Palgrave Macmillan.

Cultural Workers Organize. n.d. "Digital Media Unionization Timeline." https://culturalworkersorganize.org/digital-media-organizing-timeline/

Cunningham, Stuart and Craig, David. 2019. *Social Media Entertainment: The New Intersection of Hollywood and Silicon Valley*. New York: New York University Press.

Cunningham, Stuart and Craig, David (eds). 2021. *Creator Culture: An Introduction to Global Social Media Entertainment*. New York: New York University Press.

Dalla Costa, Mariarosa and James, Selma. 1975. *The Power of Women and the Subversion of the Community*, 3rd edn. London: Falling Wall Press.

Davis, Angela Y. 1983. *Women, Race and Class*. New York: Vintage Books.

Davis, Jim and Stack, Michael. 1997. "The Digital Advantage," in Jim Davis, Thomas Hirschl, and Michael Stack (eds), *Cutting Edge: Technology, Information, Capitalism and Social Revolution*. London: Verso, pp. 121–44.

Deliveroo. (n.d.). "Apply to Be a Rider." https://riders.deliveroo.ie/en/apply/

de Peuter, Greig. 2011. "Creative Economy and Labor Precarity: A Contested Convergence." *Journal of Communication Inquiry* 35(4): 417–25.

de Stefano, Valerio. 2016. "The Rise of the 'Just-in-time Workforce': On-Demand Work, Crowdwork, and Labor Protection in the 'Gig Economy'." *Comparative Labor Law & Policy Journal* 37(3): 471–504.

Dickson, E. J. 2020. "Sex Workers Worry Bella Thorne's $2 Million Payday Could Ruin OnlyFans." *Rolling Stone*, August 26. https://www.rollingstone.com/culture/culture-news/bella-thorne-onlyfans-sex-workers-1050102/

Doherty, Michael and Franca, Valentina. 2020a. "Solving the 'Gig-saw'? Collective Rights and Platform Work." *Industrial Law Journal* 49(3): 352–76.

Doherty, Michael and Franca, Valentina. 2020b. "The (Non/)Response of Trade Unions to the 'Gig' Challenge." *Italian Labour Law e-Journal* 1(13). https://doi.org/10.6092/issn.1561-8048/10762

Dolan, Kerry A., Wang, Jennifer, and Peterson-Withorn, Chase. 2021. "*Forbes* World's Billionaires List: The Richest in 2021." *Forbes.* https://www.forbes.com/billionaires/

Duffy, Brooke Erin. 2017. *(Not) Getting Paid to Do What You Love: Gender, Social Media, and Aspirational Work.* New Haven: Yale University Press.

Duffy, Brooke Erin and Hund, Emily. 2015. "'Having it All' on Social Media: Entrepreneurial Femininity and Self-Branding Among Fashion Bloggers." *Social Media + Society* 1(2). https://journals.sagepub.com/doi/abs/10.1177/2056305115604337/

Duffy, Brooke Erin and Schwartz, Becca. 2018. "Digital 'Women's Work?' Job Recruitment Ads and the Feminization of Social Media Employment." *New Media & Society* 20(8): 2972–89.

Duffy, Brooke Erin, Pinch, Annika, Shannon, Shruti, and Sawey, Megan. 2021. "The Nested Precarities of Creative Labor on Social Media." *Social Media + Society* 7(2). https://doi.org/10.1177/20563051211021368

EA Spouse. 2004. "EA: The Human Story." *LiveJournal,* November 10. https://ea-spouse.livejournal.com/274.html

Edwards, Douglas. 2011. *I'm Feeling Lucky: The Confessions of Google Employee Number 59.* London: Penguin.

Eurofound. 2018. *Employment and Working Conditions of Selected Types of Platform Work.* Luxembourg: Publications Office of the European Union.

Facebook. n.d. "We are Facebook." Careers. https://www.facebook.com/careers/

Fast, Karin and Jansson, André. 2019. *Transmedia Work: Privilege and Precariousness in Digital Modernity.* Abingdon: Routledge.

Feher, Michel. 2009. "Self-Appreciation; Or, the Aspirations of Human Capital." *Public Culture* 21(1): 21–41.

Feher, Michel. 2018. *Rated Agency: Investee Politics in a Speculative Age.* New York: Zone Books.

Fisher, Eran. 2010. "Contemporary Technology Discourse and the Legitimation of Capitalism." *European Journal of Social Theory* 13(2): 229–52.

Forde, Chris, Stuart, Mark, Joyce, Simon, et al. 2017. *The Social Protection of Workers in the Platform Economy.* Brussels: European Parliament Directorate General for Internal Policies.

Fowler, Susan. 2020. *Whistleblower: My Journey to Silicon Valley and Fight for Justice at Uber.* New York: Viking.

Frayssé, Olivier. 2015. "How the US Counterculture Redefined Work for the Age of the Internet," in Olivier Frayssé and Mathieu O'Neil (eds), *Digital Labour and Prosumer Capitalism: The US Matrix*. Basingstoke: Palgrave Macmillan, pp. 30–50.

Frenette, Alexandre. 2013. "Making the Intern Economy: Role and Career Challenges of the Music Industry Intern." *Work and Occupations* 40(4): 364–97.

Friederici, Nicolas, Wahome, Michel, and Graham, Mark. 2020. *Digital Entrepreneurship in Africa: How a Continent is Escaping Silicon Valley's Long Shadow*. Cambridge, MA: MIT Press.

Fromm, Erich. 2013. "Marx's Concept of Man," in Erich Fromm (ed.), *Marx's Concepts of Man*, trans. T. B. Bottomore. London: Bloomsbury Academic, pp. 1–71.

Fuchs, Christian. 2008. *Internet and Society: Social Theory in the Information Age*. Abingdon: Routledge.

Fuchs, Christian. 2009. "Information and Communication Technologies and Society: A Contribution to the Critique of the Political Economy of the Internet." *European Journal of Communication* 24(1): 69–87.

Fuchs, Christian. 2014a. *Social Media: A Critical Introduction*. London: Sage.

Fuchs, Christian. 2014b. *Digital Labour and Karl Marx*. Abingdon: Routledge.

Fuchs, Christian and Sandoval, Marisol. 2014. "Digital Workers of the World Unite! A Framework for Critically Theorising and Analysing Digital Labor." *Triple C: Communication, Capitalism & Critique* 12(2). https://triple-c.at/index.php/tripleC/article/view/549/

Fuchs, Christian and Sevignani, Sebastian. 2013. "What is Digital Labour? What is Digital Work? What's Their Difference? And Why Do These Questions Matter for Understanding Social Media?" *Triple C: Communication, Capitalism & Critique* 11(2). https://www.triple-c.at/index.php/tripleC/article/view/461/

Gallagher, Leigh. 2017. *The Airbnb Story: How to Disrupt an Industry, Make Billions of Dollars . . . and Plenty of Enemies*. London: Virgin Books.

Gandini, Alessandro. 2016. *The Reputation Economy: Understanding Knowledge Work in Digital Society*. London: Palgrave Macmillan.

Gandini, Alessandro. 2019. "Labour Process Theory and the Gig Economy." *Human Relations* 72(6): 1039–56.

Gandini, Alessandro. 2021. "Digital Labour: An Empty Signifier?" *Media, Culture & Society* 43(2): 369–80.

Gannon, Emma. 2017. *eg* blog. http://www.emmagannon.co.uk/2017/06/05/news-im-in-the-latest-microsoft-tv-advert/

Garcia Martinez, Antonio. 2016. *Chaos Monkeys: Mayhem and Mania inside the Silicon Valley Money Machine.* London: Ebury Press.

Geissler, Heike. 2018. *Seasonal Associate.* South Pasadena: Semiotext(e).

Genuine. 2017. "Real People – Microsoft – Emma Gannon." https://www.youtube.com/watch?v=I8VwryUF5vM/

Gil, Javier and Sequera, Jorge. 2020. "The Professionalization of Airbnb in Madrid: Far from a Collaborative Economy." *Current Issues in Tourism.* https://doi.org/10.1080/13683500.2020.1757628

Gill, Rosalind. 2007. *Technobohemians or the New Cybertariat? New Media Work in Amsterdam a Decade after the Web.* Amsterdam: Institute of Network Cultures. https://networkcultures.org/blog/publication/no-01-technobohemians-or-the-new-cybertariat-rosalind-gill/

Gill, Rosalind. 2011. "'Life as a Pitch': Managing Self in New Media Work," in Mark Deuze (ed.), *Managing Media Work.* London: Sage, pp. 249–62.

Gill, Rosalind. 2014. "Unspeakable Inequalities: Post Feminism, Entrepreneurial Subjectivity, and the Repudiation of Sexism among Cultural Workers." *Social Politics* 21(4): 509–28.

Gill, Rosalind and Pratt, Andy. 2008. "In the Social Factory? Immaterial Labour, Precariousness and Cultural Work." *Theory, Culture & Society* 25(7/8): 1–30.

Gill, Rosalind and Scharff, Christina. 2011. "Introduction," in Rosalind Gill and Christina Scharff (eds), *New Femininities: Postfeminism, Neoliberalism and Subjectivity.* Basingstoke: Palgrave Macmillan, pp. 1–20.

Gillespie, Tarleton. 2014. "The Relevance of Algorithms," in Tarleton Gillespie, Pablo J. Boczkowksi, and Kirsten A. Foot (eds), *Media Technologies: Essays on Communication, Materiality, and Society.* Cambridge, MA: MIT Press, pp. 167–94.

Global Entrepreneurship Monitor (GEM). 2020. *Global Entrepreneurship Monitor 2019/20 Global Report.* https://www.gemconsortium.org/report/gem-2019-2020-global-report/

Google. n.d. "Our Hiring Process." Careers. https://careers.google.com/how-we-hire/?src=Online%2FHouse%20Ads%2FBKWS_Cloud_EMEA/

Gopinath, Swetha. 2021. "Deliveroo Sinks 31% in Setback to London Effort to Lure IPOs." *Bloomberg*, March 31. https://www.bloomberg.com/news/articles/2021-03-31/deliveroo-ipo-raises-2-1-billion-in-biggest-u-k-deal-this-year

Gorz, André. 2010. *The Immaterial*, trans. Chris Turner. India: Seagull Books.

Govindarajan, Vijay, Rajgopal, Shivaram, and Srivastava, Anup. 2018.

"Why Financial Statements Don't Work for Digital Companies." *Harvard Business Review*, February 26. https://hbr.org/2018/02/why-financial-statements-dont-work-for-digital-companies/

Graeber, David. 2018. *Bullshit Jobs: A Theory*. New York: Simon and Schuster.

Graham, Mark, Hjorth, Isis, and Lehdonvirta, Vili. 2017. "Digital Labour and Development: Impacts of Global Digital Labour Platforms and the Gig Economy on Worker Livelihoods." *Transfer: European Review of Labour and Research* 23(2): 135–62.

Gray, Anne. 2003. "Enterprising Femininity: New Modes of Work and Subjectivity." *European Journal of Cultural Studies* 6(4): 489–506.

Gray, Mary and Suri, Siddharth. 2019. *Ghost Work: How to Stop Silicon Valley from Building a New Global Underclass*. Boston and New York: Houghton Mifflin Harcourt.

Gregg, Melissa. 2010. "On Friday Night Drinks: Workplace Affects in the Age of the Cubicle," in Melissa Gregg and Gregory K. Seigworth (eds), *The Affect Theory Reader*. Durham and London: Duke University Press, pp. 250–68.

Gregory, Karen. 2021. "'My Life is More Valuable than This': Understanding Risk Among On-demand Food Couriers in Edinburgh." *Work, Employment and Society* 35(2): 316–31.

Gregory, Karen and Sadowski, Jathan. 2021. "Biopolitical Platforms: The Perverse Virtues of Digital Labor." *Journal of Cultural Economy* 14(6): 662–74.

Grove, Robert, Malone, Michael S., and Dillion, Patrick. 2001. "The Little People vs. America Online." *Forbes.com*, February 19. http://www.forbes.com/asap/2001/0219/060.html/

Guo, Lei and Lee, Lorin. 2013. "The Critique of YouTube-based Vernacular Discourse: A Case Study of YouTube's Asian Community." *Critical Studies in Media Communication* 30(5): 391–406.

Handy. (n.d.). "Handy Pro." https://www.handy.com/apply/

Hardt, Michael and Negri, Antonio. 2000. *Empire*. Cambridge, MA: Harvard University Press.

Hardt, Michael and Negri, Antonio. 2005. *Multitude*. London: Penguin.

Hardt, Michael and Negri, Antonio. 2009. *Commonwealth*. Cambridge, MA: Harvard University Press.

Hardy, Kate and Barbagallo, Camille. 2021. "Hustling the Platform: Capitalist Experiments and Resistance in the Digital Sex Industry." *South Atlantic Quarterly* 120(3): 533–51.

Harvey, David. 1990. *The Condition of Postmodernity: An Enquiry into the Origins of Cultural Change*. Cambridge, MA: Blackwell.

Hearn, Alison. 2008. "'Meat, Mask, Burden': Probing the Contours of the Branded Self", *Journal of Consumer Culture* 8(2): 197–217.
Heidelkamp, Birte and Kergel, David. 2017. "Media Change – Precarity within and Precarity through the Internet," in Birte Heidelkamp and David Kergel (eds), *Precarity Within the Digital Age: Media Change and Social Insecurity*. Wiesbaden: Springer, pp. 9–27.
Hern, Alex. 2019. "Verizon Sells Tumblr Just Two Years after Acquiring Social Network." *Guardian*, August 13. https://www.theguardian.com/technology/2019/aug/12/verizon-tumblr-sale-automattic/
Hernandez, Antonia. 2019. "'There's Something Compelling about Real Life': Technologies of Security and Acceleration on Chaturbate." *Social Media + Society* 5(4). https://journals.sagepub.com/doi/10.1177/2056305119894000
Hesmondhalgh, David. 2007. *The Cultural Industries*, 2nd edn. London: Sage.
Hesmondhalgh, David. 2010. "User-generated Content, Free Labour and the Cultural Industries." *ephemera* 10(3/4): 267–84.
Hill, Stephanie. 2019. "Empire and the Megamachine: Comparing Two Controversies over Social Media Content." *Internet Policy Review* 8(1). http://dx.doi.org/10.14763/2019.1.1393
Hochschild, Arlie. 2003 [1983]. *The Managed Heart: Commercialization of Human Feeling*. Berkeley: University of California Press.
Hou, Mingyi. 2019. "Social Media Celebrity and the Institutionalization of YouTube." *Convergence: The International Journal of Research into New Media* 25(3): 534–53.
Hubspot. n.d. "Careers." https://www.hubspot.com/careers/
Huws, Ursula. 2003. *The Making of a Cybertariat: Virtual Work in a Real World*. New York: Monthly Review Press.
Huws, Ursula. 2010. "Expression and Expropriation: The Dialectics of Autonomy and Control in Creative Labour." *ephemera* 10(3/4): 504–21.
Huws, Ursula. 2014. *Labor in the Global Digital Economy: The Cybertariat Comes of Age*. New York: Monthly Review Press.
Huws, Ursula. 2019. *Labour in Contemporary Capitalism: What Next?* London: Palgrave Macmillan.
Huws, Ursula, Spencer, Neil H., and Joyce, Simon. 2016. *Crowd Work in Europe: Preliminary Results from a Survey in the UK, Sweden, Germany, Austria and the Netherlands*. Foundation for European Progressive Studies. https://researchprofiles.herts.ac.uk/portal/services/downloadRegister/10749125/crowd_work_in_europe_draft_report_last_version.pdf/
Instagram. n.d. "About." https://about.instagram.com/
ILO (International Labour Organization). 2015. *World Employment*

Social Outlook 2015: The Changing Nature of Jobs. Geneva: International Labour Office.
ILO (International Labour Organization). 2020. *World Employment Social Outlook: Trends 2020*. Geneva: International Labour Office.
Irani, Lilly. 2015. "The Cultural Work of Microwork." *New Media & Society* 17(5): 720–39.
Isaac, Mike. 2019. *Super Pumped: The Battle for Uber*. New York: W. W. Norton.
Jaffe, Sarah. 2021. "Union Bargaining at a Podcasting Giant." *American Prospect*, March 11. https://prospect.org/labor/union-bargaining-at-podcasting-giant-gimlet-media/
Jamieson, Dave. 2015. "The Life and Death of an Amazon Warehouse Temp." *Huffington Post*, October 21. https://highline.huffingtonpost.com/articles/en/life-and-death-amazon-temp/
Jarrett, Kylie. 2008. "Interactivity is Evil! A Critical Investigation of Web 2.0." *First Monday* 13(3). http://dx.doi.org/10.5210/fm.v13i3.2140
Jarrett, Kylie. 2016a. *Feminism, Labour and Digital Media: The Digital Housewife*. New York: Routledge.
Jarrett, Kylie. 2016b. "Queering Alienation in Digital Media." *First Monday* 21(10). https://doi.org/10.5210/fm.v21i10.6942/
Jarrett, Kylie. 2017. "Le travail immatériel dans l'usine sociale: une critique féministe." *Poli: Politique de l'Image* 13: 12–25.
Jarrett, Kylie. 2018. "Laundering Women's History: A Feminist Critique of the Social Factory." *First Monday* 22(3). https://firstmonday.org/ojs/index.php/fm/article/view/8280/
Jarrett, Kylie. 2021. "Digital Ireland: Leprechaun Economics, Silicon Docks and Crises," in Renée Fox, Mike Cronin, and Brian Ó Conchubhair (eds), *Routledge International Handbook of Irish Studies*. Abingdon: Routledge, pp. 188–98.
Jhally, Sut and Livant, Bill. 1986. "Watching as Working: The Valorization of Audience Consciousness." *Journal of Communication* 36(3): 124–43.
Jordan, Tim. 2020. *The Digital Economy*. Cambridge: Polity Press.
Kagan, Noah. 2014. *How I Lost 170 Million Dollars: My Time as #30 at Facebook*. Austin: Lioncrest Publishing.
Kalleberg, Arne L. and Vallas, Steven P. 2018. "Probing Precarious Work: Theory, Research, and Politics," in Arne L. Kalleberg and Steven P. Vallas (eds), *Precarious Work*, Research in the Sociology of Work 31. London: Emerald Publishing, pp. 1–30.
Kanai, Akane. 2019. *Gender and Relatability in Digital Culture: Managing Affect, Intimacy and Value*. Cham, Switzerland: Palgrave Macmillan.

Kantor, Jodi and Streitfeld, David. 2015. "Inside Amazon: Wrestling Big Ideas in a Bruising Workplace." *New York Times*, August 15. https://www.nytimes.com/2015/08/16/technology/inside-amazon-wrestling-big-ideas-in-a-bruising-workplace.html/

Karatzogianni, Athina and Matthews, Jacob. 2020. "Platform Ideologies: Ideological Production in Digital Intermediation Platforms and Structural Effectivity in the 'Sharing Economy.'" *Television & New Media* 21(1): 95–114.

Karp, Paul. 2019. "Food Delivery Bike Couriers in Australia Being Underpaid by Up to $322 a Week." *Guardian*, November 19. https://www.theguardian.com/australia-news/2019/nov/20/food-delivery-bike-couriers-in-australia-being-underpaid-by-up-to-322-a-week/

Kashyap, Rina and Bhatia, Anjali. 2018. "Taxi Drivers and *Taxidars*: A Case Study of Uber and Ola in Delhi." *Journal of Developing Societies* 34(2): 169–94.

Kenney, Martin. 2003. "What Goes Up Must Come Down: The Political Economy of the US Internet Industry," in Jens Froslev Christensen and Peter Maskell (eds), *The Industrial Dynamics of the New Digital Economy*. Cheltenham: Edward Elgar, pp. 33–55.

Kepka, Alex. 2020. "Business Startup Statistics UK (2020 Update)." *fundsquire*, July 31. https://fundsquire.co.uk/startup-statistics/

Kerr, Aphra and Kelleher, John D. 2015. "The Recruitment of Passion and Community in the Service of Capital: Community Managers in the Digital Games Industry." *Critical Studies in Media Communication* 32(3): 177–92.

Kim, Jin. 2012. "The Institutionalization of YouTube: From User-Generated Content to Professionally Generated Content." *Media, Culture & Society* 34(1): 53–67.

Kirchner, Lauren. 2011. "AOL Settled with Unpaid 'Volunteers' for $15million." *Columbia Journalism Review*, February 10. http://www.cjr.org/the_news_frontier/aol_settled_with_unpaid_volunt.php?page=all/

Korczynski, Marek. 2003. "Communities of Coping: Collective Emotional Labour in Service Work." *Organization* 10(1): 55–79.

Kotamraju, Nalini. 2002. "Keeping Up: Web Design Skills and the Reinvented Worker." *Information, Communication & Society* 5(1): 1–26.

Kücklich, Julian. 2005. "Precarious Playbour: Modders and the Digital Game Industry." *fibreculture* 5. https://five.fibreculturejournal.org/fcj-025-precarious-playbour-modders-and-the-digital-games-industry/

Kuehn, Kathleen and Corrigan, Thomas F. 2013. "Hope Labor: The

Role of Employment Prospects in Online Social Production." *Political Economy of Communication* 1(1). http://www.polecom.org/index.php/polecom/article/view/9/

Kumar, Sangeet. 2019. "The Algorithmic Dance: YouTube's Adpocalypse and the Gatekeeping of Cultural Content on Digital Platforms." *Internet Policy Review* 8(2): 1–21.

Laglisse, Erica. 2014. "Gossip as Direct Action," in Lynne Phillips and Sally Cole (eds), *Contesting Publics: Feminism, Activism, Ethnography*. London: Pluto Press, pp. 112–37.

Lazzarato, Maurizio. 1996. "Immaterial Labor," in Paolo Virno and Michael Hardt (eds), *Radical Thought in Italy: A Potential Politics*. Minneapolis: University of Minnesota Press, pp. 132–46.

Leaver, Tama, Highfield, Tim and Abidin, Crystal. 2020. *Instagram*. Cambridge, UK: Polity Press.

Lei, Ya-Wen. 2021. "Delivering Solidarity: Platform Architecture and Collective Contention in China's Platform Economy." *American Sociological Review* 86(2): 279–309.

Lenaerts, Karolien, Kiljoffer, Zachary, and Akgüç, Mejtap. 2018. "Traditional and New Forms of Organization and Representation in the Platform Economy." *Work Organisation, Labour & Globalisation* 12(2): 60–78.

Li, Miao, Tan, Chris K. K. and Yang, Yuting. 2020. "*Shehui Ren*: Cultural Production and Rural Youths' Use of the *Kuaishou* Video-Sharing App in Eastern China." *Information, Communication & Society* 23(10): 1499–514.

Lin, Jian and de Kloet, Jeroen. 2019. "Platformization of the Unlikely Creative Class: *Kuaishou* and Chinese Digital Cultural Production." *Social Media + Society* 5(4). https://doi.org/10.1177/2056305119883430

Liu, Alan. 2004. *The Laws of Cool: Knowledge Work and the Culture of Information*. Chicago: University of Chicago Press.

Liu, Wendy. 2020. *Abolish Silicon Valley: How to Liberate Technology from Capitalism*. London: Repeater Books.

Lorenz, Taylor. 2019. "Instagram Memers are Unionizing." *Atlantic*, April 17. https://www.theatlantic.com/technology/archive/2019/04/instagram-memers-are-unionizing/587308/

Lorey, Isabell. 2015. *State of Insecurity: Government of the Precarious*, trans. Aileen Derieg. London: Verso.

Lorusso, Silvio. 2019. *Entreprecariat: Everyone is an Entrepreneur. Nobody is Safe*. Eindhoven: Onomatopee.

Losse, Katherine. 2012. *The Boy Kings: A Journey into the Heart of the Social Network*. New York: Free Press.

Luckman, Susan. 2018. "Online Selling and the Growth of Home-Based

Craft Micro-enterprise: The New 'Normal' of Women's Self-(under) Employment," in Stephanie Taylor and Susan Luckman (eds), *The New Normal of Working Lives: Critical Studies in Contemporary Work and Employment*. Cham, Switzerland: Palgrave Macmillan, pp. 19–39.

Lukács, Georg. 1971. *History and Class Consciousness: Studies in Marxist Dialectics*. Pontypool, Wales: Merlin Press.

Lynch, Dónal. 2020. "Thiago Cortes: 'He Shouldn't Have Worked. It Was His Day Off'." *Independent*, September 6. https://www.independent.ie/irish-news/thiago-cortes-he-shouldnt-have-worked-it-was-his-day-off-39506683.html

Lyons, Dan. 2016. *Disrupted: Ludicrous Misadventures in the Tech Start-up Bubble*. London: Atlantic Books.

Mahr, Alex. 2020. "Startup Failure in Europe – Indepth Analysis." *Startup World*, April 23. https://stryber.com/truth-about-startup-failure/

Malekmian, Shamim. 2020. "Deliveroo Rider Thiago Osorio Cortes Killed in Hit and Run in Dublin." *Hot Press*, September 2. https://www.hotpress.com/culture/deliveroo-rider-thiago-osorio-cortes-killed-in-hit-and-run-in-dublin-22826627/

Marcuse, Herbert. 1991 [1964]. *One-Dimensional Man*. Abingdon: Routledge.

Marshall, Aarian. 2021. "Gig Workers Gather Their Own Data to Check the Algorithm's Math." *Wired*, February 24. https://www.wired.com/story/gig-workers-gather-data-check-algorithm-math/

Marwick, Alice E. 2013. *Status Update, Celebrity, Publicity, and Branding in the Social Media Age*. New Haven: Yale University Press.

Marx, Karl. 1993 [1939]. *Grundrisse: Foundations of the Critique of Political Economy (Rough Draft)*, trans. Martin Nicolaus. London: Penguin.

Marx, Karl. 2013. "Economic and Philosophic Manuscripts," in Erich Fromm (ed.), *Marx's Concepts of Man*, trans. T. B. Bottomore. London: Bloomsbury Academic, pp. 73–215.

Marx, Karl and Engels, Friedrich. 2012 [1888]. *The Communist Manifesto*. Intro. and notes by Gareth Stedman Jones. London: Penguin.

Mason, Sarah. 2019. "Chasing the Pink." *Logic*, January 1. https://logicmag.io/play/chasing-the-pink/

Massanari, Adrienne L. 2015. *Participatory Culture, Community, and Play: Learning from Reddit*. New York: Peter Lang.

McDonald, Paula, Williams, Penny, and Mayes, Robyn. 2020. "Means of Control in the Organization of Digitally Intermediated Care Work." *Work, Employment and Society* 35(5): 872–90.

McDowell, Linda. 1991. "Life without Father and Ford: The New Gender Order of Post-Fordism." *Transactions of the Institute of British Geographers* 16(4): 400–19.

McDowell, Linda and Court, Gillian. 1994. "Missing Subjects: Gender, Power and Sexuality in Merchant Banking." *Economic Geography* 70(3): 229–51.

McGregor, Moira, Brown, Barry, Glöss, Mareike, and Lampinen, Airi. 2016. "On-Demand Taxi Driving: Labour Conditions, Surveillance, and Exclusion." The Internet, Policy and Politics Conference, Oxford Internet Institute, University of Oxford, September. http://blogs.oii.ox.ac.uk/ipp-conference/2016/papers.html

McRobbie, Angela. 2001. "'Everyone is Creative': Artists as New Economy Pioneers." *opendemocracy.net*, August 29. https://www.opendemocracy.net/node/652/

McRobbie, Angela. 2016. *Be Creative: Making a Living in the New Culture Industries*. Cambridge, UK: Polity Press.

McStay, Andrew. 2010. *Digital Advertising*. Basingstoke: Palgrave Macmillan.

Meehan, Eileen R. 1984. "Ratings and the Institutional Approach: A Third Answer to the Commodity Question." *Critical Studies in Mass Communication* 1(2): 216–25.

Mies, Maria, Bennholdt-Thomsen, Veronika and von Werlhof, Claudia. 1988. *Women: The Last Colony*. London: Zed Books.

Mills, C. Wright. 1951. *White Collar: The American Middle Classes*. USA: Pantianos Classics.

Morgan, George and Nelligan, Pariece. 2018. *The Creativity Hoax: Precarious Work in the Gig Economy*. London: Anthem Press.

Morini, Cristina. 2007. "The Feminization of Labour in Cognitive Capitalism." *Feminist Review* 87: 40–59.

Morini, Cristina and Fumagalli, Andrea. 2010. "Life Put to Work: Towards a Life Theory of Value." *ephemera* 10(3/4): 234–52.

Morris, Chris. 2021. "Facebook Outage Cost the Company Nearly $100 Million in Revenue." *Fortune*, October 4. https://fortune.com/2021/10/04/facebook-outage-cost-revenue-instagram-whatsapp-not-working-stock/

Moulier Boutang, Yann. 2011. *Cognitive Capitalism*, trans. Ed Emery. Cambridge, UK: Polity Press.

Mowlabocus, Sharif. 2010. "Look at Me! Images, Validation and Cultural Currency on Gaydar," in Christopher Pullen and Margaret Cooper (eds), *LGBT Identity and Online New Media*. Abingdon: Routledge, pp. 201–14.

Murphy, Andrea, Haverstock, Eliza, Gara, Antoine, Helman, Chris, and Vardi, Nathan. 2021. "Global 2000: How the World's Biggest Public Companies Endured the Pandemic." *Forbes Magazine*, May 13. https://www.forbes.com/lists/global2000/#5f84471f5ac0

Nakamura, Lisa. 2009. "Don't Hate the Player, Hate the Game: The Racialization of Labor in World of Warcraft." *Critical Studies in Media Communication* 26(2): 128–44.

Nayar, Kavita Ilona. 2017. "Working It: The Professionalization of Amateurism in Digital Adult Entertainment." *Feminist Media Studies* 17(3): 473–88.

Ndemo, Bitange and Weiss, Tim (eds). 2017. *Digital Kenya: An Entrepreneurial Revolution in the Making*. London: Palgrave Macmillan.

Neilson, Brett and Rossiter, Ned. 2008. "Precarity as Political Concept, or, Fordism as Exception." *Theory, Culture & Society* 25(7/8): 51–72.

Neff, Gina. 2012. *Venture Labor: Work and the Burden of Risk in Innovative Industries*. Cambridge, MA: MIT Press.

Neff, Gina, Wissinger, Elizabeth, and Zukin, Sharon. 2005. "Entrepreneurial Labour among Cultural Producers: 'Cool' Jobs in 'Hot' Industries." *Social Semiotics* 15(3): 307–34.

Newton, Casey. 2016. "Why Vine Died: Closing the Loop." *The Verge*, October 28. https://www.theverge.com/2016/10/28/13456208/why-vine-died-twitter-shutdown/

Newton, Casey. 2020. "Facebook Will Pay $52 Million in Settlement with Moderators Who Developed PTSD on the Job." *The Verge*, May 12. https://www.theverge.com/platform/amp/2020/5/12/21255870/facebook-content-moderator-settlement-scola-ptsd-mental-health/

Niebler, Valentin and Kern, Annemarie. 2020. *Organising YouTube: A Novel Case of Platform Worker Organising*. Friedrich Ebert Stiftung. https://www.fes.de/e/organising-youtube-building-workers-power-in-big-tech/

Nieborg, David, Poell, Thomas, with Deuze, Mark. 2019. "The Platformization of Making Media," in Mark Deuze and Mirjam Prenger (eds), *Making Media: Production, Practices, and Professions*. Amsterdam: Amsterdam University Press, pp. 85–96.

Noor, Poppy. 2020. "A Thorne in the Site: The Bella Thorne and OnlyFans Controversy Explained." *The Guardian*, August 31. https://www.theguardian.com/media/2020/aug/31/bella-thorne-onlyfans-what-happened-explained/

OECD. 2019. *Compendium of Productivity Indicators 2019*. Paris: OECD Publishing. https://doi.org/10.1787/b2774f97-en

Ola. n.d. "Drive with Ola." https://partners.olacabs.com/

O'Brien, Sara Ashley. 2020. "One Year after the Google Walkout, Key Organizers Reflect on the Risk to Their Careers." *CNN Business*, January 9. https://edition.cnn.com/2019/11/01/tech/google-walkout-one-year-later-risk-takers/index.html

O'Neill, Christopher. 2017. "Taylorism, the European Science of Work, and the Quantified Self at Work." *Science, Technology & Human Values* 42(4): 600–21.

Ongweso, Edward Jr. 2021. "Organized DoorDash Drivers #DeclineNow Strategy Is Driving Up Their Pay." *Vice*, February 19. https://www.vice.com/en/article/3anwdy/organized-doordash-drivers-declinenow-strategy-is-driving-up-their-pay/

O'Reilly, Tim. 2005. "What is Web 2.0? Design Patterns and Business Models for the Next Generation of Software." *O'Reilly Media*, September 30. http://oreilly.com/web2/archive/what-is-web-20.html

Paasonen, Susanna, Jarrett, Kylie, and Light, Ben. 2019. *NSFW: Sex, Humor, and Risk in Social Media*. Cambridge, MA: MIT Press.

Pager, Tyler and Palmer, Emily. 2018. "Uber Driver is Latest to Kill Self in Industry." *New York Times*, October 8. https://www.nytimes.com/2018/10/07/nyregion/uber-driver-suicide-for-hire-taxis-new-york.html/

Palmer, Amanda. 2015. "No, I Am Not Crowdfunding This Baby (An Open Letter to a Worried Fan)." *Medium*, August 26. https://medium.com/we-are-the-media/no-i-am-not-crowdfunding-this-baby-an-open-letter-to-a-worried-fan-9ca75cb0f938/

Pasquinelli, Matteo. 2009. "Google's PageRank: Diagram of the Cognitive Capitalism and Rentier of the Common Intellect," in Konrad Becker and Felix Stalder (eds), *Deep Search: The Politics of Search Beyond Google*. Innsbruck: Studienverlag, pp. 152–62.

Pein, Corey. 2018. *Live Work Work Work Die: A Journey into the Savage Heart of Silicon Valley*. London: Scribe.

Pennell, Stella. 2019. *Trouble in Paradise: Contradictions in Platform Capitalism and the Production of Surplus by Airbnb Hosts in Regional Tourist Towns*. Unpublished doctoral thesis. Albany, NZ: Massey University.

Pennell, Stella. 2021. "Airbnb and the Paradox of the Body: The Biopolitical Management of Hosts in Four Tourist Towns in New Zealand." *Journal of Sociology*. https://doi.org/10.1177/14407833211000122

Peoples Dispatch. 2019. "Uber and Ola Drivers in India Threaten Massive Agitation if Their Demands Are Not Met." July 15. https://peoplesdispatch.org/2019/07/15/uber-and-ola-drivers-in-india-threaten-massive-agitation-if-their-demands-are-not-met/

Peoples Dispatch. 2020. "Trade Unions and Progressive Movements Across the World Unite to #MakeAmazonPay." November 28. https://peoplesdispatch.org/2020/11/28/trade-unions-and-progressive-movements-across-the-world-unite-to-makeamazonpay/

Perlin, Ross. 2012. *Intern Nation: How to Earn Nothing and Learn Little in the Brave New Economy*. London: Verso.

Pesole, Annarosa, Brancati, Cesira Urzí, Fernández-Maciás, Enrique, Biagi, Federico, and Vasquez, Ignacio Gonzalez. 2018. *Platform Workers in Europe Evidence from the COLLEEM Survey*. EUR – Scientific and Technical Research Reports. Luxembourg: Publications Office of the European Union. https://publications.jrc.ec.europa.eu/repository/handle/111111111/52393/

Pfannebecker, Mareile and Smith, J. A. 2020. *Work Want Work: Labour and Desire at the End of Capitalism*. London: Zed Books.

Pham, Minh-Ha T. 2015. *Asians Wear Clothes on the Internet: Race, Gender, and the Work of Personal Style Blogging*. Durham and London: Duke University Press.

Pisoni, Adam. 2017. "In Defense of Diverse Founding Teams." *Medium*, January 12. https://medium.com/@adampisoni/in-defense-of-diverse-founding-teams-e9f0b5b81f25/

Pollak, Sorcha. 2020. "Deliveroo Cyclists: 'We Want to Deliver Food Without Thinking We Might Be Robbed or Run Over.'" *Irish Times*, September 5. https://www.irishtimes.com/news/ireland/irish-news/deliveroo-cyclists-we-want-to-deliver-food-without-thinking-we-might-be-robbed-or-run-over-1.4347707/

Postigo, Hector. 2003. "Emerging Sources of Labor on the Internet: The Case of America Online Volunteers." *International Review of Social History* 48: 205–23.

Postigo, Hector. 2009. "American Online Volunteers: Lessons from an Early Co-Production Community." *International Journal of Cultural Studies* 12(5): 451–69.

Prassl, Jeremias. 2018. *Collective Voice in the Platform Economy: Challenges, Opportunities, Solutions*. Report to the European Trade Union Confederation. https://www.etuc.org/en/publication/collective-voice-platform-economy-challenges-opportunities-solutions/

Purcell, Christina and Brook, Paul. 2020. "*At Least I Am My Own Boss!* Explaining Consent, Coercion and Resistance in Platform Work." *Work, Employment and Society*. https://doi.org/10.1177/0950017020952661

Qiu, Jack Linchuan. 2016. *Goodbye iSlave: A Manifesto for Digital Abolition*. Urbana: University of Illinois Press.

Raval, Noopur and Dourish, Paul. 2016. "Standing Out from the Crowd: Emotional Labor, Body Labor, and Temporal Labor in Ridesharing." Proceedings of the 19th ACM Conference on Computer-Supported Cooperative Work & Social Computing, February, pp. 97–107. https://doi.org/10.1145/2818048.2820026

Ray, Aditya. 2019. "Unrest in India's Gig Economy: Ola-Uber Drivers' Strikes and Worker Organisation." *Futures of Work* 10. https://futuresofwork.co.uk/2019/12/09/unrest-in-indias-gig-economy-ola-uber-drivers-strikes-and-worker-organisation/

Roberts, Sarah T. 2019. *Behind the Screen: Content Moderation in the Shadows of Social Media*. New Haven and London: Yale University Press.

Robinson, Cedric J. 2021 [1983]. *Black Marxism: The Making of the Black Radical Tradition*, 3rd edn. London: Penguin.

Rose, Nikolas. 1998. *Inventing Our Selves: Psychology, Power and Personhood*. New York: Cambridge University Press.

Rose, Nikolas. 1999. *Powers of Freedom: Reframing Political Thought*. Cambridge, UK: Cambridge University Press.

Rosenblat, Alex. 2018. *Uberland: How Algorithms are Rewriting the Rules of Work*. Oakland: University of California Press.

Rosenblat, Alex, Kneese, Tamara, and boyd, danah. 2014. "Workplace Surveillance." Data & Society Working Paper, October 8. https://datasociety.net/library/workplace-surveillance/

Rosenblat, Alex and Stark, Luke. 2016. "Algorithmic Labor and Information Asymmetries: A Case Study of Uber's Drivers." *International Journal of Communication* 10: 3758–84.

Ross, Andrew. 2003. *No-Collar: The Humane Workplace and its Hidden Costs*. Philadelphia: Temple University Press.

Ross, Andrew. 2009. *Nice Work if You Can Get It: Life and Labor in Precarious Times*. New York: New York University Press.

Ross, Andrew. 2013. "In Search of the Lost Paycheck," in Trebor Scholz (ed.), *Digital Labor: The Internet as Playground and Factory*. New York: Routledge, pp. 13–32.

Sanders, Teela. 2012 [2005]. *Sex Work: A Risky Business*. Abingdon: Routledge.

Sandoval, Marisol. 2020. "Entrepreneurial Activism? Platform Cooperativism between Subversion and Co-optation." *Critical Sociology* 46(6): 801–17.

Scharff, Christina. 2016. "The Psychic Life of Neoliberalism: Mapping the Contours of Entrepreneurial Subjectivity." *Theory, Culture & Society* 33(6): 107–22.

Schiffer, Zoe. 2021a. "The Google Union Just Passed 700 Members." *The*

Verge, January 11. https://www.theverge.com/2021/1/11/22224926/google-union-700-members/

Schiffer, Zoe. 2021b. "Exclusive: Google Workers across the Globe Announce International Union Alliance to Hold Alphabet Accountable." *The Verge*, January 25. https://www.theverge.com/2021/1/25/22243138/google-union-alphabet-workers-europe-announce-global-alliance/

Schneider, Nathan. 2016. "Denver Taxi Drivers Are Turning Uber's Disruption on Its Head." *Nation*, September 7. https://www.thenation.com/article/archive/denver-taxi-drivers-are-turning-ubers-disruption-on-its-head/

Scholz, Trebor (ed.). 2013. *Digital Labor: The Internet as Playground and Factory*. New York: Routledge.

Scholz, Trebor. 2016. *Uberworked and Underpaid: How Workers are Disrupting the Digital Economy*. Cambridge, UK: Polity Press.

Schrier, Jason. 2017. *Blood, Sweat, and Pixels*. New York: Harper Collins.

Scolere, Leah, Pruchniewska, Urszula, and Duffy, Brooke. 2018. "Constructing the Platform-Specific Brand: The Labor of Social Media Promotion." *Social Media + Society* 4(3). https://doi.org/10.1177/2056305118784768

Scott, James C. 1990. *Domination and the Arts of Resistance: Hidden Transcripts*. New Haven: Yale University Press.

Sengul-Jones, Monika. 2017. "'Being a Better #Freelancer': Gendered and Racialised Aesthetic Labour on Online Freelance Marketplaces," in Ana Sofia Elias, Rosalind Gill, and Christina Scharff (eds), *Aesthetic Labor: Rethinking Beauty Politics in Neoliberalism*. London: Palgrave Macmillan, pp. 215–30.

Siapera, Eugenia. 2019. "Online Misogyny as Witch Hunt: Primitive Accumulation in the Age of Techno-capitalism," in Debbie Ging and Eugenia Siapera (eds), *Gender Hate Online: Understanding the New Anti-feminism*. Cham, Switzerland: Palgrave Macmillan, pp. 21–43.

Simply Wall St. 2021. "Is Twitter's (NYSE:TWTR) 169% Share Price Increase Well Justified?" January 12. https://simplywall.st/stocks/us/media/nyse-twtr/twitter/news/is-twitters-nysetwtr-169-share-price-increase-well-justified/

Smythe, Dallas W. 2014 [1977]. "Communications: Blindspot of Western Marxism," in Lee McGuigan and Vincent Manzerolle (eds), *The Audience Commodity in a Digital Age: Revisiting a Critical Theory of Commercial Media*. New York: Peter Lang, pp. 29–53.

Sobande, Francesca. 2020. *The Digital Lives of Black Women in Britain*. Cham, Switzerland: Palgrave Macmillan.

Soriano, Cheryll Ruth, Cabalquinto, Earvin Charles and Panaligan, Joy

Hannah. 2021. "Performing 'Digital Labor *Bayanihan*': Strategies of Influence and Survival in the Platform Economy." *Sociologias* 23(57): 84–111.

Sperber, Amanda. 2020. "Uber Made Big Promises in Kenya. Drivers Say It's Ruined Their Lives." *NBC*, November 29. https://www.nbcnews.com/news/world/uber-made-big-promises-kenya-drivers-say-it-s-ruined-n1247964/

Srnicek, Nick. 2017. *Platform Capitalism*. Cambridge, UK: Polity Press.

Stabile, Susan J. 2008. "Google Benefits of Google's Benefit?" *Journal of Business and Technology Law* 3(1): 97–108.

Standing, Guy. 2016. *The Precariat: The New Dangerous Class*. London: Bloomsbury Academic.

Stanford Crowd Research Collective. 2015. "Daemo: A Self-Governed Crowdsourcing Marketplace." Conference paper, ACM UIST, November 8–11. http://dx.doi.org/10.1145/2815585.2815739

Streeter, Thomas. 2011. *The Net Effect: Romanticism, Capitalism, and the Internet*. New York: New York University Press.

Stripe. n.d. "Jobs." https://stripe.com/ie/jobs

Styhre, Alex. 2019. *Venture Work: Employees in Thinly Capitalized Companies*. Cham, Switzerland: Palgrave Macmillan.

Surie, Aditi. 2018. "Are Ola and Uber Drivers Entrepreneurs or Exploited Workers?" *Economic and Political Weekly* 53(24). https://www.epw.in/engage/article/are-ola-and-uber-drivers-entrepreneurs-exploited-workers/

Swarme. n.d. "Work." https://swarme.co.uk/work/

Sybert, Jeanna. 2021. "The Demise of #NSFW: Contested Platform Governance and Tumblr's 2018 Adult Content Ban." *New Media & Society*. https://doi.org/10.1177/1461444821996715

Szeman, Imre. 2015. "Entrepreneurship as the New Common Sense." *The South Atlantic Quarterly* 114(3): 471–90.

Tan, Chris K. K. and Xu, Zhiwei. 2020. "The Real Digital Househusbands of China: The Alienable Affects of China's Virtual Male Lovers." *Journal of Consumer Culture*. https://doi.org/10.1177/1469540519899968

Taplin, Jonathan. 2017. *Move Fast and Break Things: How Facebook, Google and Amazon Have Cornered Culture and Undermined Democracy*. London: Pan.

Tarnoff, Ben and Weigel, Moira (eds). 2020. *Voices from the Valley: Tech Workers Talk About What They Do – and How They Do It*. New York: FSGO/Logic.

TaskRabbit. n.d. "Become a Tasker." https://www.taskrabbit.co.uk/become-a-tasker

Tassinari, Arianna and Maccarrone, Vincenzo. 2020. "Riders on the Storm: Workplace Solidarity Among Gig Economy Couriers in Italy and the UK." *Work, Employment and Society* 34(1): 35–54.

Terranova, Tiziana. 2000. "Free Labor: Producing Culture for the Digital Economy." *Social Text* 18(2): 33–58.

Thrift, Nigel. 2001. "'It's the Romance, Not the Finance, that Makes the Business Worth Pursuing': Disclosing a New Market Culture." *Economy and Society* 30(4): 412–32.

Thrift, Nigel. 2005. *Knowing Capitalism*. London: Sage.

Ticona, Julia and Mateescu, Alexandra. 2018. "Trusted Strangers: Carework Platforms' Cultural Entrepreneurship in the On-Demand Economy." *New Media & Society* 20 (11): 4384–404.

Tiidenberg, Katrin. 2019. "Playground in Memoriam: Missing the Pleasures of NSFW Tumblr." *Porn Studies* 6(3): 363–71.

Tiidendberg, Katrin and van der Nagel, Emily. 2020. *Sex and Social Media*. Bingley, UK: Emerald Publishing.

Tiqqun. 2012. *Preliminary Materials for a Theory of the Young Girl*. South Pasadena, CA: Semiotext(e).

Todericiu, Ramona and Stănit, Alexandra. 2015. "Intellectual Capital – The Key for Sustainable Competitive Advantage for the SME's Sector." *Procedia Economics and Finance* 27: 676–81.

Tokumitsu, Miya. 2014. "In the Name of Love." *Jacobin* 13. https://www.jacobinmag.com/2014/01/in-the-name-of-love/

Trapmann, Vera, Bessa, Ioulia, Joyce, Simon, Neumann, Denis, Stuart, Mark and Umney, Charles. 2020. *Global Labour Unrest on Platforms: The Case of Food Delivery Workers*. Friedrich Ebert Stiftung. http://library.fes.de/pdf-files/iez/16880.pdf

Tronti, Mario. 1973. "Social Capital." *Telos* 17: 98–121.

Tsing, Anna. 2009. "Supply Chains and the Human Condition." *Rethinking Marxism* 21(2): 148–76.

Tubaro, Paola, Casilli, Antonio A., and Conville, Marion. 2020. "The Trainer, the Verifier, the Imitator: Three Ways in Which Human Platform Workers Support Artificial Intelligence." *Big Data & Society* 7(1). https://doi.org/10.1177/2053951720919776

Turkopticon. n.d. https://turkopticon.ucsd.edu/

Turner, Fred. 2009. "Burning Man at Google: A Cultural Infrastructure for New Media Production." *New Media & Society* 11(1/2): 73–94.

Upwork. n.d. "Find Jobs." https://www.upwork.com/i/how-it-works/freelancer/

Vaclavik, Marcia C. and Pithan, Liana H. 2018. "The Agency Search: The Meaning of Work for App Drivers." *R. A. M Revista de*

Administração Mackenzie 19(5). https://doi.org/10.1590/1678-6971/eramg180080

van Doorn, Niels. 2017. "Platform Labor: On the Gendered and Racialized Exploitation of Low-Income Service Work in the 'On-Demand' Economy." *Information, Communication & Society* 20(6): 898–914.

van Driel, Loes and Dumitrica, Delia. 2021. "Selling Brands While Staying 'Authentic': The Professionalization of Instagram Influencers." *Convergence: The International Journal of Research into New Media Technologies* 27(1): 66–84.

Varghese, Sanjana. 2020. "Gig Economy Workers Have a New Weapon in the Fight Against Uber." *Wired*, February 17. https://www.wired.co.uk/article/gig-economy-uber-unions

Veen, Alex, Barratt, Tom, and Goods, Caleb. 2019. "Platform-Capital's 'App-etite' for Control: A Labour Process Analysis of Food-Delivery Work in Australia." *Work, Employment and Society* 34(3): 388–406.

Wajcman, Judy. 2010. "Feminist Theories of Technology." *Cambridge Journal of Economics* 34(1): 143–52.

Wakefield, Jane. 2021. "Amazon's Algorithms Taken to Task in Landmark Bill." *BBC News*, September 29. https://www.bbc.com/news/technology-58719675/

Wang, Xiaowei. 2020. *Blockchain Chicken Farm and Other Stories of Tech in China's Countryside*. New York: FSGO/Logic.

Warin, Robbie and McCann, Duncan. 2018. *Who Watches the Workers? Power and Accountability in the Digital Economy Part 2: Data, Algorithms and Work*. New Economics Foundation. https://neweconomics.org/2018/06/who-watches-the-workers/

Wartenberg, Thomas E. 1982. "'Species-being' and 'Human Nature' in Marx." *Human Studies* 5(1): 77–95.

Waxman, Olivia B. 2018. "How Internships Replaced the Entry-Level Job." *Time*, July 25. https://time.com/5342599/history-of-interns-internships/

Weiss, Tim. 2017. "Entrepreneuring for Society: What is Next for Africa?" in Bitange Ndemo and Tim Weiss (eds), *Digital Kenya: An Entrepreneurial Revolution in the Making*. London: Palgrave Macmillan, pp. 461–85.

Wen, Shawn. 2014. "The Ladies Vanish." *The New Inquiry*, November 11. https://thenewinquiry.com/the-ladies-vanish/

Whyte, William H. 2002 [1956]. *The Organization Man*. Philadelphia: University of Pennsylvania Press.

Wiener, Anna. 2020. *Uncanny Valley: A Memoir*. London: 4th Estate.

Willis Garcés, Andrew. 2016. "How Uber and Lyft were Driven

from Austin and Replaced with a Worker Cooperative." *Waging NonViolence*, November 8. https://wagingnonviolence.org/2016/11/austin-uber-worker-coop/

Wilson, Sloan. 2005 [1955]. *The Man in the Gray Flannel Suit*. London: Penguin.

Wong, Julia Carrie. 2021. "Revealed: Google Illegally Underpaid Thousands of Workers across Dozens of Countries." *Guardian*, September 10. https://www.theguardian.com/technology/2021/sep/10/google-underpaid-workers-illegal-pay-disparity-documents/

Wood, Alex J. 2020. *Despotism on Demand: How Power Operates in the Flexible Workplace*. New York: Cornell University Press.

Wood, Alex. J., Lehdonvirta, Vili, and Graham, Mark. 2018. "Workers of the Internet Unite? Online Freelancer Organisation among Remote Gig Economy Workers in Six Asian and African Countries." *New Technology, Work and Employment* 33(2): 95–112.

Wood, Alex J., Graham, Mark, Lehdonvirta, Vili, and Hjorth, Isis. 2019. "Good Gig, Bad Gig: Autonomy and Algorithmic Control in the Global Gig Economy." *Work, Employment and Society* 33(1): 56–75.

Woodcock, Jamie. 2019. *Marx at the Arcade: Consoles, Controllers, and Class Struggle*. Chicago: Haymarket Books.

Woodcock, Jamie. 2020. "The Algorithmic Panopticon at Deliveroo: Measurement, Precarity and the Illusion of Control." *ephemera* 20(3): 67–95.

Woodcock, Jamie. 2021a. "Game Workers Unite: Unionization among Independent Developers," in Paolo Ruffino (ed.), *Independent Videogames: Cultures, Networks, Techniques and Politics*. Abingdon: Routledge, pp. 163–74.

Woodcock. Jamie. 2021b. *The Fight Against Platform Capitalism: An Inquiry into the Struggles of the Gig Economy*. London: University of Westminster Press.

Woodcock, Jamie and Cant, Callum. 2019. "The End of the Beginning." *Notes from Below*, June 8. https://notesfrombelow.org/article/end-beginning

Woodcock, Jamie and Graham, Mark. 2020. *The Gig Economy: A Critical Introduction*. Cambridge, UK: Polity Press.

Xia, Bingqing. 2014. "Digital Labor in Chinese Internet Industries." *Triple C: Communication, Capitalism & Critique* 12(2): 668–93. https://doi.org/10.31269/triplec.v12i2.534

Xia, Bingqing. 2018. "Capital Accumulation and Work in China's Internet Content Industry: Struggling in the Bubble." *Economic and Labor Relations Review* 29(4): 501–20.

Xia, Bingqing. 2019. "Precarious Labour in Waiting: Internships in the Chinese Internet Industries." *Economic and Labor Relations Review* 30(3): 382–99.

Yadav, Anumeha. 2017. "With Few Formal Unions, Ola and Uber Drivers Draw on Informal Networks to Enforce Strikes in Delhi." *Scroll.in*, February 14. https://scroll.in/article/829284/with-few-formal-unions-ola-and-uber-drivers-draw-on-informal-networks-to-enforce-strike-in-delhi/

Yin, Ming, Gray, Mary L., Suri, Siddharth, and Wortman Vaughan, Jennifer. 2016. "The Communication Network within the Crowd." WWW'16: Proceedings of the 25th International Conference on World Wide Web: 1293–1303. https://doi.org/10.1145/2872427.2883036

Zelizer, Viviana A. 2005. *The Purchase of Intimacy*. New Jersey: Princeton University Press.

Zelizer, Viviana A. 2011. *Economic Lives: How Culture Shapes the Economy*. New Jersey: Princeton University Press.

Zhao, Elaine Jing. 2016. "Professionalization of Amateur Production in Online Screen Entertainment in China: Hopes, Frustrations, and Uncertainties." *International Journal of Communication* 10: 5444–62.

Zhao, Elaine Jing. 2019. *Digital China's Informal Circuits: Platforms, Labour and Governance*. Abingdon: Routledge.

Zhou, Namaan. 2020. "Hungry Panda Fails to Appear before NSW Inquiry Looking into Death of Food Delivery Rider." *Guardian*, November 16. https://www.theguardian.com/business/2020/nov/16/hungry-panda-fails-to-appear-before-nsw-inquiry-looking-into-death-of-food-delivery-rider/

Zou, Sheng. 2018. "Producing Value Out of the Invaluable: A Critical/Cultural Perspective on the Live Streaming Industry in China." *Triple C: Communication, Capitalism & Critique* 16(2): 805–19.

Zuboff, Shoshana. 1988. *In the Age of the Smart Machines: The Future of Work and Power*. New York: Basic Books.

Index

Adkins, Lisa 155–6, 160, 163–4, 204–5
adpocalypse 55–6, 188
　see also YouTube
AdSense 51–2
　see also advertising; YouTube
advertising 17–20, 23, 44–5, 51, 55, 73, 140
affect 43, 47, 50, 71, 106–8, 115, 136, 140–4, 158, 196
　and discipline 93, 149–50, 152–4
　see also passion
Airbnb 61, 152–3, 161
algorithms 52–4, 56, 88–92, 181, 199
　and management 53, 89–91, 95, 188
　and visibility 53–4, 148, 193
Alibaba 21, 144
　see also GAFAM/BAT companies
Alienation 33, 102–5, 121–3, 134–6, 154, 158–9
　definition of 103–5
　dis-alienation 102–3, 105–8, 111
Alphabet *see* Google
　see also GAFAM/BAT companies
Amazon 18, 19, 20–1, 84, 86, 128
　fulfillment centers 26, 36, 76, 92, 94, 108
　industrial action at 180, 191
　Mechanical Turk 174–5, 194
　see also GAFAM/BAT companies
AOL 18, 36, 177–8
Apple 18, 20–1, 146
　see GAFAM/BAT companies
artistic critique 121–3, 128
artists 127–8, 183
Arvidsson, Adam 108–9, 125–6, 131, 140, 203–4, 211
assetization 33, 159–65, 211
　assetized worker 34, 160–3, 165, 197–8, 205
assets 17, 111, 114, 138, 154
　vs. commodities 161–2, 165
Atari 128–9
audience commodity 44–45
autonomy 34, 70–7, 95–6, 106–7, 130, 137, 170, 182, 209–10
　and entrepreneurialism 114–15, 120, 126
　as management tool 86–96
　contractual 72–7

Baidu 21, 25
　see also GAFAM/BAT companies
Berlant, Lauren 96
Bhattacharya, Tithi 30
Bhattacharyya, Gargi 204, 207–8, 211, 214
Bishop, Sophie 54, 193–4
Boltanski, Luc 116–21
brand value 43–4, 140–1, 145, 149
Braverman, Harry 69–71, 95, 110, 122

Index

Bulut, Ergin 48, 62, 83, 96, 132, 168, 171
Burawoy, Michael 72, 96, 191, 197

Campbell, Colin 123–6
Cant, Callum 172–3, 199
carework 9, 23, 27, 75, 93
  see also domestic work
Chang, Emily 82, 83–4, 85, 144, 146, 147
cheap labor 64–8, 131, 202–3, 205–8
Chen, Julie Yujie 91, 181
Chiapello, Eve 116–21
China 46, 65
  social media platforms in 52, 121
  see also entrepreneurialism in China
class 40–1, 109, 122, 162, 166, 170, 188
  composition 209–11, 213–4
  see also inequality
Cockayne, Daniel 111, 130, 142
Cohen, Nicole S. 71, 171, 179–81, 186
commodification 17, 136–7, 158–9, 162, 163–4, 165
  definition of 135
  of subjectivity 134–6, 153–4, 157–9
commodities *see* assets vs. commodities
consumption 13, 19, 104, 123–6, 156–7, 207
content moderators 76, 88, 179
contracts *see* labor contracts
Cortes, Thiago 1–3
counterculture 13, 121–2, 128–30
Craig, David 21, 46, 51–2, 62, 79, 106
creative industries 17, 21, 47, 50, 61–2, 122, 137
cruel optimism 96–9
cultural industries *see* creative industries

cults 144
Cunningham, Stuart 21, 46, 51–2, 62, 79, 106

Deliveroo 1, 45, 74–5
  industrial action at 172–3, 196–7
de Peuter, Greig 40–1, 171, 179–81, 187
Didi Chuxing 91, 181
digital labor 6–11
  definition of 28
  individualizing nature of 130, 167, 169–70
digital media industries 11–2
discrimination *see* inequality
domestic work 24, 29–30, 66, 204–5
  see also carework
DoorDash 181
Duffy, Brooke Erin 47–8, 54, 100, 106, 111, 128

Edwards, Doug 145
Enspiral 183
entrepreneurial imaginary 76, 83, 86, 109, 110–13, 115–16, 119–27, 129–32, 203–4
entrepreneurialism 50, 96, 107, 110–15, 131, 137, 149, 150, 160
  and affect 141–3
  and labor struggle 170–2, 184, 188, 189, 198
  in Africa 50, 112
  in China 112–13
Etsy 27, 96, 132
Eurofound 190
exploitation, definition of 36–8
  see also commodification of subjectivity; self-exploitation

Facebook 20–1, 44, 49, 59, 97–8, 106–7, 129, 141, 145–7, 179
  see also GAFAM/BAT companies

Index

Fairmondo 183
Feher, Michel 138–9, 144, 154, 160–1, 165, 196, 197, 211
feminist theory 29–30, 157
feminization 155–8, 165, 204–5
financialization 15, 61–2, 67, 159–60, 197–8
Fisher, Eran 102–3, 119
Fiverr 45
Foodora 190
Fordism 13–14, 69–70, 102–3, 122, 207
  see also post-Fordism
FOSTA-SESTA laws 54, 133
Fowler, Susan 78
freelance workers 26, 38, 49–51, 53, 61, 73–4, 78–79, 210
  and autonomy 74–5
  and emotional labor 151–2
  and solidarity 169–70, 174, 190
  unions 185
Fuchs, Christian 23, 31, 44–5, 139

GAFAM/BAT companies 20–2, 25, 129, 169, 203
games industry 48, 62–4, 132, 168
gamification 170
Gandini, Alessandro 6, 11, 71, 149, 152, 212–13
Gannon, Emma 100–1, 120, 127, 132
Garcia Martinez, Antonio 143
Geissler, Heike 108
gender 24, 34–5, 51, 65–7, 78, 83, 145–8, 151, 156–8
  see also feminization; inequality, gender
gig economy 23, 24
  see also platform work
Gill, Rosalind 50–1, 83
Gimlet Media 185, 188
Global Entrepreneurship Monitor 113, 115
Glovo 178

Google 18, 19, 20–1, 36, 55–6, 76, 85, 128, 145–6, 155
  Books 163
  industrial action at 179
  Ngram Viewer 4
  unionization at 186–7
  see also AdSense; GAFAM/BAT companies; YouTube
gossip 84, 193–5, 198, 205
Graham, Mark 9, 50, 174
Gray, Mary 90, 96–7, 107–8, 194

hackers 83, 143, 145–6, 171
  and entrepreneurialism 129–30
hacking 180–2
Handy.com 75
harassment, online 57, 148
  sexual 78, 147, 179
  see also inequality
Hesmondhalgh, David 17, 38
hiring practices 15, 38, 73, 81–3, 151, 155
  see also inequality
Hubspot 144
human capital 137–40, 142, 145, 153, 165
  self-investment in 114, 154–6, 160–1
human resources 77–8, 138
Hungry Panda 80
Huws, Ursula 5, 40–1, 71, 75, 84, 96, 101

immaterial labor see labor, immaterial
Independent Workers of Great Britain 173, 185
industrial action 173, 175–7, 179–80, 191
  informal 192–8
industrious capitalism 108–10, 125–6, 142, 203–4, 211
inequality 51, 56–7, 78, 82–3, 145–7, 151–2, 179–80, 207–8
  ability 57

Index

age 84, 145
class 179–80
gender 51, 57, 78, 83, 146–7, 151–2
racial 51, 57, 83, 146–7, 151–2
sexual 57, 146
in Silicon Valley 81–5
see also harassment
influencers 46, 49, 54, 106, 148, 181, 185, 194–5
informal contracts 47, 73–4, 77, 80–1
workplaces 48–9, 77–9, 81, 85–6, 96, 98, 128–9, 145–6
see also industrial action; labor contracts
insecurity 39–42, 108
employment 42, 60–4, 77–8, 81–5
income 42, 46–64
job 42, 57–64
skill reproduction 42, 49, 56, 77–9
work 42, 77–8, 79–80
Instagram 44, 106, 148
International Labour Organization 15–16, 101, 210
internships 46–8, 180
Isaac, Mike 78, 82, 97, 130, 144

Kagan, Noah 59
Kalanick, Travis 78, 82
Kantor, Jodi 59, 84–5, 86, 128
Kuaishou 132

labor contracts 15, 37–8, 43, 72–7
division of 66, 69–70, 208
hope 47, 111
immaterial labor 40–1, 135–6, 137, 141
process theory 69–72
relational 52
theory of value 36–8, 39, 211
see also digital labor; domestic work; self-employment
Lei, Ya-Wen 189

Liu, Wendy 98–9, 147–8, 171–2
live-streamers 46, 52
Lorde, Audre 180, 184
Losse, Katherine 97–8, 129, 145, 146
LucasArts 62–4
Luckman, Susan 96, 132
Lukács, Georg 135, 165
Lyft 90, 184
Lyons, Dan 84, 85, 144

Marwick, Alice 150
Marx, Karl 6, 29, 31, 36–7, 65, 69, 103–5, 121, 123, 136, 161, 163, 165, 209–11
Mateescu, Alexandra 93
McRobbie, Angela 122, 126, 127
Mechanical Turk *see* Amazon, Mechanical Turk
Microsoft 20–1, 100–1
see also GAFAM/BAT companies
microwork 24, 107–8, 174, 194
see also Amazon, Mechanical Turk
multi-homing 181
MySpace 149

Neff, Gina 50, 61, 120
neoliberalism 15, 40–1, 80–1, 108, 113–14, 126, 142, 205
networking 47, 49–51, 82–3, 111, 144–5, 150, 204

occupational health and safety 1, 79–80, 176–7, 180
see also insecurity, work
Ola Cabs 107, 176
O'Neill, Christopher 94
OnlyFans 133–4, 153–4, 164

Palmer, Amanda 52
passion 48, 103, 105, 125–9, 136, 137, 141–2, 144
in job ads 149–50, 155
patronage 52, 133

Pennell, Stella 152–3
Perlin, Ross 46
Pham, Minh-ha 57, 65–6, 202, 205
platform cooperatives 182–5
platform work 5, 9–10
  definition of 23–5
platformization 21, 27
post-Fordism 14–17, 40, 80–1, 102–3, 105, 155, 165
  see also Fordism
precariat 40–1, 206
precarity 39–42
  see also insecurity
projective spirit of capitalism see spirit of capitalism
Proposition 22 178
Protestant ethic 109, 123–6

race 51, 57, 65–7, 83, 131, 151, 203–4, 206, 207, 208, 211
  see also inequality
Rappi 79, 185
ratings on platforms 57, 92–4, 95, 150–2, 175, 204
  on TV 44
Razorfish 129
reflexive modernity 155–6, 159
risk 41, 64, 120, 177, 203
  and entrepreneurs 110–14, 120, 132
  and stock options 58–62
  see also occupational health and safety
Romanticism 123–7, 128–32
Rose, Nikolas 113–14, 126
Rosenblat, Alex 53, 93, 95, 107
Ross, Andrew 48, 129, 171

Scholz, Trebor 182–3
Schrier, Jason 62–4
scientific management see Taylorism
self-branding 150–2, 155–6
  see also commodification of subjectivity; networking

self-employment 10, 24, 38, 73–4, 95, 163, 177, 209
  see also labor contracts
self-exploitation 37–8, 137, 163, 209
self-expression 102–3, 106, 120, 124–5, 127
self-reflexivity 155–7, 204
  see also reflexive modernity
Sengul-Jones, Monika 151–2
SESTA-FOSTA laws see FOSTA-SESTA laws
sex 146
  work 133–4, 158, 162, 178
sexual content 54, 55–7, 87–8, 195–6
  see also FOSTA-SESTA laws
shadowbanning 54, 56–7
Silicon Docks 1–2
Silicon Valley 38, 67, 76, 77–8, 81–6, 98, 128–31, 144, 210
  business model 60–2, 119
  hiring practices 81–2
  as imaginary 111–13, 131, 132
  unionization in 172
  work culture 144–7
Smythe, Dallas 44
Sobande, Francesca 57
social factory 136, 162–3, 212
social reproduction 24, 204–5, 158
  theory 30, 101, 191–2
solidarity 168–9, 192, 194
spirit of capitalism 116–21, 123, 125, 131
Spotify 146, 188
Srnicek, Nick 73
Stabile, Susan J. 85, 145–6
stakeholders 160–1
Standing, Guy 40, 41–2, 194, 206
startups 67, 77–8, 81–2, 97–9, 111, 142, 144–5, 147
  business model of 58–60, 97, 160
  founders 129–31, 132, 143
  unionization within 170–2
stock options 58–9, 77, 97–8, 144, 146, 161

Stocksy 183
Streitfeld, David 59, 84–5, 86, 128
Stripe 107
suicide 61
Suri, Siddharth 90, 96–7, 107–8, 194
surveillance 91–2, 95
Swarme 75
Sybert, Jeanna 195–6
Szeman, Imre 110–1, 113

TaskRabbit 132, 188
Taylorism 70–1, 75, 88, 94–5
Tencent *see* GAFAM/BAT companies
Thévenot, Laurent 116–21
Thiel, Peter 82, 98
Thorne, Bella 133–4, 135, 153–4, 163–5
Ticona, Julia 93
tipping *see* patronage
Tiqqun 156–8
transmedia work 8
Trilogy 144
Tumblr 195–7
Twitter 60, 73, 89, 140

Uber 45, 54–5, 61, 78, 80, 82, 85, 93–4, 95, 107, 144, 169–70, 184
 algorithmic management at 53, 90
 Eats 80, 182
 industrial action at 176, 178, 182

unionization 171–2, 177, 185–7, 189–90
Upwork 75, 91
UrbanSitter 150–1
user labor 10–1, 23
 as rent 10

value *see* brand value; labor theory of value
Vine 60
visibility *see* algorithms and visibility
vlogging *see* YouTube

wage theft 36, 46–8
 see also insecurity, income
Wang, Xiaowei 65, 112–13
Web 2.0 18–19
Weber, Max 109, 123–6
WeChat 173
WhatsApp 44, 173
Wiener, Anna 82, 83
Wood, Alex 77, 81, 174
Woodcock, Jamie 9, 128–9, 170–1, 172, 173, 175, 199
worker forums 153, 173–5, 192–3

Young Girlification 156–8, 162, 165, 204
YouTube 49, 51–2, 53–4, 55–6, 79, 181, 185–6, 193
 Partner Program 55–6, 87
 see also adpocalypse; AdSense

zhubos *see* live-streamers